Guy Arnold

Modern Nigeria

Longman

LONGMAN GROUP LIMITED
LONDON
Associated companies, branches and
representatives throughout the world

First published 1977

SBN 0582 64642-1 (cased)
64643.X (paper)

Filmset by Keyspools Limited, Golborne, Lancashire
Printed in Great Britain by
Lowe & Brydone (Printers) Ltd, Thetford, Norfolk

Contents

Acknowledgements

The publishers are grateful to the following for permission to reproduce photographs:

between pages 2 and 3:
Associated Press Ltd. for plates 5 and 7; Camera Press for plates 1, 3, 4, 6; Keystone for plate 8; Popperfoto for plate 2.

between pages 56 and 57:
Camera and Pen International for plate 11 (bottom); Camera Press for plate 11 (top); Alan Hutchison for plate 9 (top); Keystone for plate 10 (top); Nigeria Information Services for plate 10 (bottom); Ministry of Information, Enugu, for plate 12 (top); Popperfoto for plate 9 (bottom); the United Africa Company Limited for plate 12 (bottom).

between pages 94 and 95:
Camera Press for plate 15; David Hill for plates 14 (bottom) and 16 (top); John Hillelson for plate 13 (bottom); Alan Hutchison for plate 16 (bottom); Popperfoto for plate 13 (top).

between pages 128 and 129:
Associated Press Ltd. for plates 18 (top and bottom) Camera Press for plates 17, 19 (top) and 20 (top and bottom); Keystone for plate 19 (bottom).

Cover transparencies by kind permission of Alan Hutchison and David Hill.

Maps

Between pages 179 and 180: maps showing
(1) the twelve states of Nigeria created in 1967;
(2) the nineteen new states created in 1976;
(3) the member countries of the Economic Community of West African States.

Foreword

One of the difficulties in writing an appraisal of any modern country is that of finding a suitable cut-off point. This problem is increased significantly when writing about a country as vital as Nigeria.

While the author was collecting material in Nigeria there occurred the bloodless coup which toppled Gowon. Within weeks of the book's completion a number of developments took place which could not be omitted: the creation of seven new states; the attempted coup which resulted in the death of the Head of State; the decision to move the capital from Lagos; and some dramatic revisions to the Third Plan.

As it happened, 1975 was an ideal point at which to examine modern Nigeria. It was fifteen years after independence—long enough for the colonial era to have begun to recede into history; it was the year of the coup which ended nine years of Gowon's rule and brought in the reforming regime of Mohammed; it was—as a result of the oil boom—the year in which Nigeria launched its, and Africa's, greatest development plan.

Nigeria has the population, the land, the resources and the leadership that go with world power. During the five years that it implements the giant Third Plan (1975–1980) it will also lay the foundation of a modern industrial state and so begin to develop the power commensurate with its size and potential influence.

Guy Arnold
August 1976

Introduction

At the beginning of 1976 Nigeria had an estimated population of 78.7 million people (based upon the 1963 census figures) and an annual growth rate of 2.7 per cent. It was, by far, the most populous country of Africa. Its estimated GDP for the year was ₦16 000 million, giving it a per capita income of approximately ₦200 ($330), The country's economy had come to be dominated by oil.

The country has scores of languages, the most prominent being Hausa-Fulani in the north, Ibo in the east and Yoruba in the west. At independence in 1960 when the country was divided into regions, each of these (north, east and west) was sufficiently large and distinct to form a nation on its own, while the Middle Belt region of the north and the Niger Delta in the east could also have been made into separate nations. Therein lay the newly independent state's most basic and intractable problem.

Nigeria's size ensures dramatic changes of climate from south to north: on the coasts are swamps and then a 160-kilometre belt of rain forest leading into open woodlands and finally the grass savannahs of the north merging in their turn into the sandy scrubland on the borders with Chad and Niger, and stretching on into the Sahara. Of key economic and social importance is the fact that 80 per cent of the population live in rural areas and are still among some of the poorest people anywhere in the world. Nonetheless, Nigeria is well endowed in resources, more than able to take care of its huge population. The staple foods are cassava, millet, yams, rice, peppers, palm and groundnut oils, kola, meat and fish or stockfish. Unemployment has been a major problem since independence: finding jobs for the increasing number of school leavers or those who consistently leave the countryside for the towns in search of better opportunities.

A considerable number—about 50 000—of expatriates still work in Nigeria: in commerce and industry; as teachers; and in other posts under various aid schemes. Yet their presence is not obvious in the way it is in smaller African countries, for against the vast backdrop of Nigeria they tend simply to disappear. There is an able and highly trained civil service (heavily purged for corruption in the months September–November 1975 under the new reforming government of

Murtala Mohammed), and a larger trained output of graduates and other personnel benefiting from higher education than in any other African country, though proportionately Nigeria needs them all. The country enjoys a widely varied and remarkably free press.

The two main religions (accounting for perhaps 60 per cent of the population) are Islam and Christianity. Islam, the stronger influence of the two, is of overwhelming importance in the north while Christianity predominates in the south: the western part of the country is mainly Protestant (and also increasingly Muslim) while the east has been much influenced by Catholicism. In the nineteenth century the religious reformer Uthman dan Fodio did much to spread Islam and unite the north. The country has great ethnic diversity and rests upon a wide mixture of cultures, the earliest known being the Nok culture of pre-history. It was in the twelfth century that Nigeria was drawn into the mainstream of events to the north when the ruler of Kanem, Ummejilami, was converted to Islam. The Benin Kingdom in the mid-west grew up in the twelfth century; it was to flourish for five hundred years. In the late thirteenth century there emerged in the south the Yoruba kingdom of Oyo.

The first Europeans to impinge upon Nigeria were the Portuguese. In the fifteenth century their explorers and traders came to the Guinea coast; they monopolised West African trade until well into the sixteenth century when, with the growth of the Atlantic slave trade, other European powers came to challenge their monopoly. There followed the rise of the trading city states of the Niger Delta, first as a result of the slave trade and then, in the nineteenth century, for the palm oil trade. The nineteenth century saw growing contacts between the Muslim north and the southern kingdoms and the emergence of the British as the dominant European power in the area.

The British annexation of Lagos in 1861 might be taken as the beginning of the colonial period although British traders, missionaries and government representatives had been involved on the coast long before. By 1871 Lagos with £500 000 of trade annually had become self-sufficient. Already in 1860, however, a British consul had been established at Lokoja at the confluence of the Niger and Benue rivers, and the trade of the Delta region was then worth £1 million annually to Britain. By the late 1870s four companies were operating in the Delta alone and it was then that the figure of Taubman Goldie emerged to consolidate the companies into the United African Company. It was Goldie's ambition to add the region to the British Empire and this he duly accomplished. In its early days the UAC had the power to make treaties and controlled its own fleet of gunboats. To ensure that the company could combat French competition Goldie 'went public', so increasing the capital from £100 000 to £1 million.

In the meantime the 'Scramble for Africa' had got under way in earnest: in 1884 a German Protectorate was proclaimed over neighbouring Cameroon and at the Berlin Conference of 1884–1885 the powers recognised that British influence was paramount in the Delta area. Britain granted a Royal Charter to the Niger Company in 1886 and gave it political authority in the areas it controlled. The company took over Nupe and Ilorin in 1898 and founded the West African Frontier Force to protect its acquisitions from the French. In southern Nigeria the Benin empire was the last to hold out, but by the turn of the century it had succumbed to British power.

In 1900 the British Government took over all the company territories and established three protectorates: the Niger Coast Protectorate; the Lagos Colony Protectorate; and the Protectorate of Northern Nigeria. Sir Frederick Lugard was appointed High Commissioner for the northern protectorate, where he introduced his system of indirect rule and carried out the subjugation of the area. The name Nigeria was coined in 1897 by Flora Shaw in an article in *The Times* of London and it stuck. In 1914 the three protectorates were united to become the Colony and Protectorate of Nigeria. Effectively British rule over Nigeria, starting with the creation of the three protectorates in 1900, lasted for exactly 60 years.

Nationalist agitation began to grow in the 1930s and was given a tremendous boost by the events of the Second World War. From the mid-1940s onwards a series of constitutions (and the politics surrounding their attainment) took steps towards self-government and then independence, and this process dominated the last fifteen years of British rule. The British Governor from 1943 to 1947, Sir Arthur Richards, was not progressive and was politically unpopular. His successor Sir John Macpherson, with Hugh Foot as his Chief Secretary, reviewed the Richards Constitution of 1946 and speeded up the movement towards self-government. In the period 1945 to 1960, five constitutions were enacted, leading first to self-government and then to independence. The last governor of this period was Sir James Robertson. During the 1950s some of the wide divergences of outlook between north and south emerged: the Sardauna of Sokoto, for example, argued that the process of independence should be held back because the north was not ready for it—and he had some grounds for this attitude since at independence in 1960 there were only 41 secondary schools to serve the whole of the north.

The 1954 constitution officially made Nigeria a federation of three regions. In 1957 a prime minister was appointed to head the Council and an upper chamber, the Senate, was created. The success of the three regionally based parties in the elections of 1959 demonstrated the strength of regional loyalties and pulls as against the centre or a more national concept of politics and this fact provided the main political problem for the first six years following independence. The north was dominated by the NPC (Northern People's Congress) led by Sir Ahmadu Bello; the east was dominated by Dr Nnamdi Azikiwe's

NCNC (National Council of Nigeria and Cameroons); and the west by Chief Obafemi Awolowo's Action Group.

Though it always resisted colonialism, Nigerian nationalism did not have to fight as, for example, Kenya or Ghana did. The modern nationalist struggle could perhaps be dated from 1937 when Dr Azikiwe returned home, already famous from his activities abroad, to found his *West African Pilot*, which for the next fifteen years was to be identified with the struggle towards independence. The Second World War gave a major boost to nationalism in Nigeria as it did elsewhere. During the war and after the passing of the 1940 Commonwealth Development and Welfare Act by Britain, which stipulated among other things that unions should be formed, there was a major advance in the Nigerian trades union movement. From 12 unions with 5 000 members in 1940 the figure rose to 85 unions with 30 000 members by the end of the war. This promising growth of unions and union activity was to lapse for a long period after the war. First, however, came the general strike in 1945 which was a landmark in terms of new labour pressures upon the colonial government.

After Dr Azikiwe the second major nationalist figure to emerge was Chief Awolowo. He went to study law in London in 1944, returning home in 1949 to found the Action Group and so counter the political success up to that time of Azikiwe's NCNC. By 1950 the two major southern parties—the NCNC and the Action Group—with their respective Ibo and Yoruba bases came to be balanced in the north by the Northern People's Congress (NPC).

Thus by the beginning of the 1950s the stage had been set for the political struggles and regional rivalries that were to dominate Nigeria both up to independence and for the six years after it, until the political collapse that produced military rule and the civil war.

The decade and a half from 1950 to 1965 was a period of intense political activity in Nigeria: extreme diversity and regional pulls demanded the politics of compromise while in fact the process that took place led to the emergence of the north as the preponderant political power within the federal situation. Nationalism in these years became a dual process: the nationalism that led to independence and the end of the colonial era; and the tribal nationalisms of Yoruba, Ibo and Hausa-Fulani that constantly threatened the weak federal centre. The key political figures during this period were the Sardauna of Sokoto in the north, and his principal lieutenant, Sir Abubakar Tafawa Balewa, who became Federal Prime Minister; Chief Awolowo in the west, and his principal political rival there, Akintola; and Nnamdi Azikiwe in the east. These, however, were only the top names; the extravagance and corruption of politicians became notorious so that when the crisis that swept them aside came in January 1966 many Nigerians felt that a new era had dawned.

During the 1950s the three leading political figures (the Sardauna,

Awolowo and Azikiwe) concentrated upon their regions as the bases of their political power—though Azikiwe especially attempted to establish a national following—and the centre remained weak and ineffective. The 1954 constitution deprived the central government of its right to approve regional legislation and the small list of exclusive federal subjects was confined to defence, foreign policy and communications. There was a concurrent legislative list—affairs that both the central and regional governments could deal with—that included commerce, agriculture, labour and industrial development while all the other subjects were regional. While regional premiers were created at this time, there was as yet no Federal Prime Minister, and the Federal Government continued to be run by the Governor General. Nonetheless, the 1954 election for the Federal Government was the first on a national scale. No party obtained a majority: the NPC won 79 out of 184 seats, the NCNC got 61 seats and the two formed a coalition while the Action Group made up the opposition. Then in 1957 the eastern and western regions became self-governing, though the north did not do so until 1959. Sir Abubakar became the first Federal Prime Minister (he was the deputy leader of the NPC) while the Sardauna of Sokoto preferred to remain as regional prime minister. The period up to independence was dominated by the question of the minorities and the possibility of more regions. A further divisive development at this time was the tendency for a majority political party in one region to lend its political support to minority groups in the other regions. Shortly before independence the Minorities Commission produced a list of civil rights to be written into the constitution. The elections of 1959—the year before independence—gave a majority to the NPC–NCNC coalition which was to last until 1964; Awolowo and his Action Group became the opposition. Then on 1 October 1960, Nigeria became independent and celebrated the event in suitably lavish and splendid style.

With independence Nigeria embarked—apparently—upon a democratic British pattern of politics both at the centre and in the regions. But the federal structure was too weak to bear the strains of the powerful pulls from the regions for long: it faced emergency within two years and had broken down in disorder at the end of five. In a sense, the period 1960–1966 was a necessary prelude to the eradication of overt British political influence and set the scene for the subsequent Nigerianisation that had to come in political and other ways. In November 1960 Azikiwe became the first Nigerian Governor-General.

During the first five years of independence Nigeria was especially to find its feet in terms of foreign affairs. Although its approach to international affairs began conservatively it was soon clear that a so-called 'moderate' approach was by no means a certainty. Nigeria broke off relations with France over that country's Saharan nuclear testing to find itself the only African nation to have done so. In

December 1962 it abrogated the defence treaty with Britain. In terms of the divisions within Africa at that time it was to emerge in 1961 as the leader of the moderate Monrovia group of states as opposed to the more radical Casablanca group, led by Nkrumah of Ghana and Sekou Touré of Guinea. In January 1962, however, when representatives of the two groups met in Lagos they did come near to finding agreement and their deliberations foreshadowed the later creation of the Organisation of African Unity. The last major Nigerian initiative in foreign affairs in this period was the Commonwealth Conference on Rhodesia held in Lagos literally on the eve of the first military coup that toppled the civilian government: it was the first Commonwealth conference ever to be held outside London.

The first six years of independence were deeply troubled ones for Nigeria. In the western region the deep rift in the Action Group between the supporters of Awolowo and those of Akintola threatened by 1962 to split the region disastrously. Attempts to dismiss Akintola as premier led to disturbances in the Assembly and the Federal Government declared a state of emergency in the region. Restriction orders were then served on the leading politicians; the regional governor was suspended for exceeding his constitutional powers; there was a major inquiry into corruption. Then came the treason trial of Awolowo and 27 others which was to last eight months and provide major controversy as to its rights and wrongs then and subsequently. Awolowo was found guilty of treason and sentenced to ten years' imprisonment, reduced to seven on appeal. Chief Anthony Enahoro was repatriated from Britain to face charges of complicity in the same plot and he was sentenced to 15 years, later reduced to ten. Akintola then became the head of a reconstituted western government. These troubles destroyed the regional power of the Action Group. The Federal Government then created the fourth region of the Mid-West.

An attempt at a census in 1962 was cancelled because of distorted figures. A new census was carried out in 1963 (still the basis for calculations in Nigeria): when published in 1964 the figures showed that Nigeria had a population of 55.6 million making it the tenth most populous country in the world. More controversial was the fact that it gave the population of the north as 30 million which, since seats in the federal house were allocated according to population, meant that the north had a built-in political majority over the south.

There was a successful general strike in 1964 when more than 800 000 workers came out and the government was forced to accept higher wage levels than it had previously been willing to concede. Then came the federal elections of 1964; election day was set for 30 December and by the time the elections took place mammoth malpractices had been revealed. In the new year a crisis followed when in his capacity as President (Nigeria had meanwhile become a republic) Azikiwe held back as long as he could before calling upon

Abubakar again to form a government. Towards the end of the year the western region elections produced near chaos and another major crisis loomed as 1966 opened. The Commonwealth Conference in Lagos in January 1966 provided a brief interregnum, but even as the Commonwealth prime ministers departed the storm broke.*

The first republic collapsed in January 1966: that year was to see two military coups and the polarising of the eastern region from the rest of the country until the secession of Biafra was proclaimed in May 1967 by Colonel Ojukwu, and civil war became inevitable. The military plot of the majors over 14–15 January 1966 swept away the old political system and eliminated Abubakar, Akintola and the Sardauna of Sokoto. The Army Commander, Major-General Aguiyi-Ironsi, then became temporary Head of State and tried to hold a deteriorating position for the next six months. His most decisive action was the abolition of the regions on 24 May 1966, when he proclaimed a unitary Republic of Nigeria. There followed the first massacres of Ibos in the north at the end of May and the possibility of northern secession was then widely discussed.

At the end of July 1966 came the second military coup that overthrew Ironsi, though his death was not confirmed for six months. Major-General Yakubu Gowon then became Supreme Commander and effectively Head of State on 29 July 1966, a position he was to hold for exactly nine years. In the following months acrimonious discussions took place between the Federal Government and Ojukwu for the eastern region; in September–October the second wave of massacres of Ibos took place in the north and resulted in the trek back to the eastern region from many parts of Nigeria of perhaps a million Ibos while in the east the demand for secession grew. In January 1967 the Aburi meeting took place in Ghana in an attempt to settle the deadlock. On 26 May 1967, Gowon announced the division of the country into twelve states and on 30 May Ojukwu announced the secession of Biafra. Civil war swiftly followed, and was both bitter and bloody. It ended in the collapse of Biafra and a total federal victory in January 1970. With the reconciliation and rehabilitation policies that followed in the early 1970s the second phase of Nigeria's independence began.

In many ways 1975 was a key year for Nigeria. It was fifteen years after independence and long enough for the country to feel genuinely free of British colonial ties. It was the year in which—as a result of the huge new oil wealth—the country launched the largest development plan in its (or Africa's) history. And it was the year of the third coup that brought to an end nine years of the Gowon regime and ushered in the new reforming government of Mohammed. Thus 1975 represents a turning point in Nigerian history; it is an ideal place at which to attempt an assessment of the country's development and potential.

* For a detailed account of the period 1960–1966 see Walter Schwarz, *Nigeria*, Pall Mall, 1968.

Chapter one

Coup—1975

Throughout July 1975 the Nigerian media and most especially the press had been carrying almost unceasing and mounting criticisms of the Gowon government. They attacked it over port congestion; they lambasted its failure to ensure proper distribution of petrol throughout the country; they raised the worn but explosive issue of the replacement of the state governors (the young soldiers, one policeman and one civilian who had been ruling the twelve states into which Nigeria had been divided in 1967, and whose continued tenure of power without change since then was a major cause of political discontent); they examined aspects of corruption; and leading figures on the political or journalistic front such as Aminu Kano or Tai Solarin kept alive the question of a return to civil rule.

On Sunday 27 July 1975 Nigerian television showed the boyish figure of General Gowon running up the steps of his plane and turning to salute into the cameras as he set out for Kampala and the Organisation of African Unity (OAU) Summit Meeting of Heads of State. The next day Brigadier Theo Danjuma made an unusual remark for a top Nigerian soldier: he said he did not blame people agitating for a return to civilian rule—it seemed quite legitimate.

Then in the early morning of Tuesday 29 July Nigerians learnt of their third military coup in nine years; it was, indeed, the anniversary of the day Gowon had become Head of State. On the radio at 6 am, instead of the normal news broadcast, a relatively unknown soldier—Colonel Garba—broadcast a brief message to the nation. He informed it that a bloodless coup had taken place; that only essential workers should report for duty; that the borders were closed till further notice.

The colonel's voice sounded nervous and fraught with emotion: he had been a close personal friend of Gowon and, as Commander of the Guards he had a special, indeed precise, responsibility to prevent any coup or attempted coup against the Head of State. Instead, he was on the air announcing the coup. The fact that Garba, a Yergam from one of the small middle belt tribes, announced the coup rather than a northerner or westerner was possibly vital in forestalling any early violence since it helped to allay the fears of the country's smaller groups.

Thereafter the broadcast went out every half-hour and in between the radio played martial music. Troops were to be seen at strategic points in Lagos and elsewhere: the airports, bridges, radio stations—all the normal places deemed essential in any coup operation. Nigerians who did go out that first day went about their business quietly and, indeed, what most characterised the day of the coup was an extraordinary calm across the country. People, however, were holding their breath: would there be bloodshed or could the transfer of power be achieved without this?

That evening, in a brief news summary, the name of the new Head of State was announced: Brigadier Murtala Mohammed who had been Federal Commissioner for Communications. Other key posts announced were: Alhaji M. D. Yusuf, Inspector-General of Police; Brigadier Olusagun Obasanjo, Chief of Staff Supreme Headquarters (replacing Vice-Admiral Wey); Brigadier Theo Danjuma, Chief of Staff of the Army (replacing Major-General David Ejoor); Commodore Adelanwa, Chief of Naval Staff (replacing Rear-Admiral Nelson Soroh); Colonel Yisa Dokko, Chief of Air Staff (replacing Brigadier Emmanuel Ikwe). These for the moment were to form the Supreme Military Council. Meanwhile all Majors-General, military governors (including the Administrator of the East Central State) and former heads of services were to go on retirement. Only Brigadier I. D. Bissala of the former Supreme Military Council was not retired.

Speaking over Nigerian radio the next evening the new Head of State, Brigadier Mohammed, said that General Gowon had been removed from office because despite the resources available to the nation the aspirations of the people were not being met. Other reasons for his removal included: his inaccessibility to the people; his disregard of responsible opinion including that of traditional rulers and intellectuals; his insensitivity to the feelings and yearnings of the people; the indecision and indiscipline of his administration; his neglect of the administration of the armed forces. As a result, Brigadier Mohammed said, the people and the members of the Armed Forces had become disillusioned with his regime as a corrective one. The new Head of State then outlined government changes. Three organs of government at Federal level were to be: the Supreme Military Council; the National Council of States; and the Federal Executive Council. The SMC—the key body in the state—was to comprise the following: the military heads already announced plus the GOC First Division, Brigadier Julius Alani Akinrinade; the GOC Second Division, Brigadier Martin Adamu; the GOC Third Division, Brigadier Emmanuel Abisoye; the Commander Lagos Garrison Organisation, Brigadier John Obada; also Colonel Joseph Garba; Lieutenant-Colonel Shehu Yar Adua; Brigadier James Oluleye; Brigadier Iliya Bisalla; Colonel Ibrahim Babangida; Lieutenant-Colonel Muktar Mohammed; Colonel Dan Suleman; Captain Oluf-

1 Nigeria's Head of State, Lieutenant General Olusegun Obasanjo

2 The Sardauna of Sokoto, first premier of the Northern Region

3 Sir Abubakar Tafawa Balewa, first federal prime minister of Nigeria

4 Dr Nnamdi Azikiwe, Nigeria's first President

5 Major-General Aguiyi Ironsi became Head of State after the military coup of January 1966

6 General Yakubu Gowon was Nigeria's Head of State for nine years, from July 1966 to July 1976

7 It was while he was attending the 1975 summit conference of the OAU at Kampala that General Gowon received the news that he had been deposed. His successor was Brigadier Murtala Mohammed

8 Brigadier Murtala Mohammed took control of the government of Nigeria in July 1975. Seven months later he was assassinated in an abortive coup

emi Olumide; Captain Husaini Abdullahi; Mr Adamu Suleman; Lieutenant-Colonel Alfred Aduloju and Lieutenant-Commander Godwin Kanu.

After further announcing the new state governors and the composition of the SMC, Brigadier Mohammed said that a political programme was to be reviewed and would be announced later. Meanwhile the new regime was to set up a panel to advise on the question of new states and another to advise on the question of the federal capital. The controversial 1973 census was cancelled and for planning purposes the government would continue to use the 1963 figures. A further panel was established to advise on the future of the Interim Common Services Agency (ICSA) and the Eastern States Interim Assets and Liabilities Agency (ESIALA), which had been made necessary because of the division of the former Nigeria into states. The Black Arts Festival, due to be held in Nigeria that November, was postponed. There followed a reaffirmation of friendship with all foreign countries and an assurance that foreign nationals and investments would be safeguarded; the government would honour all obligations entered into by its predecessors and would continue to give active support to the OAU, the UN and the Commonwealth. It was a short businesslike speech of a man—or men—who intended to get down to work at speed. (See Appendix I for full text).

Meanwhile in Kampala the drama of Gowon's fall had seriously affected the usefulness of the OAU summit. Gowon received the news with dignity and declared his support for and acceptance of the new military leadership of the country. (Brigadier Mohammed had said that Gowon would be free to return to the country as soon as conditions permitted.) It was confirmed that Gowon's wife and two children were already in London. At a brief press conference in Kampala, Gowon said that he accepted the change and would gladly serve Nigeria in any capacity, and appealed to all citizens to co-operate with the new government 'to ensure the preservation of peace, unity and stability'.

The new Head of State, Brigadier Murtala Mohammed, was born in 1938 in Kano and educated at the Government College, Zaria, after which he joined the army as a cadet in 1958. A good deal of his training was in England at Sandhust and Catterick. He was part of the Nigerian military contingent that served in the Congo peace keeping force at the beginning of the 1960s. By 1965 he had risen to become acting Chief Signal Officer of the Nigerian Army; he was promoted to Lieutenant-Colonel in April 1966 and then became Inspector of Signals. During the civil war he was GOC 2 Infantry Division and was one of the most successful commanders that emerged. He was appointed Federal Commissioner of Signals in August 1974. Married with five children, he was particularly interested in Arabic studies.

The immediate reaction of Nigerians to the coup was one of cautious waiting: for 24 hours, possibly 48, people trod delicately and wondered whether or not violence was to follow. This tension was heightened at least in the first day because there was no news. After the Garba broadcast—repeated every half-hour—twelve hours were to elapse before anyone knew who was to be Head of State. Forty-eight hours later a great collective sigh of relief was beginning to spread across the country as it became clear that it really had been a bloodless coup. The papers still held their breath, however, wondering perhaps where they stood and how far they could go in comments. Thus the editorial of the *Daily Times* for Thursday 31 July was 'Promoting Safety at Work'—a long rather dull piece starting: 'Industrialisation is a necessary pre-requisite to economic growth.' No doubt, the country's premier newspaper had its tongue in its cheek. By the weekend, however, the press had returned to its own inimitable form and was busy proffering advice to the new rulers. Two days after the coup, some of the now sacked state governors were still occupying their residences with their families. In Lagos, the soldiers on the streets ordered 'molue' bus conductors to slash fares from 10 to 5 kobo with the result that a large number of such buses simply withdrew from the streets altogether, making the traffic chaos even worse than normal. From all over the country came expressions of support for the new government from trade unions, students and other groups. At this early post-coup stage the general attitude was one of accepting that the change had been inevitable, of saying that the Gowon regime had run out of steam and come to a stop, of cautiously accepting the programme announced by Mohammed, and of a resigned 'wait and see' what the performance would be.

It is ritualistic with new regimes following coups to insist upon the need for national discipline. Certainly, in this respect, the regime did not differ from other military takeovers elsewhere. Equally, however, it did indeed have a case. In his speech to the nation Brigadier Mohammed had stressed the breakdown of discipine: the press were not slow to take up this theme; nor were the new members of the SMC or the new state governors as they went to their various capitals. Demands for discipline and threats against slackers became *de rigueur* over the following days and weeks.

It was, however, a mark of the astonishingly smooth operation of the coup that progressively for the remainder of that week internal flights were first resumed, the curfew was lifted, the borders with ECOWAS (the newly created Economic Community of West African States) neighbours were reopened and finally by the weekend international flights were resumed, so that by the following Monday, 4 August, the country was back to normal. That weekend the press, resuming its usual occupation of pointing out what problems the new government should tackle and how, warmly welcomed one key innovation of the new regime: the fact that the state governors were not also to be members of the Supreme Military Council—a restraint whose absence before had contributed possibly the most crippling inhibition upon the Gowon regime. The welcome this received was commensurate with the frustrations that had gone with the previous position of power of the governors.

The immediate sacking and replacement of the 12 former governors helped set the tone of the new regime. Addressing the new governors before they set out for their several seats from Lagos only two days after the coup, Brigadier Mohammed denounced the conduct of their predecessors and enjoined the new governors to be fair, firm and decisive. He emphasised that their appointments were military and that they were responsible through the Chief of Staff Supreme Headquarters to the Head of State. Most of the new governors took up their posts in the state capitals the weekend after the coup and the public demonstrations of approval indicated very clearly that whatever else the people thought of the coup—at that stage—they welcomed the change of governors and their public brief to stamp out corruption and crush indiscipline. There was also a growing chorus of demands that all advisers of the old regime should be changed.

As Nigerians reviewed the previous twelve months and tried to assess the new regime it was clear that the change was potentially popular. Not only had the Gowon regime come to a virtual standstill but its last year had been increasingly criticised because of its failure to tackle a whole host of problems: corruption, port congestion, traffic chaos in Lagos, petrol distribution, the broken promise to change the state governors, and above all Gowon's announcement (in October 1974) that there would not, after all, be a return to civilian rule in 1976 as Gowon had promised in 1970. By July 1975 the country was more than ready to welcome a change. This it did soon enough after the coup. Then it waited to see what difference the new men would in fact produce. Most of the major questions that had long bothered politically conscious Nigerians—a new federal capital, the cost as well as the chaos surrounding the coming Black Arts and African Festival, the 1973 census, the question of more states—had been included in Brigadier Mohammed's initial speech after the coup, so at least it appeared that the new government had its priorities right and was about to tackle those questions of greatest public and political concern.

An important feature of the public reaction to the coup was one of near self-congratulation accompanying the relief that it had been bloodless. As the editorial of the *Nigerian Herald* put it: 'When in the early morning of July 29, an announcement was made that a change was effected in the leadership of the Federal Military Government, our foreign detractors felt we would shed blood.' That may well have been true; yet it was also true that many Nigerians wondered whether blood would not be shed. Fortunately none was, and so it became possible to hail the change-over as one of maturity—as indeed it was in the manner in which it occurred. The same paper spoke of the maturity with which the change-over had been effected: there were no bitterness, rancour or trials. The new regime had recognised the services of those who had been ousted—something almost unique in the history of modern coups in which normal practice is to decry and denigrate everything to do with the ousted regime. Finally the paper paid tribute to the realistic, calm and mature way Gowon had accepted the change.

Once the excitement had died down, however, and the country took stock of its new rulers—as they took stock of their position—both had to face the fact that Nigeria—populous, rich and the potential leader of the continent—faced enormous problems. These are, and must remain, daunting to even the most able of governments. There were immediate ones: port congestion, traffic chaos in the capital, fuel shortages round the country. There were the longer term problems: how to implement effectively and fairly the mammoth Third Plan so as to spread the new oil wealth to all the nation's citizens; how to put universal primary education (UPE) into operation; and how to overcome shortages of manpower. And then came the ultimate questions. How, when and in what fashion to return to civilian rule? How to deal with fundamental issues such as resolving—or tackling—the corruption that seems endemic to public life? And, ultimately, what sort of society does Nigeria wish to become?

Initial fears in the south that with the coming to power of Mohammed there had been too great a shift towards northern predominance were allayed partly by the appointment to two of the top posts of Brigadiers Obasanjo (a westerner) and Danjuma (from the middle belt); and partly by the political masterstroke of cancelling the 1973 census that (however accurate or inaccurate it may have been) seemed overwhelmingly to weight things in favour of the northern states. The speed of initial actions and the problems singled out for attention at the start also helped to reassure the public about the new regime's intention of tackling tasks in the right order.

Nigeria's first fifteen years of independence from 1960 to 1975 were stormy and traumatic, including one of the most devastating civil wars of modern times as well as an unprecedented economic boom based upon oil. Psychologically the 29 July 1975 coup came at the right moment: following the smooth way the new regime sought to establish itself in control came the widespread hope that a new period for the country had begun.

Unfortunately, the transition from Gowon to Mohammed was not to go down in history as quite the bloodless coup it had appeared to be in July 1975. There was to be a tragic second phase: the bloody attempted counter-coup led by Lieutenant-Colonel Dimka in February 1976 in which the Head of State, General Murtala Mohammed, lost his life. General Mohammed, who had dispensed with protective guards, was driving himself to Dodan barracks on the morning of Friday 13 February 1976 when he and his aide-de-camp were shot and killed. Afterwards Lieutenant-Colonel Dimka, accompanied by two officers in uniform and four others, arrived at the Nigerian Broadcasting Corporation where he recorded a message to the nation: the Mohammed regime was overthrown; all the 19 state governors had ceased to exercise power; the states would be run by brigade commanders; there was to be a dusk-to-dawn curfew.

Two hours later loyal troops had arrived to seize control of the broadcasting station. The plotters were on the run. In the north in Kaduna Major-General Julius Akinrinade, commander of the First Infantry Division, said in a broadcast that what had happened in Lagos had 'nothing to do with the rest of the country'. A similar broadcast was made from Enugu, when it appeared that the attempted coup had been by a handful of officers who were then being rounded up.

Whatever had been planned had gone badly wrong, but at that stage it was not at all clear just how extensive a plot had existed. On the Monday following the coup attempt the police closed down the Reuters' office in Lagos: Reuters' chief correspondent, Colin Fox, a Briton, and his two Nigerian assistants were taken away for questioning. Later Fox was deported to Benin; the two Nigerians were released. The Reuters' offices were in the same building as the British High Commission and this may have had some connection with the next most curious aspect of the affair.

There were two suggestions at the time that foreign powers were involved: on the Sunday following the coup attempt, demonstrating students headed for the American Embassy bearing placards which implied a link between the Dimka affair and the CIA. At the same time a tennis match involving the American Arthur Ashe was stopped by troops without explanation.

ˈ Far more important, by implication and result, was the way the coup attempt was linked to Britain. First, on the Friday itself, Colonel Dimka with three armed soldiers arrived at the British High Commission and told the High Commissioner, Sir Martin LeQuésne: 'I am the new Head of State'. He wanted to telephone London from the High Commission to talk with Gowon. The British High Commissioner refused either to allow this or to forward a message to Gowon. Sir Martin spoke with Dimka for about a quarter of an hour before the latter left. Dimka's visit to the High Commission led to students' attacking the High Commission the following Tuesday and doing extensive damage to it. The mere fact that Dimka was known to have gone there produced a natural enough reaction in the tense mood of Lagos at the time. Shortly afterwards Sir Martin was withdrawn from Lagos by Britain at Nigeria's request.

Events leading to this diplomatic quarrel are complicated, and the

British and Nigerian versions differ substantially. According to the British High Commissioner, he made a report to the Nigerian police immediately following the Dimka visit. Three days later he informed the Nigerian Foreign Ministry and asked if he could release a full account of the affair. This he was requested not to do. In the meantime, however, the Reuters' correspondent (who shared the High Commission building) had seen Dimka enter. He subsequently approached the High Commissioner who explained what had happened but emphasised that he was not to publish. When the Reuters' man had confirmed the story from independent sources, however, he did file it in London. The result was Nigerian anger, the attack on the Reuters' office and the expulsion of Fox, although how much for this offence as opposed to the Reuters' report of tribal rioting in Kano is not clear.

The Nigerian version of the affair was different. First, the Nigerians were upset because the British High Commissioner put in an early claim for the damages resulting from the students' attack upon the High Commission. Though the claim may have been technically justified, it showed insensitivity to Nigerian feelings so soon after the death of the Head of State: it was undiplomatic in the extreme. The Nigerian Government said that the demonstration which wrecked the High Commission was in any case the result of the story of Dimka's visit being leaked to the press. The British Foreign Office claimed that the whole business was a misunderstanding. Nigeria, however, asked that Sir Martin LeQuésne should be withdrawn on the grounds of his personal unacceptability and to this Britain agreed. There were further undercurrents to the affair for Nigerians had accused Sir Martin of adopting towards them attitudes reminiscent of the days of the British Raj; apparently he had become unacceptable before the Dimka coup attempt.

While this particular drama between Nigeria and Britain was being played out, investigations into the background of the coup attempt continued and showed it to be far wider based than just a handful of irresponsible men around Dimka. First, within five days of the coup attempt the Nigerian Government issued a statement to the effect that Gowon had known and approved of the attempt. The statement claimed that investigations showed that the coup aimed at restoring Gowon to power. One of the plotters, it was alleged, had several times visited Britain to brief Gowon on the coup plans. The main reason given for the attempt was the contention that the Nigerian Government was going communist and so the coup was intended to 're-establish the policy of non-alignment'. In Britain Gowon denied any connection with the coup attempt, saying: 'I deny it emphatically. I know absolutely nothing about it. . . . If it was their plan to carry out the coup and then ask me to go back, well, that is their own look-out.'

Meanwhile the round-up of suspects and the investigation proceeded and three weeks after the event Dimka was found and arrested in eastern Nigeria. A total of 125 people were arrested, of whom 40 were later released: they included both soldiers and civilians. On the day of the attempted coup an investigation panel was set up under Major General Emmanuel Abisoye which worked at speed. Of those investigated each defendant was given ample opportunity to call in any witness or refute evidence against him. On 11 March, less than a month after the attempt, 32 people implicated in it—at that stage not including Dimka—were sentenced to death. The most prominent of these—the revelation of whose involvement shocked Nigerians—was the former Defence Commissioner, Major-General I. D. Bisalla. These 32 were to be executed immediately and the following day thousands of Nigerians witnessed the public executions by firing squad.

By the time the executions took place the government claimed that it had ample evidence to link Gowon to the coup attempt. It claimed not only that he knew of the plot but that, by implication, he approved of it as well. The government asked that Gowon (in Britain) should 'come to defend himself' on charges connected with the coup attempt. It was not immediately clear whether Nigeria was formally asking Britain to hand over Gowon or not. In Britain Gowon was clearly shocked at the sudden turn of events. He claimed to have known nothing of the coup attempt and flatly denied any involvement. In a statement to the British *Sunday Times* he said: 'I cannot return to Nigeria now without creating more problems for my nation, and for the present I have chosen to be involved only in my studies as a student at Warwick University. Now I study politics; I do not comment or get involved in Nigeria or any other international affairs. I have learnt not to criticise leadership. I know how difficult it is to lead. The new men in my country came up with me. They know my standards and now it is up to them.'

In Lagos in mid-March the Nigerian Government issued the transcript of an alleged conversation between Gowon and Dimka in London in which Gowon apparently told Dimka to get in touch with Bisalla on his return to Nigeria. A formal request for Gowon's return to Nigeria to face charges of complicity in the plot was delivered by Colonel Garba, Commissioner for Foreign Affairs, to Britain's Foreign Secretary (then James Callaghan) on 24 March. The British answer to the request was that it would 'study and consider the request carefully'. In Nigeria the mood against the plotters was strong. Following his talks in London with Mr Callaghan Colonel Garba said: 'During our discussion we were both anxious that the matter should be resolved in a manner that would not affect the relations between our two countries. I gained the impression that the British Government was particularly conscious of the need for this.'

It was not until the second week of May that a British reply to the

Nigerian request 'to facilitate General Gowon's return' was delivered in Lagos by the Minister of State for African Affairs, Mr Ted Rowlands, in which Britain said that extradition (though this had not been applied for) was a matter for the courts to decide and not a political decision so that the government could not pursue it. Two days after Rowlands left Lagos Colonel Dimka and six other plotters were executed by firing squad. In a nationwide broadcast General Obasanjo described the British refusal as 'an unfriendly act towards the Government and people of Nigeria'.

Three months after the assassination of Mohammed, the Obasanjo government was proceeding at speed with the new measures and reforms that had been started under Mohammed, with no obvious change of direction. Perhaps the most significant long-term result for Nigeria following the coup attempt was the fact that Obasanjo, a Yoruba, and the most senior man in the government after Mohammed, automatically stepped into the dead head of state's place: this marked a major advance in a country which has always been obliged to pay so much attention to a man's ethnic origins when considering him for high office.

Chapter two

Pre-coup politics

For a country that is run by the military Nigeria displays a surprising degree of continuing political activity all the time. The political ferment that was apparent in the months before the fall of Gowon gave a clue as to both why he fell and what the successor regime needed to tackle with all its attention to avoid a comparable fate, for it was the constant expression of what the people wanted and what most angered them that forced military action to change the military men at the top. The same thing could happen again.

Up to 1975 Nigeria had passed through three main phases since independence: the period of Westminster-style democracy that was to collapse in confusion; the civil war; and a subsequent half-decade of military rule which ended in the 1975 coup. Throughout this time, it could be argued, the country had not discovered what political system it wanted. It has yet to determine the kind of society it wants to be. Part of the problem appears to be an absence of any sense of social obligation—at least at the national level. People do not feel they owe as much to the state as they do to their family, tribe or region. There are elements of a dog-eat-dog society. Before October 1974 Gowon had announced that political activity could recommence on that date in preparation for a return to civilian rule, and as the time approached increasing thought was given to what the next step would be. For example, Allison Ayida, then Permanent Secretary for Finance, and later to become head of the Federal Civil Service, said 'the most sensitive potential threat to the continued existence of Nigeria will not come from the East. The next crisis is most likely to have its origins in basic economic issues—the equitable allocation and proper management of the increased disposable resources of the Federation.'[1] This reminder of the possible claims of some form of socialism at least pinpoints one eventual outcome in a country where capitalism all too easily gets its head. Certainly by the last year of the Gowon regime there were few ideas or ideological leads from the top.

The one thing, however, that really sparked off a smouldering political awareness throughout the country was the announcement by Gowon in his speech of 1 October 1974—the fourteenth anniversary of independence—that he and his military government did not, after all, intend to hand over political power to the civilians in 1976 and return to barracks. Four years earlier, and only nine months after the end of the civil war, Gowon had announced his nine-point programme which included the return to civilian rule. Then, in 1974, although at least parts of that programme had been achieved, he reneged on its most vital aspect for no obvious reason except, it seemed, that the military wanted to stay in power. Indeed, the main subject of political debate in Nigeria, certainly since the conclusion of the civil war, had been the return to civilian rule: when and in what manner. By 1973 and 1974 debate was gathering force and there was constant discussion of the form civilian rule should take. When the preliminary results of the 1973 census became known there was widespread disbelief in the south of the population figures shown. Many southerners had thought that the previous census had been rigged and now they believed that this new census had also been rigged. As a result confidence in the impartiality of the government was undermined. Frustration and growing ferment over the census was followed by the long drawn-out affair of Joseph Tarka, one of the Federal Commissioners,[2] against whom corruption was alleged. He eventually resigned, yet further allegations against Governor Gomwalk of the Benue Plateau State were categorically rejected by Gowon in person.

The problem about being a soldier is that you do not expect fierce discussion of your orders; by October 1974 Gowon and his military government had been subjected to at least a year's very fierce discussion—about the census, Tarka and Gomwalk—all extremely sensitive issues for any government, and no doubt these helped tip the balance. In his October 1 speech Gowon said

> . . . those who aspire to lead the nation on the return to civilian rule have not learnt any lesson from our past experiences. In spite of the existence of a state of emergency which has so far precluded political activity, there has already emerged such a high degree of sectional politicking, intemperate utterances and writings which were deliberately designed to whip up ill-feeling within the country to the benefit of the political aspirations of the few. There is no doubt that it would not take them long to return to the old cut-throat politics that once led this nation into serious crises.

In these circumstances, Gowon went on, 1976 was unrealistic and it would 'amount to a betrayal of trust to adhere rigidly to that target date.' There was to follow a period of political quiet or at least quiescence, not, however, for long, for in that speech Gowon also promised a change of state governors—by then already overdue—and this increasingly became a major talking point.

When politically oriented Nigerians—which means a large number of highly articulate people—cannot discuss one topic they turn to another. Having been obliged to drop the subject of an imminent return to civilian rule, they took up instead two other subjects: the promised change of state governors, and corruption in public life. Gowon played down 'witchhunting' for corruption on the grounds that rumour flourished too easily in Nigeria. Justice, however, needs to be seen to be done and this—too evidently—was not the case. Justifying his decision to go back on the promise of a return to civilian rule, Gowon said: 'I see myself as an honourable soldier statesman. I speak for the nation. I have no constituency, my constituency is the nation.'[3] Not long afterwards the nation—or at any rate a very effective portion of it—decided that he no longer spoke for it.

Nigeria's problems are liable to crystallise in terms of the relationship between its rich and poor. There are some extremely rich Nigerians, although the great bulk of the population is very poor and knows itself to be so while observing the extent of the wealth of the minority. It is a situation that cries out for political action. The growing question as Nigeria booms is who is to control the boom for whom? How much must development rest with external capital and imported foreign companies and how much, how quickly, can be brought under the control of Nigerians? Another continuing debate in Nigeria concerns the shortage of executive capacity which in itself is used as one of the justifications for partnership with foreign business. 'Indigenisation' is by no means established yet; much of the Nigerian economy remains in the control of non-Nigerian forces. Alongside these debates of the period 1973–1975 came the Udoji awards—the Udoji Report on the Civil Service was presented to the government in September 1974 (see Chapter 11). The subsequent 'udoji' scramble drew every sector of the economy into a wage spiral demand with long-term consequences for the country that have yet to be worked out.

Of all the debates during Gowon's last months that concerning more states was perhaps one of the most significant, though often not in the sense in which it was debated. The demand for more states was one for the recognition of the claims of groups as against the centre; a Nigeria of 19 states, as it became early in 1976, effectively strengthens the centre still more in relation to the states. The Nigeria of 12 states already meant that none had the pull to break the Federal Government on its own; 19 states must still further lessen such a possibility. In retrospect the greatest political achievement of the Gowon years may be seen as the establishment of a strong and workable central government against all the divisive pulls of the regions that have so consistently played their disruptive part in the story of Nigeria.

Underneath all the debates was the ever-present question of state power; the claims of one group as against another; the extent to which the Ibos had been able to return to the parts of the country they fled at the outbreak of the civil war; the balance of representation of the different groups in the government (for example, what was the background of the permanent secretaries)? Increasingly the centre was taking power—control of university and then primary education, for example—from the states so that part of the growing debate concerned the relevance of state governments. In the days of civilian rule the regions had had great power, and those who ran them were the political representatives of the people. By 1975 the states had little power and what they had was being cut down while those who ran them were appointed by the centre—although they also appeared to be immovable. Nor surprisingly, therefore, the argument about the replacement of governors generated heat. The creation of the states in 1967 was a crucial political act of immense significance for the country: the power of the states subsequently in relation to the centre a continuing theme of the nation's political advance. Only a military government could have created them out of the old regions in the first place; by 1975, however, they had become a major part of the country's structure and so the question of creating more formed a vital aspect of the political debate. Although the constitutional powers of the states remained comparable with those of the old regions the significant difference lay in the infinitely greater power of the centre because of its increased revenue control and allocation. The system of revenue allocation determines the power relationship between the two and a new system was adopted in April 1975.

The new system deprived the states of the direct proceedings from their export duties and excise duties on petroleum products, tobacco and spirits and decreed that these were all to be paid into the Distributable Pool Account (DPA). On the crucial issue of oil the government lowered greatly the percentage of oil revenues that goes to the producer states. As a result the size of the DPA at the Federal Government's disposal was considerably increased. Currently it consists of 80 per cent onshore oil rents and royalties (only 20 per cent as opposed to an earlier figure of 45 per cent going to the state of origin) while the 5 per cent royalties that formerly went to the Federal Government also then went into the DPA. In addition, 100 per cent of offshore oil rents and royalties that had been previously retained by the Federal Government were to go into the DPA as well as 35 per cent of all general import and excise duties (the balance going direct to the Federal Government) so that, from April 1975, the DPA became a most powerful instrument of central financial control. Up to 1975 the DPA had been divided among the states according to population. From April 1975, however, 50 per cent of the DPA was to be divided equally among the states; and 50 per cent according to population, the aim being to achieve as balanced an overall development as possible. The new financial division ensured that all states received a secure revenue for general and development purposes; and also, by abolishing the derivation principle of revenue, it gave greater controlling power to the centre—both in taking revenue away from the states (the oil money) and in reallocating it.

In the last months of the Gowon regime the press expressed frustration at a government that appeared to be increasingly negative; and called, at all levels, for greater participation of the people—in effect, a return to civilian rule. As the *Nigerian Herald* commented in July 1975: 'The perpetuation of a state of emergency tends to suggest that the people are being coerced into obedience to the government, and this impression does no good to the government. It is, therefore, in the best interest of the Federal Government, and indeed of the federation, that the Supreme Military Council reviews the whole issue of "state of emergency" in the country.' This call, in effect, was for a total revision of the then military-political set-up.

Nigeria's press is the liveliest in Africa. Less than three weeks before the coup that toppled Gowon in July 1975, the press was criticising the government on virtually all the major issues then bothering Nigerians: the question of changing the state governors; what the government intended to do about the census issue; whether or not new states were to be created. There were reminders that corruption was rampant and that the government had done nothing to eradicate it from public life. And the issue of a return to civilian rule was more and more openly debated despite the fact that the government had ruled out a return to it in 1976. There was also the telling and courageous complaint that 'The lion's share of the oil revenue still goes to maintaining the 250000 strong armed forces with no enemies but the Nigerian people who, after many rough encounters with the swaggering troops, no longer regard them as saviours.'[4] The paper also pointed out that despite arrests of journalists the press maintained a courageous and open opposition to the government.

The breadth of the criticisms offered to the government provide an excellent overall picture not only of the questions that most exercised the country at the time but also of the ways in which a government— stale by any political standards—was laying itself increasingly open to criticism. More and more that month—though whether with foresight or not is another matter—the press called for the army to reconsider its role and get out. On the fateful weekend when Gowon departed for Kampala one paper (*The Sunday Times*) speculated on nine years of military rule and how much of its programme the government had accomplished, clearly having Gowon's nine-point programme in mind. Sarcastically the paper suggested that when the military were well into their second decade of power the country might then begin to get some answers to its questions.

The issue of a return to civilian rule rightly dominates all political discussions. Debates upon the subject show high sophistication: they also show a lack of any startlingly new ideas and as much disagreement as Nigeria has ever had. The only thing the politically minded agree upon is that there should be a return to civilian rule; thereafter, questions of how, the form of government, the powers of states as opposed to the centre remain as divisive as ever. Back in 1973 Aminu Kano, then Commissioner for Health, said: 'Nigerians must be allowed to discuss quite openly, stoutly and without fear, the future of their country. Frank discussion on the country's future constitution is necessary and should begin now at all levels.' A year later debate focused attention upon whether the contradictory interests in the country were still so strong that they would overthrow any attempt at civilian government. Then came Gowon's speech of 1 October 1974, and the clamp-down on all political discussion, which did not last long. Despite the indefinite postponement, much of the public discussion kept pointedly to a return to civilian rule in 1976 as though it was going to happen anyway. One of the complications clearly seen by everybody (though not its answer) was whether the return to civilian rule should foster federal-national politics or state politics.

Speaking in mid-July 1975, Michael Ogon, a former Commissioner for Economic Development in the South Eastern State government, condemned the current cry for a return to civilian rule and instead called for a review of the constitution that would make it possible 'for local councils and state parliaments to be elected within one year with full powers to legislate for subjects within the competence of state governments.' He suggested that a stage by stage approach could lead to the withdrawal of the military by 1979. Many who took part in the debate made it clear that they feared any civilian administration following the military would face deep problems unless it had a well thought out constitution.

Other groups of individuals called upon Gowon to honour his pledge of 1 October 1970, and return the country to civilian rule by 1976 despite his 1974 retraction. The national president of the Social Reformers' Movement, Akin Omoboriowo, said 'with ports congestion, biting inflation and fuel shortage in an oil-rich nation, the Nigerian Army should re-examine their efforts and see whether they are in fact better substitutes for civilian politicians.'[5] An article in the *New Nigerian*,[6] ignoring Gowon's statement of October 1974, began:

> Now that the Nigerian public is approaching the year 1976, it is important that some form of programme has to be drawn to enable the country to have a smooth return to a civilian administration.

Thereafter followed practical suggestions as to how the handover could be accomplished. There was also plenty of comment and advice (which Nigerians are not slow to offer) in the letter columns of the popular press.

This weight of opinion that would not be silenced must have carried a clear enough warning to the Gowon regime that it had over-reached itself in attempting to prolong its life. Equally, public dissatisfaction with an apparently endless military commitment to rule must have had a powerful influence upon the new regime that took over on 29

July 1975. Indeed, the *Daily Times* of 30 July carried a deadpan piece suggesting ways in which a smooth return to civilian rule could be effected by 1 October 1976—without once mentioning that a coup had taken place the day before and a new set of military rulers had installed themselves. It was a nice technique. The point, no doubt, was taken by the new men.

The rising crescendo of calls—from past politicians, students, labour leaders, newspapers, educationists—for a return to civilian rule would not be stilled, and without doubt this was the major issue at the time of Gowon's fall. Two months later, on 1 October 1975, Mohammed was to announce his government's plans for a return to civilian rule—although not until 1979.

Other issues, closely related, were almost as important. They received the same kind of vociferous debate. One was the replacement or change of the state governors. It was to be a feature of the July coup to separate Gowon as Head of State from the misdemeanours of the governors. Before the coup, however, they were singled out for attack as a means of getting at the whole government, including the Head of State. Gowon's failure to change them despite repeated promises to do so gave rise to a number of speculations. One of these was that he could not change them and in a sense was their prisoner—and, certainly, there was a fair amount of truth in this. The *Daily Times* of 12 July said: 'The present governors have served this government for so many years and we now need fresh hands, fresh administration and new outlook in the scheme of things.' Perhaps it was the simple desire for new men as much as anything else that ensured a contining pressure to change the governors. Papers reviewed the possible reasons for delay in making the change: that the governors wanted to remain until after the Queen's visit (then scheduled for October) or until after the Black Arts Festival (then scheduled for November). The week before his fall Gowon, addressing a Regimental Sergeants-Major Convention in Lagos, was asked when he would replace the governors and replied that he would do so before the end of the year. It was instructive that by then soldiers were putting the question to the Head of State; by implication, however veiled, they were asking when Gowon himself would go. Ironically, one of the governors, David Bamigboye of Kwara State, announced that he had packed his bags ready to be reassigned at any time. And before that Major General Hassan Usman Katsina the Commissioner for Establishments, had said that even the Head of State did not know when the governors would go. At the time this remark was treated as a joke; in retrospect it appeared that he knew what he was talking about. The point at issue throughout— apart from particular criticisms of particular governors—was the power they enjoyed and their accountability, or lack of it. As the *Nigerian Tribune* said four days before the coup: 'No one compelled the Supreme Military Council to decide to change the governors; but, having taken the decision and having announced it from the highest possible pedestal, the Council is in honour bound to fulfil a promise so freely made to the nation.'

Another topic that received equal debate at this time was the question of whether to retain Lagos as the federal capital or move it elsewhere. Kaduna was widely canvassed as a possible site—certainly more geographically central than Lagos but inevitably raising fears of northern dominance, always a highly sensitive issue. Perhaps this debate could be described as slightly less political in an overt sense— yet only slightly so: plenty of excellent technical reasons were advanced for moving the capital from an overcrowded seaport but in fact nothing in Nigeria can escape a political connotation and whatever the possible justifications for moving the capital from Lagos the question of an alternative site—wherever that might be— brimmed with explosive political possibilities.

Then that July there erupted the extraordinary series of press attacks upon one Federal Commissioner, Edwin Clark, of Information. Mr Clark was unwary enough to make a statement on Radio Kaduna's weekly television programme 'Meeting Point' to the effect that the government had not returned the country to civilian rule because the old politicians had not learnt their lessons after the civil war. Thereafter the press unleashed a barrage of criticism upon the poor man, who in his capacity as Commissioner for Information had managed to upset the press corps generally anyway; they were certainly merciless in his pursuit after his weak defence of the government's action. He was fully reported in almost every paper; then his remarks were analysed at length. It was not only an occasion for an attack upon an individual who lacked charisma and popularity but also and more generally, an excuse to air a whole series of grievances against the regime at large. Some of the attacks were reasoned: thus the *Sunday Times*[7] first quoted his remark that there was no breed of politicians coming up and then went on to say that even if true that in itself should not be used as an excuse to delay a return to civilian rule. Thereafter the paper went on at length to discuss the possible political models the military might adopt in returning the country to civilian rule. In this case Clark's remark became the peg upon which to hang a familiar argument.

Naturally enough the regime attempted to defend itself in face of this gathering barrage of criticism, but it was hardly convincing. Most officials simply said, in effect, that the country was not ready for a return to civilian rule—and presumably they spoke to a common brief. The universities came in for a share of government rebuke for they too had been busy demanding change. The Secretary to the Kwara State Military Government advised universities to practise what they preach: 'If democracy is the model government which they advocate, and the students and the outside world are made to realise this, governmental activities in the universities should reflect practical features of democracy.'[8] Another defender of the regime, the President General of the United Labour Congress of Nigeria, Alhaji Yunusa Kaltungo, went so far as to call for the expulsion of all civilian commissioners from the government and their replacement by men from the armed forces. The civilian commissioners, he suggested, were not representing the people's interest; yet he too then called upon Gowon to ensure that military rule did not go beyond 1976. It was, indeed, a topsy-turvy debate.

The Benue Plateau State Commissioner for Information, Chia Surma, did not disguise the fact that the regime was a direct dictatorship and suggested that Nigerians should count their blessings after taking a critical view of the gigantic development brought about by the presence of the military in the political scene of Nigeria.[9]

This fierce debate in the weeks before Gowon's fall revealed many things: first, that no military regime in Nigeria can for long stifle political debate. Second, that the issues which concern the politically motivated are fundamental enough: who runs the country and how. Third, that any regime which attempts to put off civilian rule for too long is storing up trouble for itself. And fourth, and most disturbing, the absence of any obvious political ideology. All the talk was of a return to civilian rule, a change of men, the power of the centre as opposed to the states, the techniques of government. There was no comparable discussion of what sort of Nigeria, what kind of aims— such as socialism or capitalism the country was after. Such discussion was to take place when the panel on the new constitution had been established by the government of Murtala Mohammed which replaced Gowon's. Delivering a lecture on 'Teachers' Education and the Third National Development Plan' to an annual convention of the Advanced Teachers Colleges Students' Association, the deputy editor of the *Nigerian Observer*, Andy Akporugo, said that the nation should set itself a goal and follow it: 'It could be capitalism or socialism. What we need is an ideological orientation.'[10] This need for orientation appears all the more important in a society which has such obvious extremes of wealth and poverty and where, moreover, these are likely to become more pronounced during the present era, when vast wealth is accruing so rapidly to the nation and yet Nigeria remains predominantly a nation of have-nots.

As Chief Obafemi Awolowo (one of the old politicians) said in an address to Ife University as its Chancellor in October 1973: 'A situation such as we now have, under which (the) good things of life are assured to a small minority of Nigerians and almost totally denied to the vast majority of our countrymen is pregnant with unpredictable dangers for all of us, if allowed to continue for much longer.'[11] No politician—either military or civilian—has as yet come up with an answer to that.

Notes

1   Quoted in *African Development*, April 1974
2   Federal Commissioner: the title used under the military government for posts equivalent to Cabinet Ministers under civilian rule
3   In an interview with Bridget Bloom, *Financial Times*, 9 June 1975
4   *Nigerian Tribune*, 10 July 1975
5   *Daily Times*, 24 July 1975
6   *New Nigerian*, 24 July 1975
7   *Sunday Times*, 20 July 1975
8   *Nigerian Herald*, 16 July 1975
9   *Daily Times*, 26 July 1975
10   *Nigerian Observer*, 11 July 1975
11   See *Africa Contemporary Record*, 1973–1974, page B723

Chapter three

Gowon and his regime

Gowon's fall shook Africa: not because the end of his regime by coup was particularly different from any other—though it had special elements of its own—but because his well-known persona had come to be identified with the greatest black power on the continent. His fall, too, gained added significance since it took place when the continent's leaders were gathered in Kampala for the OAU Summit. What could happen in Nigeria, it was felt, could certainly happen elsewhere. Several other leaders hurried home early.

The most immediate and subsequently most persistently applied justification for the coup given by Mohammed and his new men was that indiscipline and indecision had developed in the government and had penetrated the ranks of the federal and state civil services so that the affairs of the country had been brought to a standstill. There was a good deal to support the charge which inevitably recoiled upon the leadership.

Soon after the coup General Gowon himself admitted that he knew he was going to fall some ten days earlier. He told the Nigerian press in Kampala: 'I did not act because I didn't want heads to roll', and he went on to say he preferred 'pleading guilty to the oft-repeated charge of weakness to being a murderer.'[1] It was a not untypical remark as he departed from his high office, retaining a marked degree of personal dignity, enhanced as always by his particular brand of charm. There was certainly a great deal of speculation at the time that he did know about the coup in advance and that the manner of his going had been worked out with his successor, though the truth or otherwise of this is unlikely to be made public for some time.

The coup took place on Tuesday 29 July 1975 when Gowon was in Kampala. After the news became known he retired to his hotel suite where, except for his one press conference, he remained until 1 August when he left for Lome, the capital of Togo where he was to remain for two weeks. Then he went to London to join his wife, Victoria, who had gone there on holiday on 25 July before Gowon left Nigeria. The British said he was welcome to stay; Gowon had said he wanted to go back to Nigeria at a future date when it was acceptable to the new regime for him to do so as a private citizen. Six weeks after the coup it was announced that Gowon was to become a student of politics at one of Britain's new universities, Warwick: there was the inevitable press photograph of the ex-General, ex-Head of State queuing with a tray in the students' cafeteria for his lunch and then he settled down to his course on politics. Nigeria in its own way, meanwhile, was digesting the Mohammed government.

Assessments of Gowon will be made for many years to come, for he presided over the affairs of Africa's largest state for nine crucial years of its history. Within forty-eight hours of his overthrow he himself admitted that those who accused him of being weak 'are probably right'[2] and he was to tell the Nigerian delegation in Kampala: 'A colleague once joked to me that I was Nigeria's prisoner number one because of the complicated process one got through before seeing me in Dodan Barracks.' In all the press comments upon the coup and the fall of Gowon, few of Nigeria's papers made outright attacks upon the General. They blamed him for weakness, for surrounding himself with the wrong people and then failing to discipline them, yet, again and again, they ended by saying that the General himself was a good man who had made errors—rather than anything else. In a post-coup situation, in any country that in itself is quite an epitaph to a fallen leader. As one newspaper put it: 'It is gladdening and highly mature of the new rulers for the way they have treated the fallen General Gowon. Whatever anyone may say General Gowon has some achievements creditable to his rule. The retirement of the General with full benefits by the new military rulers in appreciation of what he has done for the nation is indeed highly commendable.'[3] What seemed clear in the aftermath of the coup was that while many had a deep loyalty to Gowon they had very little time for much of his regime.

Gowon came to power after the interregnum following the disappearance of General Aguiyi-Ironsi who was murdered in the counter-coup of July 1966. At the time he said his coming to power was an interim measure and that in due course there would be a return to civilian rule. He was to introduce the division of the country into twelve states, preside over the civil war, rehabilitation and the great oil boom. But in 1974 he announced that, after all, the promise to return to civilian rule in 1976 had been premature and that the military would stay in power for the time being. This prompted Tai Solarin, one of Nigeria's best known and most pungent commentators, to write an article entitled 'The Beginning of the End'—prophetic enough of what was to come.

The main events of Gowon's regime can be enumerated easily enough: the creation of the states; the war; reconstruction and rehabilitation; indigenisation of the economy and the take-over of the oil industry; the abortive census of 1973; the announcement of Universal Primary Education (UPE); the launching of the giant Third Plan. In foreign affairs the first five years of the 1970s led Nigeria to assume a radical image on the African stage and culminated in the signing in Lagos of the Treaty of the Economic Organisation of West African States (ECOWAS) just two months before the coup. One comment on Gowon's exit, after an enumeration of the various stages of his nine-year reign, ended bitterly enough:

> And as the General bows out his exit, he would be remembered as a Nigerian who had the finest opportunity in recorded history, but who through indecision, inaction and idiosyncratic preoccupation made little use of that opportunity. And now that the stage has been cleared, everybody in the generalismo's operatic party taking his 'exit', may this nation never know another tomfoolery.[4]

More generous assessments, however, suggest that his downfall began in July 1974 over his indecision in the case of Joseph Tarka, the then Federal Commissioner for Communications, who was accused of corruption and later resigned. In the year that followed there was an almost total seizing up of affairs of state. Gowon's broken promise about restoring civilian rule; his failure to tackle the question of the creation of more states and reassign the state governors; rising inflation; the growing chaos at the ports and traffic congestion in Lagos; maldistribution of petrol round the country; the disorganisation surrounding the Black Arts Festival—it seemed that nothing could go right in Nigeria and that its leader could no longer tackle the problems properly.

Gowon's achievements, however, will stand high whatever the collapse at the end. He showed some able political judgements—as, for example, his release (although it had been ordered by Ironsi before his death but not carried out) of Chief Awolowo who had been imprisoned for treason in 1963 by the old civilian government. Gowon went to the airport to meet the popular Awolowo to tell him: 'We need you for the wealth of your experience.' His handling of the civil war must be open to endless debate, yet who would have handled it better—and how? More important was what has been called his three-R theory of reconstruction, rehabilitation and reintegration afterwards.[5] At the end of the war Gowon issued his nine-point programme and it is, perhaps, upon this that his later reputation as head of state must rest. His programme was to include: the reorganisation of the armed forces; the implementation of the Second National Development Plan; the eradication of corruption in the country's national life; the creation of more states; the preparation and adoption of a new constitution; the introduction of a new revenue allocation formula; the carrying out of a new national census; the organisation of genuinely national political parties; and the organisation of elections and subsequent installation of popular governments at both state and federal levels.

Of these nine points five got nowhere. Corruption surely got worse; the question of more states was ignored, as was the preparation of a new constitution; while the organisation of national political parties and elections for popular governments were set aside by Gowon in his 1 October 1974 speech. Of the rest: the census, perhaps not surprisingly in terms of Nigeria's history, was so fraught with explosive political possibilities that it was the first thing the Mohammed regime cancelled on coming to power. The Second Plan—one way and another—was partially fulfilled, the failures here being due mainly to lack of sufficient executive capacity. The army was supposedly reorganised, though not according to Gowon's successors. A new and on the whole sound system of revenue reallocation was introduced. But in terms of putting into operation a political programme it was hardly an exciting or successful record.

Possibly Gowon's biggest contribution over this five-year post-war period was his activity in foreign affairs. Here Nigeria was to take the lead in an African approach to negotiations with the EEC; in asserting African independence against European and especially French man-oeuvres in West Africa; in establishing ECOWAS; and, more generally, in giving Nigeria a new and progressive international image following the trauma of the civil war. The country was greatly helped in this by the new-found wealth that came from oil. Given the nature of politics—whether by a civilian or a military government—the record of the Gowon regime is reasonable: half achievements, half failures. Had Nigeria held democratic elections in 1975 Gowon would certainly have been voted out of power; he lost anyway, but to a new set of military men, and this was following a year when, at worst, almost everything went wrong, or, at best, simply stagnated.

It is one of the curiosities of his regime that Gowon had the ability to win respect for himself while his lieutenants were seen as increasingly corrupt; that at his fall his own passing should be regretted while that of his governors and principal supporters welcomed with relief. Throughout his nine years only one state governor—Brigadier Robert Adebayo of the West—was ever moved, and he was transferred. Indeed, one of the problems at the end was that the SMC included the twelve state governors who to all intents and purposes formed Gowon's cabinet: thus, whatever he might have wanted to do Gowon could hardly remove or change them without seriously jeopardising his own position. But from 1 October 1974 onwards there appeared a growing military arrogance as though the army ruled by right and could do as it pleased. And though for a short time after the October bombshell the press dropped the debate about a return to civilian rule, they were to resume it again with great force in 1975, and in the weeks preceding the July coup it appeared that a tidal wave of political pressures were being released which only dramatic action could contain. Then came the coup and Mohammed's subsequent promise of a return to civilian rule in 1979.

Perhaps the strongest criticism of Gowon was that when faced with increasingly complex and difficult problems he resorted to inaction rather than try to break deadlocks; he did not wish to be ruthless with previously appointed colleagues, so they stayed on long after they ought to have been sacked or at least transferred. His cautious approach was probably right for the civil war and the immediate aftermath with its essential humanitarian problem of rehabilitation. But then new approaches to development were needed. Although the nine-point programme looked good enough on paper, in practice it was not to be implemented (or only in part) while, towards the end of his period of rule, Gowon appeared increasingly reluctant to take firm action over an ever-widening range of subjects. This indecision was made worse by the behaviour of many of his lieutenants who acted more and more as though they were laws unto themselves—the more so when it was obvious that the Head of State would not (or could not) check them. Thus, some months before his fall, it was clear that Gowon's regime had reached stalemate. The problems piled up, the General was increasingly inaccessible, and nothing was done. The result was that when Mohammed and his men carried out their coup they did so at a time which gave them an enormous initial psychological advantage: everyone was ready for a change.

Notes

1   *The Sunday Times*, 10 August 1975
2   *New Nigerian*, 8 August 1975
3   *Nigerian Observer*, 14 August 1975
4   *The Sunday Times*, 3 August 1975
5   *The Sunday Times*, 10 August 1975

Chapter four

New government 1975

The government which took over from the Gowon regime after the 1975 coup certainly faced enough urgent problems to keep it busy and, for a time, merely announcing what it was going to do about these problems, rather than actually doing anything, constituted a programme. Top of the list was the question of a return to civilian rule: but replacement of governors, and then establishing how the new men should act, dealing with the problems of port congestion, petrol distribution and traffic chaos were more than sufficient to keep the government at full stretch. Then came the question of corruption. The new men—mostly high-ranking army officers—looked able enough, but this may have been due to their rank. In its early days Gowon's regime had become known as a corrective regime. What Nigerians asked themselves in August after the coup was whether the Mohammed regime was also to be a corrective regime—of the faults and sometimes simply the non-performance of their predecessors, or was it to be something more?

It is an interesting reflection upon the state of Nigerian political life at the time when Mohammed took over that two of the first and most welcome things that he did were negative: the cancellation of the 1973 census results, and the postponement of the Second World Black and African Festival of the Arts and Culture. There were immediate calls for a clean-up operation: a weeding-out of corrupt or deadwood officials from ministries and elsewhere, and soon enough it looked as though the new men were determined to tackle this delicate problem, too. Some problems, such as the decongestion of the ports, were not really difficult to solve, being largely a question of administration, although the results of successfully dealing with them were likely to be spectacular. But, always, the question came back to civilian rule and from the outset it was remembered what one of the principal new men—Brigadier Danjuma—had said the day before the coup: that the military had outstayed their welcome. To whom, it was asked, did he refer? The Gowon men who were to go the next day; or *all* the military?

Enough at least was announced in the first few days to elicit the optimistic remark from the newly appointed Kwara State Governor,

Ibrahim Taiwo, that the Mohammed take-over was the 'first Nigerian revolution'. He told a meeting of journalists at Government House: 'The revolution has its objectives and we must not fail in carrying out the objectives.' He did not elucidate what these were, although he added that the new regime would soon reveal its strategy.

The press was not slow to lecture the new government upon its duties and, as the *New Nigerian* pointed out: 'The Armed Forces by their very nature and profession do not represent the totality of the way of life of this society. A civil government on the other hand emerges from the guts of the society it rules. It is therefore illogical for the military, however intelligent and dedicated, to perpetuate its rule.'[1] The paper went on to make the point that a civilian elected government is directly accountable to the people it rules. Like the rest of the press, the *New Nigerian* was feeling its way with the new regime: writing as though it assumed they intended a return to civilian rule although at that early stage no one, in fact, knew anything of the sort.

Corruption is a dominant theme when the public life of Nigeria is under discussion and in one of his early statements to his newly formed Supreme Military Council Brigadier Mohammed said that his government would not condone the misuse or misappropriation of public funds at federal or state levels. He said the 'timely intervention' of the new regime had provided the country with another opportunity to start again the task of rebuilding the nation.

The SMC early appointed the members of the Federal Executive Council and allocated ministerial responsibilities: the council was made up of 14 military and police personnel and 11 civilians (see Appendix 2). The new men undoubtedly gave the impression that they had the will to tackle the country's tasks as they took up their jobs. A point made by a number of Nigerian commentators and taken up by the new government was the need for a code of conduct for men in public affairs. Among the reasons Brigadier Mohammed had given for the change of government were insensitivity to the yearnings of the people, lack of consultation, indecision and indiscipline by the former leadership. He now called for sacrifice and self-discipline at all levels of Nigerian society. Both the justification for the coup and the call for discipline were to be expected of a new regime; more to the point, however, would be the measures the Mohammed government actually put into operation. In its decline the Gowon government patently failed to give the nation a sense of direction; at the same time too many of its leaders were behaving too obviously like private potentates responsible to no one, least of all to the people.

The new leadership, it was suggested,[2] could only avoid the same pitfalls if it took immediate measures to establish the basis of disciplined and committed service by eliminating the ways private interests intruded into public policy. In effect, this meant the establishment of a code of conduct for the leadership—and the means of enforcing it. Here is a question central to much political discussion and thought in Nigeria: how, in a society that is moving at great speed, can a code of public conduct be established that is enforceable because generally accepted, when at the same time many aspects can be seen of a race for power and wealth? By any standards this is an exceptionally difficult proposition. Various conditions are required and were suggested at the time of the change: for example, that leaders—the SMC, governors, commissioners, permanent secretaries and others— should declare their assets and liabilities and those of their families; that while in office they should not also take part in business; that they should be forbidden to own more than two houses or plots; and forbidden to own a bank account or property outside the country. And so on. A national body would have to be set up to ensure the code is obeyed. There were plenty of other suggestions, some less obvious, others of the prurient type that are always made and seldom adopted. The point at issue, however, was fundamental enough: the leadership had to set the example and that until that was seen to have happened it was useless to talk of corruption in Nigerian society as though it could be eliminated by fiat of the government. Some of these demands which came with the new regime were accompanied by equally strong ones for investigation into the affairs of the men just ousted from office. This presented considerable difficulty for the new government in the extent to which such an investigation was justified and the degree to which this could degenerate into a witch hunt. Before the year was out a very substantial investigation into corruption and other abuses of office was to affect several thousands of Nigerians (see below pp. 32–33). One of the most persistent demands at the time was for the leadership to be accessible to the people: in other words, a demand for democratic procedures. Politicians who need to seek re-election every few years must be accessible to their voters in ways that soldiers can ignore. In its own way the discussion, once more, was back indirectly to the issue of a return to civilian rule.

In the first days of the new regime there was no lack of expressed support by a wide variety of individuals and organisations. Equally, people waited to see what the first actions would be—as opposed to early statements of aims. There was, in fact, one incident that did not reassure: it appealed in part yet at the same time it was frightening. Soldiers in Lagos launched an aggressive battle against the hoarding of consumer goods, inflation of market prices and transport fares. They raided market places, drinking houses, bus stops and motor parks, meting out instant justice to profiteers, seizing and auctioning goods sold above controlled prices. They roughed up suburban and minibus drivers who had been imposing a flat rate of 10 kobo for a trip. In Apapa the week after the coup they auctioned large quantities of gari and rice at one naira a tin and milk at 5 kobo. They drastically reduced prices for beer, soft drinks, yams and fowls. When butchers refused to bring down their prices the soldiers took over their stalls and sold the meat at reduced prices for them. One result of such action in and around Lagos was that night clubs and beer parlours closed early to avoid action by the military men. This, however, was not the way to enforce new laws—clearly the troops would not have acted this way without sanction from above—and such tactics were soon dropped.

Meanwhile the new governors had taken up their posts in the twelve states and all—obviously briefed with considerable care as to their conduct—made extraordinarily similar pronouncements about being fair and firm, not standing for corruption, respecting the traditional rulers, taking advice and not tolerating interference from members of the past regime. The new commissioners were appointed and got down to their tasks. Within two or three weeks of the coup the structure of government became clear. The SMC was the highest governing body while the Federal Executive Council had ministerial responsibility for the execution of policy. A new departure was the establishment of a Council of States as a forum for deliberations on matters affecting the states to which every state was to send representatives headed by the military governors.

A major innovation was the fact that the governors were not members of the SMC and that they had no direct access to the Head of State but were responsible to the Chief of Staff Supreme Headquarters, Brigadier Obasanjo. This emphasised the military nature of their posting and gave them far less power at the centre than their predecessors had had. The danger was that the arrangement put a great deal of power in the hands of the Chief of Staff, Supreme Headquarters, for, as the *Nigerian Observer* said: 'Our fear in this arrangement is that if the Chief of Staff Supreme Headquarters got it wrong, he could very easily send the Head of State on a holiday and assume the role of a 'super-governor', which more appropriately is the other calling of the Commander-in-Chief.'[3] Then there was the problem that some members of the SMC were also members of the Federal Executive Council. The functions of the Council of States were far from clear and there was at least the impression that it represented a sort of consolation prize for governors who were no longer to belong to the SMC.

The new regime soon got to grips with urgent problems. Its first month was impressive. What people wanted to see tackled most were: the question of a return to civilian rule; corruption; the question of abandoned properties in the Rivers State; the abolition of private primary schools and a reduction of school fees generally. Suggestions as to programmes came forth fast enough. In sheer technical terms probably the most urgent problem to be dealt with was that of Lagos and Apapa port congestion, and then that of petrol distribution. Goodwill and relief were perhaps equally mixed as the new government moved into action: otherwise people wanted to wait and see. The

General Officer commanding the Third Infantry Division, Brigadier Emmanuel Abisoye, said early in August that the new government had a programme for the return to civilian rule which would shortly be made known to the public, and this was to remain the key to public attitudes until Brigadier Mohammed set the date as 1979 in his speech of 1 October. A committee was set up under the chairmanship of Mr Justice Aguda of the Ibadan High Court to look at possibilities for a new site for the federal capital and report by 31 December 1975.

The government's next step was to release all military and security detainees. Such moves are more or less standard practice with new regimes, but the bigger question remained to be tackled: when would the detention laws be reviewed? The government retained the state of emergency and the detention laws, but most people would like to see a return to a situation where in all respects at all times all men are subject to the law.

In mid-August an anti-inflation task force was set up to examine the current inflationary tendencies in the economy of the nation and identify their causes, and in that context to review the fiscal, monetary and other anti-inflationary measures being pursued, and finally to recommend (bearing in mind the economic and social objectives of the country) short- and long-term policies and measures that would effectively contain inflationary pressures in the national economy. At the same time Brigadier Mohammed curtailed the practice which had grown up under the previous regime whereby permanent secretaries attended Executive Council meetings. He endorsed the Third Plan which the regime accepted in full as a target. In the middle of August the government announced measures to overcome the cement shortages: it took over entire cement consignments awaiting offloading in the ports and established a controlled price. As it happened the new regime had exactly two months (from the coup to 1 October—Nigeria's fifteenth anniversary of independence) to implement some of its most important immediate measures before Brigadier Mohammed announced plans for a return to civilian rule.

Reflection upon the merits and faults of the Gowon regime became an inevitable pastime in the weeks that followed his fall. These reflections contained much to instruct his successors. As one paper put it: before Gowon came to power there was widespread corruption in the country but 'During his regime, its density may have increased so much so that the general had reason to say "We've never had it so bad".'[4] When the press had taken up this and other issues under Gowon they had been threatened and intimidated. In other words, people said that Gowon had to take the blame for what went on under his name. The implications were clear enough for the new men.

The problem of running a country the size and complexity of Nigeria must always be formidable. In a post-coup situation when a steady demand for change—or at least action—was building up into a crescendo the need for the government to prove itself was great indeed. Massively affected by inflation, attempting to mount one of the greatest ever development plans, spread the effects of oil wealth, decongest the ports, get even distribution of petrol, decide whether to move the federal capital and whether to create more states, start a breakthrough in the agricultural revolution, deal with new in-dustrialisation and transform Nigeria into a socially conscious state in terms of welfare, the government faced no kind of sinecure. Above all this was the demand and need to move back towards civilian rule.

There was no difficulty naming the country's problems: these everyone could agree upon even if there were different ideas about priority. Most people wanted a speedy return to civilian rule. But then came the difficulties. What kind of civilian rule should it be? What kind of constitution should it have? What sort of society was Nigeria to develop into? There were calls for greater work. As one paper put it: 'There is only one thing which Nigerians know how to do best—enjoy themselves '[5]

As early as 10 August one paper in demanding that the new government kept 1976 as the date for a return to civilian rule said: 'In the fourth place, the success of the coup of July 29, 1975, makes it quite clear that other coups can happen.'[6] There was clearly a need for self-examination. As the new military governor of the South-Eastern State, Lieutenant-Colonel Paul Ufuoma Omu said:

> I will expect everyone to make a careful and critical self-examination of himself to ascertain in what ways he had helped to accelerate the moral decadence of our society in the recent past. You certainly cannot plead utter innocence and there is no doubt whatsoever that you have contributed in one way or the other to the ills that continue to plague our society.[7]

It is one thing, however, to diagnose ills; it is something quite different to prescribe the cure. Debate continued in the weeks following the coup, while everyone waited to learn the intentions of the Mohammed regime.

In his address to the nation to mark Nigeria's 15th independence anniversary on 1 October, the Head of State, Brigadier Mohammed, declared that the country's military rulers would hand over power to a democratically elected government of the people on 1 October, 1979. He said that the military leadership did not intend to stay in office 'a day longer than necessary, and certainly not beyond this date.'

Politics is not an exact science and to treat it with too much neatness, as though political behaviour can be planned, may turn out to be the great weakness of the timetable announced by Mohammed. Once a timetable is set politicians are bound to become active no matter what they are told is permissible at any given stage in the

timetable. In the period up to 1979, therefore, the greatest requirement of the regime is likely to be flexibility as excitement mounts and
attempts at growing 'participation' in the political rejuvenation
process run ahead of the announced schedule.

Mohammed then spelt out the details of a five stage-programme.
First, the issue of the states had to be determined. This was entirely
logical: if Nigeria's twelve states were to be redefined into 14, 17 or
more it could only lead to chaos if that process were still under way
when the next part of the programme was started. The aim was to
complete the preliminary steps for the establishment of new states by
April 1976 and thereafter set them up if that was the decision.
Meanwhile a drafting committee was given until September 1976 to
complete the first draft of a new constitution. Stage two was designed
to provide time for the new states to settle down while, at the same
time, the whole Federation was to embark upon an extensive
reorganisation of local government. There were to be elections 'at local
government level of individual merit without party politics. Arising
from this, there will then be a Constituent Assembly partly elected and
partly nominated.' The purpose of this Assembly was to draft the new
constitution after which it was to be dissolved. This second stage was to
last until 1978. Stage three was scheduled to start in October 1978 when
the ban on political activities was to be lifted and parties could be
formed in preparation for stages four and five to consist of elections to
the state legislatures and finally to the new Federal Government.

The biggest criticism that could be levelled at this programme was
the soldierly ignorance it displayed of political behaviour. Thus the
most vital part of all—the coming back into the open of democratic
politics—was telescoped into the last year of a four-year process.
Politically active Nigerians, anxious for a return to democratic
practices, argued that four years was too long to wait especially as
political activity could gather momentum only in the last year.
Further, in 1975, after nine years of military rule, a large number of
young Nigerians had no experience of the political process whatsoever,
so that there were very strong arguments indeed for allowing political
activity to start again earlier than 1978. Nonetheless the regime had
made plain its intentions and the country had a new target to work
towards.

The attack on corruption and abuse of office produced a major
purge in the months following the coup. Immediately there were a
number of sackings and retirements—of governors and top military
personnel. Then the government turned its attention in very much
greater detail to the whole civil service—both federal and state. As the
Sunday Times said towards the end of the purge:

Corruption, indiscipline and needless arrogance not only abound in
the Nigerian civil service; it has become an abode for mediocrity,

laziness, apathy, avoidable narrow-mindedness, nepotism, favour-
itism and tribalism on a stupendous and incredible scale.[8]

By November 21 when the purge came to an end an estimated
10 000 had lost their jobs. The dismissals ranged over a wide variety of
jobs and often came to particular groups in dozens or more: 1 500
railway staff were reorganised out of their jobs; or 76 officials of East
Central State on a variety of charges that included inefficiency,
irresponsibility, gross misconduct, financial mismanagement and
abuse of office.[9] Fifteen hundred officials of Western State were
dismissed as 'dead wood'. Those who were dismissed could fall into one
of three categories: retirement with full benefits; termination of
appointment allowing a month's pay in lieu of notice; and dismissal
with no benefits at all. Much of the purge was clearly arbitrary,
although despite its scale there does not appear to have been too much
of a witch hunt. Further, there followed relatively few indictments or
prosecutions and clearly the consideration here was to 'clean house'
rather than create an embittered and—in the circumstances—sizable
group of highly disgruntled 'out-of-works' who might well be a source
of future discontent to the government. A variety of panels was created
to investigate, one of the first of which was an Assets Investigation
Panel. Other panels were created to look into specific scandals or
allegations of abuse such as the cement over-ordering scandal. The
panels were given wide briefs and the power to compel people to give
evidence. The government resisted the calls for stiff penalties and
many whose misdemeanours were obvious suffered no more than
dismissal. The new government's aim was not so much retribution as to
ensure that such misuse of position would be discouraged in future.
The Head of State regarded the process as corrective and checks were
designed to prevent the recurrence of such abuses. Most important of
these checks was the establishment of a permanent corrupt practices
bureau and a public complaints commission to investigate complaints
against public servants.[10]

By the end of 1975 the government of Murtala Mohammed had
certainly made an impact. Nigeria's first fifteen years of independence
had been traumatic enough. Now 1975 marked a turning point. As
1976 began Nigeria faced a bewildering variety of problems. It had
the money (from oil) and more skilled and trained people than any
other African country. It would need both for the tasks it faced.

Notes

1   *New Nigerian*, 4 August 1975
2   *New Nigerian*, 6 August 1975
3   *Nigerian Observer*, 18 August 1975

4   *Sunday Chronicle*, 10 August 1975
5   *Nigerian Herald*, 18 August 1975
6   *Sunday Times*, 10 August 1975
7   *Sunday Chronicle*, 10 August 1975
8   *Sunday Times*, 9 November 1975
9   See Patrick Gilkes, *African Development*, pp 24–25, for a detailed examination of
     the corruption purges
10   *Ibid.*

Chapter five

A period of transition

Nigeria in the mid-1970s was a state in transition. It had emerged from the post-colonial era of reliance upon the old metropolitan power though still having some colonial hang-ups. It had passed through a devastating civil war. It had discovered and begun to reap the benefits of vast oil resources. Now it was embarking, often with great uncertainty if superficial confidence, upon a new era in its history. In the key year of 1975 the mammoth Third Development Plan was launched; a bloodless coup toppled Gowon and brought in the Mohammed regime—with its October promise of a return to civilian rule in 1979. After 15 years of independence Nigeria was moving forward with increasing confidence in its position in Africa as a whole.

Nigeria is a highly complex state to run. By African standards it is quite remarkably free; there is no omnipresent military and criticism of the government is commonplace. Its problems stem partly from the sheer difficulty of holding together a state of so many diverse parts, and partly from the expectations of the people which—after half a generation of freedom—are still remarkably high. Oil has ensured that everyone wants and intends to share in the new wealth bonanza. Nigeria is on a different scale from the rest of Africa: with a population of 70 million-plus, huge oil resources and vast land potential it can be described as a multi-racial rather than multi-tribal society because of its enormous ethnic diversity. Altogether it has more than 140 tribes but the three dominant groups are the Hausa-Fulani, the Yoruba and the Ibo. Its geographical size—900.000 square kilometres—as well as its population and resources, and the large numbers (by African standards) of trained and experienced people available all ensure that Nigeria is in a commanding position on the continent. Properly developed and with a sound political system, Nigeria could provide decisive leadership for the continent as a whole, as well as consolidating a powerful West African regional organisation in ECOWAS. Thereafter, it might be able to give the OAU the sort of backing that would begin to make that body an effective organisation in world terms.

The country's problems of growth, however, are formidable. As a result of the oil boom, Nigeria has some similarity with a pools winner unsure of what to do with his winnings. The country's infrastructure is groaning under the strains it has so suddenly had to meet, while generally the society is attempting to change at too great speed for at least some institutions and people to be able to cope adequately. There are manpower restraints and shortfalls, endless problems of port congestion, poor communications and inefficiency. None of this should have been unexpected in the circumstances and none ought to be more than a passing irritation that has to be taken into account during a time of almost fevered change. Structural changes in the 1970s have included the process of participation in various other industries such as banking and the 'indigenisation' programme that has transferred some foreign business concerns—or parts of them—into Nigerian hands.

The country has been badly affected in the 1970s by world inflation (as well as its own arising out of the oil boom) and these in turn have been exacerbated still more by the Udoji awards and the subsequent round of wage demands that spread over the country (see Chapter 11).

A fairly typical newspaper headline in 1975 was: 'Milk becomes scarce as over 5000 litres wait at the port' and such delays and breakdowns in the efficient running of the country reflected as much as anything the booming conditions that Nigeria had, by then, to cope with. Telephones often do not work, electricity keeps being cut off, the water is turned off, streets can be reduced to chaos as a result of huge potholes left by the rains—potholes that may not be repaired for a month afterwards.

Many of the country's problems must be related to the question of population. Again and again this goes to the heart of Nigerian affairs—whether political or economic—and few events in the independent history of Nigeria have caused greater controversy than the two censuses of 1963 and 1973.

Over a ten-year period conflicting and irreconcilable figures have been returned for Nigeria: in 1953—31.5 million; in 1962—45.6 million or 54 million; in 1963—55.6 million (the figure that is currently taken as the working one for the country). Then in 1970 the UN Demographic Year Book gave Nigeria's population as 55 074 000.[1] The 1973 census figures were the subject of immediate controversy of a potentially lethal kind and Brigadier Mohammed made it one of his first actions after he came to power simply to cancel the results outright. At the start of 1974, for example, taking the 1963 census figures and assuming a 2.6 per cent annual growth rate the Nigerian population then stood at 72.2 million. Part of the problem with regard to the 1973 census was that it appeared to shift the population balance still further away from the south and to the north than had been shown in the 1963 census. Political fears of northern dominance were reinforced by the economic fact that the revenue allocations to states are based upon population. Nonetheless, the provisional total population figure for the country according to the

1973 census was 79 758 969, making Nigeria eighth in rank in the world.

Complications surrounding the population question are a key to many other things in Nigeria. Nigerian political loyalties, for example, are largely those of family and tribal grouping and since political power goes with numbers the census automatically becomes an instrument of politics and not, as elsewhere, no more than an instrument of statistical record to assist in general administration. Therein lies the problem. The 1962 figures were cancelled because of the controversy that surrounded them. The 1963 figures, it was widely believed in the south, had been inflated in the north to assist the Northern People's Congress. The 1973 census was carried out with the assistance of more than 150 000 of Nigeria's 220 000 soldiers while the rest were placed on general alert for the census period which lasted a week. There were 120 000 enumerators, each accompanied by a soldier. The results showed a phenomenal rise in the country's total population as well as in that of certain states (see Appendix 3). More important and part of the controversial nature of the result was the fact that it showed the six northern states (the former northern region) to have increased to 51.38 million from the 1963 figure of 29.80 million, while the other six states had only increased to 28.28 million from a figure of 25.86 million in 1963. These overall figures were more than enough to make the census invalid in southern eyes. The southern six states had hardly increased their numbers at all, the northern six had very nearly doubled theirs! Not only does the size of an individual state's population govern the amount of revenue it receives from central funds, it is also likely to govern the proportion of its representation in the central assembly or legislature when a return to civilian rule takes place. Following the July 1975 coup and Mohammed's immediate cancellation of the 1973 census figures Nigeria returned for practical purposes to calculations based upon the 1963 figures.

Another key to Nigeria is found in the army. The civil war meant that a small-scale colonial style army was turned into one of the largest in Africa (indeed, in the world). Its officers and men emerged from the civil war with a sense of battle competence that gave them assurance in the post-war years. The views of the officers and men of this huge army form an important factor in determining the future of the country. Only Egypt and South Africa on the continent have larger armed forces than Nigeria, and by 1975 there was guarded but growing talk of the possibility that Nigeria could use her forces outside her own borders: should this happen it would almost certainly be in a conflict in southern Africa. Defence forms the biggest item of recurrent expenditure, amounting to ₦309 million in 1973–74, although that was still only 40 per cent of the figure spent on defence in South Africa. A quote from an army officer gives an indication of the elitist attitude of the army: to the suggestion, made in 1971, that the army should be deployed to produce more food, he replied: 'The army is an elite force for the defence of the fatherland against internal disorder and external aggression and not a labour gang; if we farm, what will the farmers do?'[2]

Throughout the 1970s, following the end of the war, a major problem has been that of containing—or attempting to contain—the level of military expenditure. Thus in 1970–71 military expenditure exceeded estimates by three times to over £100 million, as opposed to £32 million the previous year. In 1972—apart from allocations to the states—defence was the highest item of recurrent expenditure. Over 200 000 men in arms is a heavy load for any country to carry. One of the problems in the period 1970–1975 was that the huge wartime army had not been provided with the standard of accommodation required for a peacetime force and during that time there was no question of reducing its size. Vast sums, therefore, had to be found for providing barracks. Meanwhile, the policy was not to demobilise men until they had been trained in a trade or craft and there was a job for them to go to—and this simply did not happen. There were fears of troubles if too many soldiers were to be demobilised. A total of over 200 000 men made Nigeria's the ninth largest standing army in the world.

In the post-war years every major Nigerian city has had at least a battalion stationed in or near it and this presence at each centre of population has meant, of course, that, provided the army acts as one, it is in a position to countrol the country. The army is not too overtly in evidence, though from time to time incidents involving troops or arrogance and bullying have polarised civilians and soldiers. Yet, considering the size of the army and the way in which it was expanded during the civil war, it has remained, on the whole, a remarkably well behaved one. Road blocks at the entrances to towns, soldiers stopping and searching vehicles and generally carrying out 'police' roles have meant that the people have become suspicious and sometimes afraid of soldiers who in turn have become arrogant. It is not good for any country to give too much power to its soldiers for potentially they have too much anyway.

Views upon the Nigerian army vary widely. The bulk of the Nigerian people want the soldiers to be soldiers and leave them alone. They would prefer a return to civilian rule. Against this is the often expressed view of soldiers (advanced particularly by some expatriates) that they get things done. Then there are those of a dictatorial turn of mind (especially if their own positions happen to be secure) who argue that the army is a good thing for the country and that any return to civilian rule would be chaotic. These, however, appear to be a minority.

Certainly in the period just before the 1975 coup there was a growing feeling in Nigeria that the army was too arrogant and acted too much as it pleased, appearing to think it was only answerable to itself.

A crucial element in the army's power and a factor making demobilisation especially difficult for any government—military or not—is the soldiers' pay scale. In mid-1975 military pay scales were increased following the Udoji awards. Recruits and ordinary seamen in the army, navy and airforce were to receive ₦816 a year; army and air force captains and naval lieutenants were to get ₦5 510; majors and lieutenant commanders ₦5 960; colonels and naval captains ₦10 044; while brigadiers and commodores got ₦11 556. The increases were backdated to April 1974.[3] There was a different, somewhat lower scale, for officers in special branches—such as pharmacists, physiotherapists and short-service and concessional commissioned officers. Leaving aside the officers altogether, the bulk of the 200 000 soldiers at a minimum of ₦816 a year (and on substantiation a recruit's pay would increase to more than ₦1 100) are far better off than the great majority of the population. Unless on demobilisation they can be sure of as well paid a job coming their way—which for a large number of them is unlikely—these men have a clear vested interest to remain in the army. Further, the ripple effects of the army can be substantial, especially in the rural areas of the country. Thus in central Nigeria at Abuja, for example, where a brigade of 2 500 men is stationed (amounting to perhaps 10 000 people with their dependents) the effects upon the local community of all the extra pay to be spent can be very considerable indeed. In such an area the presence of the army means that food prices go up sharply and although this is hard for many of the local people it is good for the farmers from areas possibly as much as fifty kilometres' radius from the town.

Before the 1975 coup there was growing criticism that the army government which by then had lasted longer than any of its civilian predecessors was low key, had no ideology, did not try to 'sell' its policies to the people—not even the radical ones. In mid-July, 1975, the Chief of Staff Supreme Headquarters, Vice-Admiral A. Wey, stressed the need for discipline among the members of the armed forces. This call for discipline was echoed two weeks later by Colonel I. C. Ode at a passing-out parade at Calabar when he told cadets that a good soldier could only be identified by his behaviour in society. The army was remarkably disciplined throughout the coup. Afterwards soldiers took steps to cut some prices in Lagos and, later, the Acting Director of the Military Public Relations Corps, Major Adebayo Shitta, warned that the military authorities would deal ruthlessly with any soldier caught disturbing the commercial life of Lagos.

The handover to civilian rule, when the time comes in 1979, and if no reason is found for the military to continue holding onto power, may present the army with its greatest test. Before that time, however, the army has the difficult task, which it has already embarked upon, of reducing its size.

It was early in 1976 that the Nigerian Government announced its decision to reduce the size of the army from 200 000 to approximately 100 000. The intention also is to ensure that it becomes the best equipped and effective on the continent. Recognising the impossibility of handing over the task of cutting down the army to any civilian successor government, the Army Chief of Staff, General Danjuma, said: 'We would be setting a booby-trap for that government if we refused to face the problems of demobilisation squarely, and find solutions to it before the handover.' The central problem facing the government is to keep its general assurances that the men who are demobilised will not become unemployed. Some are to be absorbed by the police force; employers are to be asked to give preferential treatment to demobilised soldiers; the oldest soldiers will simply be retired; and some corrupt or 'deadwood' (an expressively useful word) soldiers will be dismissed. Even so, it seems unlikely that the economy will be able adequately to absorb all these 100 000 men, yet it is vital that the reductions are carried out: to cut down the huge annual expense, to provide Nigeria with an army commensurate with its needs and the likely calls upon it, and to ensure that the 100 000-man army then becomes the best and most efficient possible.

As 1976 advanced and détente in southern Africa collapsed, Nigeria emerged as the leader of a new tough line towards South Africa and the possibility grew appreciably that at some time in the not too distant future units of the army might be called upon for service in southern Africa, something that would have seemed remote a year earlier.

Meanwhile the air force, mainly equipped with Soviet Mig 15s and Mig 17s, is being trained by the Russians. The Nigerian navy is still a nominal force. The government is concentrating upon re-equipping and modernising the army to make it the best fighting force on the continent.

The army's greatest achievement in power since the civil war has been in rehabilitation: this is probably a twentieth-century record. Only a handful of leaders were still in prison five years later, many soldiers were active in civilian life, some Biafran soldiers had remained in the army, there were no trials and ex-Biafrans were free to do as they pleased.

A third key to modern Nigeria must be sought in the working-out of the dilemma of centralism versus the regionalism of the states. It was the generally admitted weakness of the pre-civil war Nigeria that its centre was far too weak and the regions too strong. That system collapsed in the chaos of the civil war. The division of Nigeria into 12 states of roughly equal size in 1967 meant a reversal of the relationship between centre and regions. None of the 12 on its own was strong enough effectively to defy the centre—though the civil war had to be fought to prove the fact—and from that point onwards the central government steadily became more and more powerful, partly because no real leadership was ever allowed to emerge in the states. Individually the states were too small to become power centres opposed to the Federal Government and so could be controlled from a federal centre. With the creation of more states this will become even more the case in the future. On the other hand, there are those who have detected distinct groupings of the states: the northern states acting as a bloc, the oil states as another, and the western Yoruba-dominated states as a third.

In general terms the system of states came to be accepted and worked remarkably quickly and with success. By 1973 talk of rehabilitation since the war was largely dropped (not though many problems remained) but the eastern states were moving remarkably fast to catch up. The East Central State, which was the heart of Iboland (and Biafra), had 180 000 disadvantaged people and wide unemployment, the highest density of population in the country and great pressure on the land to contend with; yet, by July 1973 it had 1.3 million children in primary schools and 100 000 in post-primary institutions which represented a 60 per cent increase over pre-war figures. This was in the state most affected by the war. Comparable growth figures existed for the others.

The power of the governor—a military appointment and almost always a military man—has meant that everything revolved round him so that few would take independent initiatives. Instead officials wait for him to act and unfortunately, all too often, this can mean that little gets done. Another problem of the system has been deliberate state overspending. Before the 1975 coup this was a speciality of the Rivers State, based partly upon the psychology which argued that since the state was providing a large proportion of the oil wealth for the whole country it was both unrealistic and unfair to ask it to curtail its spending. When it did overspend Lagos felt obliged to meet the bill. The oil states, indeed, resent seeing their wealth taken for use in other parts of the country. On the other hand the Federal Military Government has sometimes deliberately held back funds from the states as a weapon of control. In one sense at least the civil war was about oil. In the mid-1970s—just before the July coup—the state governments just ticked along. A lot in fact was done, yet the day-to-day administration was, on the whole, of a low level. The states, it has to be remembered, possess all the factors of nation states—language, religion, customs and past histories (of the general areas) which can so easily lend themselves to divisive nationalistic tendencies—and with the creation of more states to represent more accurately ethnic divisions in Nigeria, this will become still more true in the future. The rise of populations in the northern states recorded in the 1973 census was so high as to seem both incredible and frightening to the south, hence Mohammed's decision to cancel the results after the coup which brought him to power. At that point he needed to mollify the south and show that he was unbiased, although himself a northerner. Following the coup no governors of southern origin were appointed to the northern states, although a western Yoruba was appointed to Kwara.

The behaviour of the northern states seemed likely to provide another key to the future stability of the country. The governors of the six (before the new division) northern states have always tended to vote together. There are four routes to the north: Lagos; Bonny/Warri; Port Harcourt; and Calabar, so that the north can be assured that it will not be cut off. Agriculture and rural development are the greatest boosts the north will get from the Third Plan and a most significant part of the plan will be the new producer price scheme since lack of incentive in the past has been a major drawback to higher production. Under the new price scheme, for example, benniseed is up to N264 a tonne (old price N176); soya beans are up a third, groundnuts are up N85 a tonne and so on.

When the coup took place the new state governors—all military men—were made directly responsible to the Chief of Staff Supreme Headquarters. They quickly took up their posts and there followed a great scurry of activity as they settled in. In an open letter addressed to the new governors one correspondent ironically and succinctly detailed those areas in which they should be active and where, he suggested, their predecessors had failed. They should, he argued, avoid partiality to groups, fill in the potholes on the roads, meet the people and not rely upon what the civil servants told them, maintain cordial relations with the emirs, chiefs and natural rulers, avoid misuse of office, share out offices rather than heaping them all on a few close followers, not allow advisers and commissioners too much power and abolish pomp.[4]

The new government of Mohammed early established an Assets Investigation panel which looked into the assets of the twelve dismissed state governors as well as other Federal Commissioners. The investigation subsequently revealed that 'all the ex-military governors and the former Administrator of East Central State with the exception of two were found to have grossly abused their office and (to be) guilty of several irregular practices'. Illegally acquired property worth more than N10 million was confiscated while police and law officers were instructed to 'look into the criminal aspects of their activities with a view to taking necessary legal action, if need be.' The government's main concern when it dealt with the findings of the Assets Investigation panel was to lay down 'guidelines and new standards for the conduct of public officers'. The government did not try to victimise anyone and provided adequate opportunity for those under investigation to explain how they had come by their assets.

Although in economic terms the states represent little power when compared with the centre, yet, following the oil boom, the budgets of each of the six northern states were twice as large as the total budget for the whole northern region back in 1968. In the north in the 1970s, as much as half of state income was devoted to capital works (whereas the figure in the south was only about 30 per cent). Much of this was due to educational backwardness and the consequent need to build many more schools than in the south simply to catch up. Education, indeed, was taking between 20 and 25 per cent of total expenditure and shared first place with public works. Otherwise public health received amounts ranging between 6 and 16 per cent and agriculture an average of 15 per cent of expenditure.

In state terms, however, the power factor of money controlled by the Federal Government has become of key importance. This was clear in the 1972 budget figures for the North East State, for example, where out of a total budget of £17.9 million only £3.5 million came from state sources and £14.4 million came from the Federal Government. This very lopsided dependence upon the centre for funds gives the Federal Government great power. Control of oil is the key to that situation. In 1972 the federal petroleum profits tax alone yielded £166.3 million as opposed to £2.6 million in 1968. Leaping state expenditure was illustrated in the budget speech of the East Central State Administrator, Ukpabi Asika, in 1975: from a figure of just under N 100 million recorded in the 1974 75 estimates he gave a new estimate for the following year of ₦219 million, yet while the state would raise some ₦59 million internally the big increase was almost entirely due to the change in the basis of the allocation of oil revenues by the Federal Government. In this one state—admittedly the one most seriously damaged in the war—it is proposed to spend on capital development over the 1975–1980 period more than ₦724 million.

Oil remains the key to what is happening in present day Nigeria. Not unnaturally the oil states are unenthusiastic about sharing their wealth. In the former Mid-West State (now Bendel), with a population of 3.5 million, oil is the chief economic factor (this state has the most oil) though most oil is off-shore. Otherwise, palm oil consumption has gone up as a result of greater prosperity so that the export trade (against slumping world prices) has suffered. The Mid-West (Bendel) is the main rubber producer in Nigeria and also her main timber exporter, containing the Sapele plywood plant, Nigeria's biggest industrial establishment. There is a little cocoa and a few small industries—textiles, plastics, engineering.

In the East Central State (now Imo and Anambra), however, worst hit by the war and also an oil state, though oil here plays a lesser part in its economy, great strides have been made at diversification since the 1970s—or at least at restarting the old industries. Thus by 1975 a number of war-damaged industries were back in full production. These included: Independence Brewery at Umuahia; Modern Ceramics at Umuahia; Modern Shoe Industry at Owerri; Nigeria Construction and Furniture Company at Enugu; Aba Textile Mills at Aba; Textile Printers at Onitsha; Nigeria Cement Company at Nkalagu; and the Nigersteel Company at Emene. The government has also launched other new industries in its diversification efforts, including the 'PRODA' industries which involve high quality research and emphasis upon the use of local materials.[5]

The three oil producing states—Mid-West, East Central and Rivers—found in 1975 that they had to prune their development plans while the non-oil producing states could look forward to greater cash injections into their economies.[6] Oil revenue has become the greatest source of income for the states: in 1974, for example, of a total revenue of ₦110 million for Rivers State, ₦101 million came from oil and only ₦9 million from taxes and other sources. Then on 1 April 1975, the Federal Government surrendered its right to 5 per cent oil revenue. The producing states thereafter were to take no more than 20 per cent of the oil revenues while 80 per cent went to the distributable pool. The distribution, based upon population, shows the importance yet again of the census figures. Oil which boomed during and after the war made the Rivers State particularly wealthy; before that time the state, except for Port Harcourt and its industrial area, was a little known region of swamps and creeks with a substantial population however of 2.23 million; it was also the gateway to the dense populations beyond and the route to the north.

There are many problems of imbalance as between the states. In the north, for example, the greatest problem is that of manpower. Most professional people—certainly far too many for comfort—have to be imported. They include such categories as doctors, teachers, engineers. Moreover, the more these states develop or try to do so at speed the more professional people they need so that they have to import still more which is galling to them. Thus four of the six northern states (excluding Benue Plateau and Kwara) are still mainly dependent upon expatriates for many professional and teaching skills. Further, to take the case of the North East State (now Bauchi, Borno and Gongola states), while previously it had an income of ₦6 million by 1975 this had risen to ₦150 million but all coming from the central government so that in financial terms it felt itself to be totally dependent upon and therefore in a sense at the mercy of Lagos. That is not an easy position for a poor northern state and is an inevitable cause of resentment towards the south.

Some typical state problems that were most apparent in mid-1975 help give a flavour to the more general development difficulties of the country as a whole. In the North East State (now Bauchi, Borno and Gongola), for example, the unlikelihood of being able to construct sufficient classrooms in time for the implementation of UPE looked as though it would seriously impede that programme. Building materials were not to be obtained and their lack had hopelessly retarded the programme. Even when materials in small quantities did become available they could only be transported with difficulty to some of the remoter areas of the state. Thus, by August 1975, fewer than a quarter of the 8 000 classrooms needed if the state was to embark upon UPE in 1976 had actually been built. There was further major restraint in that finance voted for the construction programme was not getting through to the local authorities while some contractors had abandoned their jobs without refunding the money paid to them for the purpose. The state complained of lack of co-ordination of federal activities, disbursement of funds, supervision of building and the non-recruitment or supply of teachers. Construction work had not started on the 17 scheduled teachers' training colleges due to open in 1976 and the consultants appointed by the Federal Government to supervise all UPE activities in the state were in Lagos and did not even have an office in the state's capital of Maiduguri.[7] All this seemed a formidable enough indictment by one state of one branch of activity in its development programme.

In the North Central State (now Kaduna) recurrent expenditure jumped from ₦10 545 000 in 1968–69 to ₦43 186 510 in 1974–75, while capital expenditure over the same period jumped from ₦3 130 700 to ₦26 215 010. In aggregate terms over this period the economy grew at 6 per cent a year while the implementation of key projects in agriculture, health and industry had a major impact. In the field of agriculture one key development concerned the establishment of farm centres for research on crops, seed multiplication and distributions, and the sale of stock and fertiliser. New extension services have concentrated upon food production, the organisation of mixed farming and tractor hiring. Irrigation, a produce inspection division, the handling and storage of foods, a grain reserve, a veterinary division, livestock improvement, range management schemes, veterinary health services, forestry, game reserves and nurseries were all being adequately afforded for the first time. When the state was created in 1967 there were in the department of agriculture 16 senior and 53 intermediate and junior staff; by 1974 these figures had increased to 53 senior and 563 junior and intermediate staff.

Two other sets of the state's budgetary statistics help to give an idea of the vast expansion of activity taking place in the north, and of the problems (especially in terms of manpower) that such expansion must produce. Thus, for works and housing recurrent expenditure in 1968–69 stood at ₦1 704 230; by 1974–75 this had increased to ₦4 298 800. Capital expenditure over the same period went up from a very modest sum of ₦385 450 to ₦14 044 255. For education the comparable figures for the same period were: recurrent expenditure jumping from ₦2 879 900 to ₦13 650 070; and capital expenditure going from ₦1 168 250 to ₦8 513 565. The state's total finances changed from a 1968–69 recurrent figure of ₦11 835 240 to ₦42 978 575; and a capital expenditure of ₦3 042 530 to one of ₦42 587 955. Such huge leaps are formidable for any state to handle; for one that is desperately short of trained manpower and heavily dependent upon skills imported from outside—either expatriate or from other parts of Nigeria—this represents a tremendous development burden to carry

The scale of Nigeria's potential for development can be understood better by examining figures relating to another of its states—Kano. With a population of over seven million people Kano state is larger than a good number of African countries. Eighty per cent of its people depend upon the land for their livelihood. In the 1970–1974 Plan, for example, the state allocated ₦33 million in its capital budget to agriculture—which was 32 per cent of the total and a greater proportion than that in any other state. Kano is striving for balanced development: it has 150 manufacturing establishments. One of its groundnut oil mills is the largest in Africa and the second largest in the world. The state itself is large—16 630 square miles—and although it is mainly agricultural it is also highly urban-oriented: that is, some 3 000 000 of its people live within 50 miles of Kano city. The value of its agricultural crops stands at approximately ₦140 million, the most important being groundnuts, although production of these in recent years has been falling.[8] After groundnuts come cotton, sugar cane, tobacco, rice, fruit, vegetables and wheat. The state also runs an estimated 750 000 head of cattle which supply both local needs and meat for Lagos. It is one of the country's major agricultural states although its productivity at ₦20 an acre is very low compared with what it could be. Much marginal land, for instance, could be made fertile by irrigation. Extension work is needed to improve agricultural practices, which comes back to the question of available trained manpower resources. Kano could achieve an agricultural revolution with two major irrigation schemes currently under way: the Kano river and the Hadejia Valley Projects. Between them these will produce many thousands of irrigated acres of land and could enable Kano to supply all the country's wheat requirements. The state has a growing number of industries which include: perfumes and cosmetics; wood and wood furniture; textiles; food and vegetable oils; candles and soap; tiles and concrete blocks; suitcases and corrugated cartons; sweets and confectionery; brewing; plastics and allied industries; iron, steel and metal; tanneries and leather works. These and some other industries command a combined capital of ₦34 884 000 and a total force of employees of 25 087.[9]

The question of more states was at once taken up by the new government of Mohammed which appointed a panel to look into the matter. A year before the coup General Gowon had sparked off an avalanche of demands for more states with his reference to the subject in his speech of 1 October, 1974. The arguments concerning the merits of more states were under full debate in the months before the 1975 coup. The dangers of too many states were obvious enough: apart from fragmentation there would be the expense of, for example, 24 state administrations as well as the central government. A figure in the region of 18 seemed the most favoured and the new government settled for 19 early in 1976.

The panel established to look at the question of more states reported back at the end of 1975. By February 1976 the Mohammed government announced that seven new states were to be created, bringing the total to 19. General Mohammed said: 'The creation of states as far as this administration is concerned is a one-time operation and future agitation on this matter will not be tolerated.' Following the announcement of the new states, their governors were immediately appointed and ordered to report to their capitals. The head of the inquiry panel, Justice Irekefe, said that had he responded to all the demands for change there would have been 200 states. Clearly the decision must disappoint some people, yet on the whole the new states answer a number of criteria well: they do not fragment the country too much (19 is a reasonable administrative total); they are fairly balanced on population grounds (the widest gap being between the biggest, Kano, with approximately 6 million people and the smallest, Rivers, with approximately 1.5 million people); they appear to come as near as is politically possible of achievement to satisfying the most obvious local-ethnic-regional demands for statehood. The regional names have been dropped in favour of new names. Seven states remain unchanged: North Central (renamed Kaduna), Kano, Rivers, Mid-Western (renamed Bendel), South-Eastern (renamed Cross River), Kwara and Lagos (with capital resited at Ikeja). Western State was split into three: Ogun, Ondo and Oyo. East Central State was split into two: Imo and Anambra. North Western State was split into two: Niger and Sokoto. Benue Plateau State was split into two: Benue and Plateau. North Eastern State was split into three: Bauchi, Borno and Gongola. (See Appendix 4.)

Another question that Brigadier Mohammed's regime had to face at once was whether to retain Lagos as the federal capital. Lagos was not designed on the scale that oil prosperity and the booming development of a huge country of 70 million people requires of its capital. Whether it could be modernised so as to make this possible was very much an open question. Everything has been concentrated in Lagos. Its biggest drawback lay in its poor communications with the rest of the country:

A country of the size of Nigeria, 372 674 square miles, extending for almost 800 miles North–South and 450 miles East–West and not blessed with adequate and efficient transport and telecommunication networks, is too big to be toyed with from a badly-situated coastal capital city of Lagos. A more centrally located capital might afford the federal decision-makers and advisers opportunity to know or reach the country much more than is the case at present.[10]

This put the case for a move succinctly enough.

The problem was, of course, a political one: in which state, in what part of the country should the capital be? There was the added problem of vast overcrowding and congestion in Lagos which could only get worse in the capital of a country expanding as fast as Nigeria when the physical limitations placed upon expansion by the city's site were so absolute, because of its island situation. For example, the 1975 population of 1 500 000 is expected to have increased to 4 000 000 by 1985. Many objections to Lagos as the capital could be overcome: its basic fault was the lack of land for replanning the roads and buildings—there is only an estimated land use area of 2 500 square kilometres which is already choked up. On the other hand, the fact that Lagos is the commercial centre of the country as well as its principal port was a powerful argument for no change.

In the event the new government decided to move the capital away from Lagos. The site chosen was about 50 kilometres south of Abuja, a position north of the confluence of the Niger and Benue rivers and at a place that is outside 'the control of any of the major ethnic groups in the country'. Here 8000 square kilometres will become a federal territory in the central part of the country. The site satisfied the criteria of the panel of 'centrality, good and tolerable climate, land availability and use, adequate water supply, low population density, physical planning convenience, security and multi-access possibility. The move is expected to take from ten to fifteen years. Meanwhile the capital stays at Lagos which in any case will remain 'the nation's commercial capital and one of its nerve centres'—a certainty for the foreseeable future. Lagos will continue to receive special federal aid as will Port Harcourt and Kaduna, all three of which are to be designated 'special areas' under the new constitution. Construction of the new capital was expected to begin within four years of the decision–that is by 1980.

The political and development problems facing Nigeria are formidable. It is in the process—far from adequately worked out—of trying to decide to what extent it will become a welfare state. Its approach to education (the introduction of free primary schooling), health services and the provision of cheap housing are three examples of this. In terms of industrialisation it has hardly begun to emerge from being a rural society— despite oil. In terms of commerce it is still overwhelmingly in the grip of big expatriate concerns. In terms of any planning it is still and must remain for the foreseeable future an overwhelmingly rural society. Therein, indeed, lies its strength. For many Nigerians the one great permanence in their lives is the traditional set-up in their villages or the rural areas in which they live. Most fundamental of all at a time of such fast-moving change is the question of philosophy: what kind of society does Nigeria want to become? It has wealth; it has a suddenly realised influence and power on the continent it may well come to dominate; it is feeling a new assurance. What direction will Nigeria take?

Notes

1   *African Development*, March 1973
2   *African Development*, November 1971
3   *West Africa*, June 30 1975
4   *Sunday Times*, 10 August 1975
5   *African Development*, March 1975
6   *African Development*, May 1975
7   *New Nigerian*, 13 August 1975
8   *African Development*, August 1973
9   *Ibid.*
10 *Africa Magazine*, November 1972

Chapter six

Oil

Oil is rapidly changing the economic, political and social life of Nigeria. Perhaps for another thirty years—a short time in historical terms but long enough politically—it will provide the means of turning the potential of this huge African country into actuality of power and influence. In the mid-1970s oil was the basis of almost all political and economic calculations: total resources and the revenue they provide; further exploitation; the role Nigeria should adopt in OPEC and, more generally, towards the outside world of its customers; what line it should take towards the rest of Africa; and, above all, how it should use its oil wealth at home. All these were questions near the centre of political debate. In the period 1967 to 1971, covering the civil war, the growth rate for oil ran at 9 per cent per annum, and oil replaced agriculture as the state's chief revenue earner.

The history of Nigerian oil falls easily into three phases. The first phase was short: the period 1958–1961 (covering independence) when the still small industry, then completely controlled by BP-Shell, exported entirely to Britain and Holland. During the second period—1962 to 1969—there was substantial diversification and Nigerian oil was also sold increasingly to West Germany, France, Canada, the USA, Argentina and Ghana while Nigeria explored sales possibilities in the giant Japanese market. The third phase from 1970 onwards saw both a rapid expansion of sales to Japan and the emergence of the USA as the largest market.[1] By 1973 Western Europe, including Britain, was Nigeria's largest customer, taking 51 per cent. Twenty-seven per cent went to the USA, 13 per cent to the West Indies and 5 per cent to Japan. The next year the American figure had risen to 30 per cent. Nigeria also controls the West African market which is virtually its captive: Ghana, Benin, Niger, Togo and Chad. Emerging from this distribution pattern is the likelihood that economic events in the OECD area will act as major determinants of Nigerian oil policy.

In 1971 Nigeria moved into ninth place as a world oil producer when output reached 1.68 million barrels per day (bpd)—23 per cent up on 1970. At that time oil revenue accounted for more than 55 per cent of foreign exchange earnings. From then on oil became the mainstay of the economy. Oil revenue doubled in 1971 and in the 1971–1972 budget petroleum revenues accounted for £166.4 million out of a total of £191.4 million. The boom continued and by April 1972 production had reached 1.8 million bpd—300 000 bpd up on the previous April. By mid-1973 Nigeria was close to Libya in production terms. That March it was averaging 1 924 133 bpd of which Shell-BP accounted for 1 233 000 bpd and it was expected that more than 2.3 million bpd would be reached by the end of the year. Then, following the October, 1973, Middle East War, came the fourfold OPEC price rise which revolutionised the oil scene.

A summary of the Nigerian oil position in March 1974—a few months after the Yom Kippur War—showed the astonishing change that oil had produced for the economy. In 1957 it produced none; in 1972 84 million tonnes, which increased to 100 million tonnes in 1973 of which only 2 million tonnes was used for local consumption, the balance being exported. By 1974 Nigerian production represented 3.5 per cent of total world production (2 598.9 million tonnes) and 6.7 per cent of OPEC output (1 330 million tonnes)—OPEC accounting for 50 per cent of world output.

By November 1974 Nigeria was producing at the rate of 2.4 million bpd and its high-priced oil (based upon its low sulphur content and short haul to its principal western markets) was providing it with the greatest cash surpluses it had ever dreamed of—enough for it confidently to produce the most ambitious development plan ever to come out of Africa. Then the world recession forced cutbacks in its production and as 1975 progressed it returned to an output of 1.5 million bpd. In mid-1975 the government was obliged to agree to requests from oil companies such as Gulf Oil to cut down production since they simply could not find markets for their supplies of crude. The first quarter of the year showed a sharp cutback in all the major companies' production figures (see Appendix 5). What Nigeria realised in mid-1975 was that, unlike the main Arab producers, it had not piled up a cash reserve over the years to fall back upon; its plan calculations were based upon a high oil income and should this fail it was in trouble. By the end of 1974 Nigeria had become by far the largest oil producer in Africa, bypassing Libya which had cut back drastically that year to a total production of 77 million tonnes while Nigeria had increased its output to 112 million tonnes.

Oil has transformed the Nigerian economy. Oil revenue accounted for 3 per cent of government revenue in 1963; 17 per cent in 1967; 75 per cent in 1972. In 1970–1971 savings exceeded estimates by N£59.6 million; in 1971–1972 the figure had risen to N233.9 million but as the Federal Commissioner for Economic Development and Reconstruction, Professor Adebayo Adedeji, said: 'This increase in savings is not due to the abstinence of individual Nigerians. It is primarily due to the larger current revenue of the public sector, which is a reflection of increased receipts from the oil industry.' Oil was reflected in every aspect of the economy: thus of the 1971–1972 12 per cent growth rate, 5.7 per cent was due to oil while manufacturing accounted for only 1.2 per cent and agriculture only 2 per cent.[2] By 1974 oil was contributing 50 per cent of government revenue and 80 per cent of foreign exchange while Nigeria found itself in the enviable though often diplomatically difficult position of having suitors for its oil favours from all over the world. It was then supplying 5 per cent of western requirements and as a result of the price per barrel leaping in 1973 from $4.29 to $8.31 and then from January 1974 to $14.69 (though this peak was not to last) it found itself facing the prospect of an additional $5,000 million and more a year in the treasury. Though the oil boom initially made Nigerians euphoric, all too soon they had to face the fact that oil is a wasting asset.

Early in the 1970s the Nigerian Government decided upon state control of the oil industry. In 1970 the Federal Government announced that it would make no more concessions to private companies and that concessions surrendered to it were reserved for NNOC (Nigerian National Oil Corporation). The basis for the government's policy was the 1959 Petroleum Profits Tax Act which had established the principle of a 50-50 sharing of profits between the government and the companies. In 1967, however, the act was amended, raising the tax to 55 per cent. In 1972 an agreement with the companies gave the government a 55 per cent net profit from the oil rather than a 50-50 split with the companies.

Participation began in 1971 when Nigeria took a 35 per cent interest in the French company, SAFRAP (now ELF) and perhaps this first choice of a company was dictated by memories of French support for Biafra during the civil war. The agreement stipulated that when production reached 260,000 bpd the Federal Government would increase its participation by three stages to reach 50-50 when production was running at 400,000 bpd. The second group to enter a participation agreement with the government were Agip-Phillips early in 1972 with the government taking $33\frac{1}{3}$ per cent.

Already at the end of 1970 the government had obtained a 51 per cent share in all companies as far as off-shore licences were concerned. Such companies—Occidental, Diminex, a Japanese consortium— were to bear all costs of off-shore exploration until oil was found. Then, if such finds were commercial the government would bear 51 per cent of the expenses and participate in the profits as a majority partner. In June 1973 agreement was reached with the oil giant Shell-BP, the Federal Government taking 35 per cent in the company, its holding being scheduled to rise to 51 per cent by 1982. The Nigerian holding was to be administered by NNOC. Similar agreements were to follow with Gulf and Mobil. A year later the government changed its policy and decided to increase its stake in Shell-BP to 55 per cent: as the *Daily Times* of 18 June 1974, said, a 55 per cent share by the government would cost N-780 million while the net receipts of government would be not less than N-5 000 million. Thus, when the oil boom was at its height, Nigeria had already acquired 55 per cent in Shall-BP, Gulf, Mobil, Agip-Phillips and Elf as well as options for majority participation in all the other companies then only at the exploration stages of activity.

Government policy in part is a reaction to the big international companies. The oil internationals are in Nigeria—as they are everywhere else—to make money. In the bustling business atmosphere of Lagos, however, they represent themselves as taking part in development as though by this they mean anything other than making money out of Nigeria. Though Shell-BP is the biggest of the companies the others are large enough, certainly in overall terms of foreign business in Nigeria. Mobil work off-shore fields in the extreme south-east and handle the largest tankers at a mooring buoy 24 miles out to sea. The West German Diminex Company started drilling in 1975 as did the Japanese consortium of Teijiu/Teikoku/Mitsui while the NNOC planned to start its own drilling in 1975 too. In 1972 Phillip Asiodu, then Permanent Secretary of the Ministry of Mines and Power, said that the oil companies were purely extractive,

> investing locally the barest minimum necessary to find oil and take it out. They and their associates have been content to contract out all the services they can to overseas companies and to make their purchases from America and Western Europe, and have not tried in any way to encourage ancillary industrial development in this country.[3]

In 1970, for example, the companies spent £65 million locally on services but less than 10 per cent of this was on services provided by Nigerian-controlled companies or on materials manufactured locally with a high local content. Between April 1970 and March 1971 the oil companies spent N-£88 million on local payments and N-£100 million plus on goods and services abroad. Thus as the post-war oil boom got under way Nigeria still faced an increasingly unfavourable balance of payments and the upsurge in this from £54 million in 1969 to £93 million in 1971 and to £235.7 million in 1972 was caused almost entirely by transfers out of Nigeria by the oil sector—in 1971 the companies transferred out £106.2 million which almost exactly matched the increased invisible deficit. As the companies found profits and dividends blocked by government policy, so they transferred out capital.

Despite government decrees the large companies are exceptionally difficult to control. The decree of 1969 laid down that companies had to achieve a 75 per cent indigenisation rate by 1979—within ten years. In 1970, of Shell's twelve managers only one was a Nigerian and of technical and professional positions Shell-BP employed twice as many expatriates as Nigerians. The involvement of the big companies is also notoriously difficult to assess: estimates of that for Shell-BP range between £200 million and £600 million. Part of the difficulty of the relationship between government and the companies is that the government has no adequate knowledge upon which to base decisions in relation to company demands. Thus, in 1974, Gulf wanted to cut back its production because it had built up surpluses, because Nigerian costs were high and because it wanted to close down 'uneconomic wells'—and in all these cases it could be asked in relation to whom or what? The government allowed a 40 per cent cutback. The orientation of Nigeria's oil industry towards the western consumers was very apparent in 1975: the previous year Nigeria had moved into seventh place as a world producer and was then supplying one third of all American imports (900 000 bpd), and 16 per cent of British imports. As one of the chairmen of a leading company smugly commented: 'Nigerian policy has always been moderate, not dictated by political pressures.'[4]

A recurring problem in Nigeria during 1975 was the shortage of oil and petroleum products round the country. It was suggested that, at least in part, the shortages had been artificially created by the companies in reaction to government set prices as a demonstration of their power, although there were real shortages too. The companies were not prepared to accommodate the government when it attempted to cut back the market price of petrol. The world recession in 1975 made Nigeria far more concerned with a policy of oil conservation. Cutbacks in production—so it was claimed—were designed partly to keep the price up and partly for reasons of conservation. With these pressures developing upon the industry, the companies withdrew about 18 rigs from the Delta area in the first half of 1975 since it was less and less worth their while to explore if they could not also subsequently exploit—and government policies of conservation inhibited this, if they did not make it impossible.

Despite such problems the major companies claimed excellent general relations with the government. In mid-1975, for example, Shell-BP had some 200 expatriates altogether in its headquarters and the field and said it was indigenising fast: Shell (National) the distribution company was quite separate from the exploration and production sides. After the cutbacks the companies protested vigorously that cutting back is not the best way to get the most out of an oil field. If too little is taken out, pressure is lost; if too much then blockages can be caused; so the companies have to find a median rate of extraction. This sounds simple, yet it is a curiosity of the oil business that the companies always manage to come up with arguments that most suit their single aim, which is maximum extraction and profits. It is not in their interest to indulge in policies of conservation: that is for the government. What the companies want all the time—something that may well often be at variance with government needs—is maximum exploitation followed by maximum extraction. Government partnership with the companies still, effectively, leaves the companies to run the business and, as they argue, they are able to provide Nigeria with basic access to world markets. In the partnership operation the government is at a disadvantage in selling its share of the oil. The companies sell their share first and only afterwards 'does what it can to sell that of the government'.[5]

The ability of the big companies to come out on top was demonstrated in 1975 by Shell which became the junior partner with the government in its operation renamed National. Thereafter, as a subsidiary part of a government company, Shell in partnership with the government could buy up parts of other companies as a part of government policy so that in each case Shell was obtaining 45 per cent of whatever portion of a company the government-controlled National bought. The result was that Shell ended up with a larger share of the distribution market than it had started with. As a director said, it was 'time to share and useful to disinvest'.[6] It is often helpful to be the junior partner.

The Nigerian counterpart to the companies is NNOC. All areas not covered by existing oil mining leases, prospecting licences or exploration licences have been vested in NNOC while concession areas surrendered under laws regulating exploration of oil and gas are also vested in NNOC. NNOC is 'the vehicle by which the government is to intervene directly in the exploration for oil, production, refining, transportation etc:, either on its own or in collaboration with suitable partners of its own choice.[7] It holds the government's shares in the nine companies where agreements had been concluded in 1975. It is the vehicle for extending government ownership of the oil industry; eventually it is intended that Nigerians will run the entire industry. In 1975 all decisions about the industry, at least nominally, were in Nigerian hands. NNOC holds 55 per cent participation in the five main producing companies. However, while NNOC and government representatives have a majority in the management committee supervising investment, management and production policies of the companies, in practice the producing companies make the day-to-day decisions. NNOC also has the rights to areas not currently allocated— on land the companies have 95 per cent of the rights but in the coastal waters about a third of the off-shore concessions are vested in NNOC. In June 1975 NNOC 'began producing its first oil with the start of production from the Izombe area in the Oguta Division of the East Central State on June 5, this year and thus becomes the seventh oil producing company in Nigeria.'[8] Here NNOC was in partnership with Ashland Oil, NNOC having the majority share of the joint company.

Like many government corporations, NNOC runs the dangers

inherent in such a political position: critics suggest it is like an octopus while at the same time being subject to ministerial decisions so that, unlike the companies, it will not be run on competitive lines. As the *Nigerian Herald* sarcastically pointed out in July 1975:

> The view has been canvassed that given the right atmosphere, the NNOC ought to have done better than now when it is just entering into an agreement with a foreign private company before it can produce 10 000 barrels of crude oil per day, four clear years after its birth into an age when almost all the oil bearing areas of Nigeria have been identified.[9]

Both the inception of the giant Third Plan and the cutbacks as a result of world recession emphasised the finite nature of Nigeria's oil resources and so increased interest in the total known reserves as well as in policies of conservation. A conservative estimate in 1975 suggested that at prevailing consumption levels Nigeria had enough oil to last for between 15 and 20 years. Presenting a paper in mid-1975 to the eleventh annual Nigerian Mining, Geological and Metallurgical Society at Nsukka University entitled 'Nigerian Oil Reserves and some considerations for effective conservation practice', Mr Moses O Kragha warned that a prolongation of the recession could mean that the smaller oilfields became unexploitable. As costs went up and new and more attractive reserves were found elsewhere as well as new sources of energy being developed, it might simply become un-economic to bother about small fields. Estimating a known reserve at a production rate of .55 billion barrels a year this meant a lifespan of between 14.4 and 16.7 years. Mr Kragha, therefore, argued for efforts at developing new reserves. By 1975 Nigeria had reached the mature stage in oil production—that is, replenishments of reserves were not keeping pace with depletions. Advising that successful exploration should be maintained, Mr Kragha suggested that for some years operations had been declining due to the 'uncertainty prevailing between companies and OPEC member countries'. As a result of increased taxation and royalty burdens the operators were becoming extra-selective of where they operated. As the managing director of a Lagos firm of consultants, Mr Kragha sounded as though he was evolving a brief for the companies; nonetheless, he made some vital points, for the Nigerian oil business is certainly not the cheapest in terms of the conditions to be met in the Delta. Despite minimum predictions of lifespan for the oil reserves, however, oil pundits think it not unreasonable that—at a rate of extraction of 2 million bpd—another five to ten years worth of oil may be discovered in the south. This is apart from any further possibilities in the north that could revolutionise the whole Nigerian situation should they be realised. Oil has now been discovered in commercial quantities in both Chad and Niger and the oil-bearing faults in those two countries run down into

9 Oil has transformed the Nigerian economy and made possible the developments envisaged in the Third Plan

10 Oil is not Nigeria's only industry. The cement factory outside Enugu maintains all-out production; the coal industry has been recovering since the civil war

11 Among Nigeria's principal exports are palm oil products—mills like this one deal with ten tonnes of fruit a day—and tin, mined at Jos (below)

12 Since the civil war great strides forward have been made in older industries such as the brewery at Umuahia, while Federated Motor Industries at Apapa is one of the newer industries vital to Nigerian development

northern Nigeria as far as Sokoto and Kano. Should these contain substantial oil deposits, the Nigerian resource picture will be substantially altered.

Company objectives and government policy of conservation also directly contradict one another in the matter of exploration. It is of course easy enough to explore for more oil and the government encourages this; thereafter, however, it does not want new discoveries to be exploited (until it is ready for new supplies to come on tap) but immediate exploitation is precisely (and only) what the companies want. As the companies put it: why should they struggle against exploration difficulties in Nigeria if they can go to Mexico and face easier exploration there as well as being able to reap the subsequent benefits of exploitation? Exploration, nevertheless, goes on all the time, yet when new oil is found permission has to be obtained from the government for every subsequent step. The government wants to maximise exploration; unfortunately exploration in the Niger Delta is exceptionally difficult and so advanced seismic systems are used. The companies claim they need a reasonable margin of profit if they are to continue exploring: the question is, what constitutes reasonable.

Nigeria's oil policy has constantly to be related to its customers. The higher cost of Nigerian oil should in normal times (when there is no recession) be offset by two advantages: the shorter and, therefore, cheaper haul to its main markets of the EEC countries and North America; and the low sulphur content of its oil which, for example, makes it especially attractive to Japan because of that country's stringent anti-pollution laws. During 1975, however, these advantages were eroded because of the slump in the tanker business and the fact that when prices are high pollution policies tend to go by the board. Apart from its main EEC and US partners and Japan Nigeria is increasing its sales in West Africa.

Oil made possible the vast developments envisaged in the Third Development Plan for 1975–1980. An early edition of the plan assumed an oil production level of 3 million bpd by 1980: this, sensibly, was later deleted. Meanwhile, as the plan got under way, output for 1975–76 was down some 20 per cent. The plan assumed an expenditure of N-30 billion of which two thirds will be spent in the public sector and one third in the private sector. As the plan was being drawn up it was confidently assumed that oil would finance it; as the recession continued through 1975 and oil production and sales were severely curtailed, it was then suggested that some aspect of the plan might have to be cut back as well.

These, however, were temporary doubts: oil can certainly finance the plan in broad terms. Between 1972 and 1974 oil transformed the economy and changed a position of chronic deficits into one of almost unmanageable surpluses so that by the latter year the surplus on balance of payments had risen to the all-time high of N-3.1 billion. The country witnessed some very rapid growth rates during the Second Plan and between 1969/70 and 1973/74 GDP grew by an average of 17.5 per cent per annum. This picture was a distorted one, however, and some sectors of the economy decreased in their absolute share. For instance transport and communications fell from 3.4 to 2.8 per cent while agriculture dropped from 49 to 40 per cent. Oil dominated the Second Plan; it will dominate the Third Plan still more.

The problem Nigeria came increasingly to face was a great deal of growth but little real development so that the challenge for the government during the Third Plan will be to see that oil not only finances it but produces real development as well. The huge expenditures envisaged will be inflationary unless they are accompanied by a corresponding increase in productivity in all sectors of the economy — something a good deal more difficult to accomplish. In the long run when the oil assets have finally dwindled and been used up, the bedrock of the Nigerian economy will be its agriculture; it is, therefore, essential that this sector above all others should be developed during the Third Plan. As the extent of the plan's dependence upon oil became apparent to Nigerians, so too did the realisation of the expendable nature of the oil — as well as the possibility that alternatives might be found to replace it. (It is not forgotten, for example, that just as arrangements were completed to sell liquefied gas to Britain, gas was discovered in the North Sea and the Nigerian deal fell through.) There are other comparable possibilities that could occur on the oil scene over the next ten years.

The Third Plan represents the first major effort at maximising the oil resources for the benefit of the whole country's development. Just as important are the long-term plans for the oil industry. In 1970 the Second Plan stated:

> Nigeria is presently so overwhelmed by her crude oil resources and the foreign exchange earnings resulting that it is often forgotten that oil is an expendable resource, and that the more it is exploited the less there is for use in the future.

By 1975 conservation had become far more a realistic part of Nigerian policy and yet the suspicion remained that in a sense this was a result of *force majeure*: conservation became fashionable, at least in part, because world recession had forced a cutback from the November 1974 production high of 2.4 million bpd to 1.5 million bpd by mid-1975. More positive, however, was the huge investment programme in the search for further resources. While known reserves could last for 30 years the Third Plan has assigned N270 million for NNOC exploration and N600 million will be used by the other companies during the plan for the same purpose. Nigeria is striving to do two things with its oil: maximise its use as the weapon to pay for development; and — at the same time — conserve it for as long as possible. It seems likely that these two equally laudable aims will be in contradiction to each other.

After the heady delights of 1973 and 1974 for the OPEC states, 1975 came as a more sobering experience, for even though OPEC maintained its solidarity and high prices it faced a continuing recession, a drop in demand and the erosion of the value of its high oil prices by western exported inflation. Nigeria, whose plan depended upon its oil sales, moved steadily from a middle of the road to a hawkish position within the councils of OPEC and by the June 1975 Gabon OPEC meeting Nigeria had reached a stand somewhere to the right of centre—a soft hawk. Three months later at the September OPEC meeting that increased oil prices by a further 10 per cent, it was a confirmed hard-liner on the issue of obtaining maximum prices.

At the same time Nigeria, which in 1971 produced all its refined requirements, discovered that the situation had altered radically for the worse by 1975 despite the huge absolute increase in the production of crude. In 1975 Nigeria faced a 50 per cent shortfall of refined products and these had to be imported at a time when its own consumption was rising at an average annual rate of 18–20 per cent. Its plan included the building of new refineries but these would not be on tap before 1977 at the earliest.

Throughout 1975 Nigeria was plagued with petroleum product shortages. These sometimes caused near riots at petrol stations where lines of vehicles had queued for days and the military controlled the pumps. Soldiers searched vehicles for illicit containers of petrol; and angry Nigerians became sarcastic against a government that could not ensure proper distribution to its own people of their modest total consumption of 2 million tons of oil products a year at a time when the country was producing in excess of 100 million tonnes. At the Ministry of Petroleum and Energy, the Permanent Secretary, Philip Asiodu, rashly promised in April 1975 that by June 30 the shortages would be at an end. This deadline was not met, though it was only partly his ministry's fault, and he was mercilessly taken to task for the failure by the press.

The problem was the result of many aspects of a booming economy. For example, in 1971 Nigeria imported 15 000 cars; in 1972, 27 000; in 1973, 38 000 and in 1974 some 45 000. In addition, growing prosperity meant that many Nigerians could afford to put back on the road old cars that had been laid up. This was only one of the reasons why traffic chaos grew. Meanwhile demands upon the home refining industry outstripped its capacity. Two factors were at work: first, that Nigeria was only refining 50 per cent of its needs; second, that port congestion and inadequate handling facilities—a result of the boom—were delaying imports of refined products. Apart from administrative difficulties the most crucial statistic was as follows: by November 1974 consumption of petrol had reached 114.3 million litres, while refinery output totalled 61.9 million litres, leaving the balance to be imported.

These shortages should have been overcome by the end of the Third Plan when Nigerian refining capacity will have been transformed. The country, however, also faced severe distribution problems.

In 1975 it was decided as a matter of urgency to increase the storage capacity of Port Harcourt refinery from 60 000 to 80 000 bpd, while other short-term emergency decisions included the building of a new jetty at Okrika near Port Harcourt and a pipeline system to link it to the existing jetty. In July 1975 a second berth at Apapa was opened up for the discharge of refined products. All sorts of problems made the distribution bottlenecks worse: thus contractors to move oil products—despite a 60 per cent increase in the fees paid them by the oil companies at the start of the year—still switched their vehicles to the transport of other more profitable dry goods such as cement.

And so the chaos mounted. Nigeria Railways failed to play a full part in distribution because it took an average of 60 days for the turn-round of a truck between Lagos and the north whereas it only took five days for a bridging truck going by road to Kano and back. Transport fleets could not be kept in service for the maximum period due to scarcity of spare parts including tyres—again a result of port congestion. While the government took a number of short-term measures to overcome—or try to overcome—the immediate crisis, the industry as a whole reviewed its long-term prospects. As with so many other developments in Nigeria, the problems the country faced were the result of the economy outrunning the ability of the infrastructure to service it properly.

Most of the problems connected with the importation of refined products that, for example, led to a reduction of duties on imported motor fuels in 1975 should fall away by the 1980s when the country is not only producing all its refined requirements but has become a net exporter of refined products as well. That is the next major step for the industry. According to one critic of government policies:

> The fact that less than 30 per cent of Nigeria's petroleum is refined in Nigeria means the country loses the numerous by-products such as lubricants, plastics, insecticides—the industries associated with such by-products could be centred in Nigeria and act as the basis of an industrial revolution.

Few Nigerians would quarrel with that. The critic continues, more controversially:

> These hard facts of brutal exploitation by the foreign oil companies and their immense and invidious political influence underline the demand for total and immediate socialisation of the petroleum sector.[10]

Nigeria plans two sorts of refinery: first, relatively small ones to ensure that with Port Harcourt the country can refine all its own needs; and second, far larger ones to refine a major part of its crude production for export purposes so as to answer at least part of the criticism quoted above. As for the first refineries, demands have been made for their siting in many parts of the country. In the end it was decided that two new refineries should be built: one at Warri on the coast, and one at Kaduna. The latter should be able to satisfy all northern needs and in addition those of Nigeria's landlocked northern neighbours—Chad and Niger. The two refineries at Warri and Kaduna will be entirely owned by NNOC; tentatively it is hoped that Warri will be on tap by 1979 and Kaduna by 1981, yet consumption by then may well make nonsense of their planned capacities. Apart from these two, however, the Third Plan also envisages two major refineries with a joint capacity of 600 000 bpd so that by 1980 Nigeria should be able to turn a substantial proportion of its crude oil into far more valuable refined exports.

The next long-term development for the industry concerns gas. The most conspicuous form of waste in modern Nigeria is the burning off of natural gas. Since the early 1970s the big oil companies have been increasingly interested in exploiting Nigeria's huge natural gas resources but the investment required would be vast. One plant (in 1975 figures) to produce 14 million cubic metres a day would require a capital investment of £250 million; the first consideration, therefore, is that of obtaining certain markets. Such markets are not easy to gauge in an energy-conscious age in which every nation is constantly investigating new possibilities of supply and becoming wary of tying its demand to any one source or commodity. Currently Nigeria burns off 56 million cubic metres of gas a day; it would take two giant plants capable of liquefying 28 million cubic metres of gas each day to account for the total Nigerian output.

By the mid-1970s the Nigerian Government was busy negotiating with Shell-BP and Agip-Phillips for two such plants to be sited at Bonny and Escravos (in the mid-west) respectively: the agreement would be for 60 per cent government participation while the government would also take a 50 per cent share in gas tanker fleets. The companies were then thinking in terms of 16 tankers, each with a capacity of 120 000 cubic metres. Each of the plants would cost an estimated $1000 million to construct and take four years to build.

This rate of gas production—or waste—will continue as long as Nigeria has oil. The gas burnt probably represents a fifth of total national energy production. Had a decision to develop natural gas been taken early in the 1970s Nigeria today could be on a par with Algeria as one of the world's major liquid gas producers; instead, it has not begun. With conservation clearly becoming of ever-increasing importance and Nigeria endeavouring to bring its huge population economically forward to join the modern world, it needs every resource at its disposal and 56 million cubic metres of gas a day for the next 15 years represents a very large resource indeed. World inflation and costs continue to escalate and the $1000 million estimated costs per plant could well double should delays continue. Most important is the question of market: probably only the USA has the capacity to absorb this amount of liquefied gas. The earliest that Nigeria may go into serious production of liquid natural gas (LNG) must now be in the early 1980s, so that the sooner these projects are set in motion the better. For the companies the order of priorities is: first, to secure their markets; second, to secure finance; and third to build the plants. Securing the market effectively means watching the evolving energy policies of the USA and the EEC: the recession of 1975 meant a zero growth in world energy demand, sometimes drops in demand, while in addition new political attitudes such as that of the USA with its Project Independence also had to be taken into account.

After these gas possibilities are others for a chemical industry. Gas could be the base for a fertiliser complex to produce nitrogenous fertilisers: an annual output of 450 000 tonnes of ammonia and 260 000 tonnes of urea. According to the plan the production of such fertiliser plants, sited near the LNG plants and using tail gas from them, could be expanded so as to meet world as well as Nigerian fertiliser demands. The plan has allocated ₦70 million to fertiliser projects and production could start in 1977. The plan has also set aside ₦300 million for a petrochemical complex. This would be to produce 40 000 tonnes each of caustic soda, vinyl chloride monomer (VCM), polyvinyl chloride (PVC) and polyethylene and as much as 250 000 tonnes annually of ethylene. Should all these plans materialise Nigeria will be well on the way to having a reasonable chemical industry of its own.

The results of the oil boom have been felt in varying degrees in all parts of the country. The greatest political problem arising from it remains that of fair distribution of wealth, while the greatest political gain for the Federal Government is an effective economic weapon of control over the states. The plan suggests (though events may alter this) that reserve accretion will end in the year 1976–1977. Meanwhile oil wealth is creating a national bourgeoisie, ensuring that inflation remains among the highest in the world, and bringing a new set of problems and social upheavals to the oil-producing areas of the country. Oil may have brought wealth to Nigeria as a whole; but it is one of the ironies of the story that the inshore areas where it has been discovered are very poor though most of the oil is offshore; their villages have been deprived of their old occupations without the majority of the people finding anything new to do; and as yet few benefits from the oil boom have filtered through to them.

There are still nothing like enough Nigerians to supervise and run the industry despite training programmes by the major companies. Oil, like most other sectors of the economy, remains over-controlled from outside. Government representatives may have a majority in the management committees which in theory supervise all major policy decisions; in practice it is the companies that still make the vital day-to-day decisions on investment, management and production. Nigeria has still a long way to travel before it controls its oil industry in fact, as well as in theory and on paper.

Nigeria needs also to give careful thought to the future of the industry in the sense that planned dependence upon it for the next twenty years could turn out to be a dangerous miscalculation. The energy crisis of 1974–1975 has highlighted other world possibilities: policies of conservation; new sources of energy; policies of self-sufficiency by major consumers like the USA. Moreover new developments occur all the time and not necessarily to the advantage of a producer like Nigeria. Thus by 1980 as a result of North Sea oil Britain, which in 1975 took 16 per cent of its oil from Nigeria, will then take none. Further, it will probably also meet at least a proportion of EEC needs so that Nigeria may lose part of that market too. All these future possibilities should persuade Nigeria to adopt a strategy of maximum diversification: to use its oil as far as possible as the means of creating alternatives so that when resources do dry up the country will at least have the beginnings of other major industries. There is probably less time in which to do this than there might seem.

As 1975 proceeded Nigeria seemed increasingly aware of this. It became an OPEC hawk and by the September meeting of that year was among those demanding a 20 per cent price rise. At the same time, one of the early actions of the new Mohammed regime in August was to reduce by a further 5 cents a barrel the price of Nigerian crude as a gesture of 'co-operation' towards the oil companies. These two curiously diverse actions emphasised the ambivalence of a policy that would be radical for development purposes yet still sees itself—in part—dependent upon the companies.

Oil wealth has brought to Nigeria vast possibilities of breaking out of an old poverty and bringing development to all its people, but it has also brought with it many problems: maldistribution of incomes and rewards with their accompanying political and social complications; rising living costs; widespread corruption; violent crime; and a spirit of indiscipline that may easily arise when a country thinks it can solve all its problems with money—in this case from oil. None of this is easy. But the opportunities that have come with oil wealth are infinitely greater than the problems.

Notes

1   *Times International*, 28 July 1975
2   *African Development*, August 1972

3 *African Development*, June 1972
4 *African Development*, March 1975
5 Private conversation with author
6 *Ibid.*
7 *African Development*, March 1974
8 *Nigerian Herald*, 5 July 1975
9 *Ibid.*
10 O. Oni and B. Onimode, *Economic Development of Nigeria*, The Nigerian Academy of Arts, Science and Technology, 1975, p. 29

Chapter seven

The plan

The Nigerian Third Development Plan is the largest and most ambitious ever launched by an African country. In 1966, on the eve of the civil war, economists were suggesting that Nigeria was then on the verge of take-off; now, certainly, it is. For the first time the plan will be financed entirely from Nigerian sources. Total financial allocations come to N 32 billion and of this N 20 billion comes from the public sector. The federal expenditure is concentrated upon the economic sector while state governments will be more concerned with social amenities. In 1974–75 Nigeria's Gross Domestic Product (GDP) stood at N 14,410 million and between 1970 and 1974 the country experienced an average growth rate of 8.2 per cent, although there were large fluctuations in that period. The Third Plan postulates a growth rate of 9 per cent and the size of the plan is meant to ensure a radical transformation of the economy. There has also been an attempt in the plan to emphasise those sectors of development that directly affect the welfare of the ordinary citizen—that is, social services—an area that has been largely neglected in Nigeria to date, so that the plan should mean the beginnings of a society where increasing state intervention for social reasons helps to balance the laissezfaire aspects of the economy. Every state government is to have sufficient funds to implement its own approved programme (readjustment in the allocations will have to be made to take account of the new states).

The N 30 000 million for the plan will be derived from estimated public and private savings over the period 1975–1980 of N 49 000 million. In 1975 agriculture and mining accounted for 72 per cent of the national income. It is expected, however, that this proportion will fall to 60 per cent by 1980 as activity in other sectors of the economy has correspondingly increased.

A comparison with the statistics of the Second Plan gives an idea of the enormous difference that oil money has made to Nigeria. Total expenditure of the Second Plan was originally to be N 3 billion; subsequently this was revised upwards to N 5.3 billion. The Second Plan, moreover, relied upon a 20 per cent foreign component while the Third expects none. At the end of that plan period only 54 per cent of the plan had been achieved. The Third Plan is to spend as much in each year of its five as the whole expenditure of the Second Plan.

Even so, the achievements of the Second Plan were by no means negligible. They included the construction of 3 520 kilometres of roads while work got under way on another 2 560 kilometres, and increases in primary school enrolment from 3.5 million in 1970 to 4.5 million in 1973, in secondary school enrolment from 343 000 in 1971 to 649 000 in 1974, and in university enrolment from 14 500 to 25 000. For the Third Plan the money restraints have gone; manpower will be the main inhibiting factor.

The plan is certainly the boldest development scheme Nigeria has ever had and as the preamble says: 'The guiding principle is the total commitment of the Federal Military Government to the provision of equal opportunities for all Nigerians regardless of the place of birth, origin or abode.'

The basic strategy of the plan is to increase the standard of living of the average Nigerian and raise Nigeria to the ranks of developed countries. The per capita income of Nigeria in 1975 was approximately N295; the aim is to increase this over the next twenty years to N700. The plan aims to raise the GDP by 9 per cent a year; with a 2.5 per cent population increase this means a 6.5 per cent increase in per capita income—if the rate is maintained—so as to achieve the N700 target in twenty years. This would mean doubling the standard of living in twelve years. The benefits of economic development have to be spread so that the average Nigerian—rather than special groups—obtains a marked improvement in his living standards.

Oil will provide the revenue, but oil is a wasting asset and its wealth must be used to develop productive capacity in other directions. During the short period the oil lasts, therefore, it is intended to create the economic and social infrastructure necessary for self-sustaining growth when the oil has dried up. The plan suggests that: 'In some sectors investment leading to what may appear to be excess capacity will nevertheless be undertaken in the expectation that demand would catch up earlier than historical trend indicates.' Thus there is to be diversification, rapid expansion and broadening of industrial activities. At the same time there is need for balanced growth which is geared to generate growth simultaneously in all areas of the country. Nigeria badly needs to achieve a balance between the urban and rural areas of the country. The 70 per cent of the population who live in the rural areas have so far benefited relatively little from the rapid economic growth of the first half of the 1970s. The plan aims to bring about a substantial increase in rural income.

Education is given special attention: 'The large programmes of expansion of secondary, technical, and university education included in the Plan are aimed at overcoming the present shortage of high level manpower.'

The plan also intends that the public sector should provide

subsidised facilities for the poorer sections of the population so as to bring about electrification, water, health, co-operatives and community developments in such communities.

All this is by way of preamble. The fundamental objectives of the plan are economic growth; price stability; and social equity. It will certainly achieve the first, but whether it will also ensure the second or make the third possible is far more open to question. The plan states five national objectives: a strong, self-reliant nation; a great, dynamic economy; a just, egalitarian society; a land of opportunities for all; and a free democratic society. At the time the plan was launched it could reasonably be argued that Nigeria was moving towards becoming a strong self-reliant nation and that its economy was also developing into a great and dynamic one, but as yet it is far from being an egalitarian society and as it is developing economically at present this possibility would seem more likely to recede than come closer. Full opportunities for all is a most debatable point—socialist opponents of capitalism would say that the plan does nothing of the sort. And until the military regime actually relinquishes power and allows a return to civilian rule Nigeria cannot claim to be a free democratic society. All this means an enormous amount has to be done before these claims will be met.

The plan has a number of other more limited objectives: to increase per capita income; to bring about a more even distribution of income; to reduce unemployment; to increase the supply of high level manpower; to diversity the economy; to achieve balanced development; and to indigenise economic activity.

The plan presents a picture of outright capitalist economic thinking and socialist ideas of state responsibility for welfare. On profits and dividends, for example, it says:

> Thus, profits should be seen, not only as an outcome of the entrepreneur's exertions and ingenuity, but also, as a function of public money. Government regulation of profits should be viewed as part of a national effort to ensure social equity in the distribution of the fruits of economic growth and development.

In terms of foreign policy the plan (which was launched before the ECOWAS Treaty of May 1975) cautiously refers to regional co-operation but lists all the difficulties, so making clear its low expectations. However, it does talk of government co-operation through a variety of inter-governmental organisations such as UNECA, the Lake Chad Basin Commission, the River Niger Commission, the Niger/Nigeria Joint Commission for Co-operation, the African Groundnuts Council and the Cocoa Producers Alliance, the African Development Bank (ADB), the African Development Fund and the Association of African Central Banks. The introduction discusses Nigeria's most favoured nation trade agreements with a number of its neighbours, and suggests other such agreements might be made. It lists its air transport agreements and says that as a result of the oil crisis Nigeria will aid African countries by selling enough crude to those with refineries to enable them to meet their internal requirements. The plan also suggests that Nigeria, despite its own demands, will do what it can whenever possible to increase its aid—technical assistance and scholarship as well as disaster relief—to its neighbours.

The projections are interesting as both forecasts and targets. Even if they are not realised, the advances envisaged are of such a nature that the change in the economy should be substantial. Allowing for a population growth of 2.5 per cent per annum and an annual inflation rate of 6 per cent, the per capita private consumption rate is estimated at 10.5 per cent per annum. If this proves correct, the standard of living should double in only seven years. The largest projected expenditure is for transport and manufacturing, each sector to have 20 per cent of the gross fixed capital formation. Agriculture, mining and building, as well as government services, are to have between 8 and 10 per cent each. The country's non-oil exports are expected to rise from ₦304 million in 1974–75 to just under ₦400 million in 1979–80. This equals an annual growth rate of 6 per cent. But this is also very modest: the non-oil primary products exports for the plan period come to only ₦1.85 billion. This low performance will be partly explained by the fact of increased domestic processing and consumption of such commodities as palm oil and cotton. Finally, when the plan reaches its last two years and the projected oil refineries come on tap, imports of refined fuel can be phased out. Capital goods and raw materials are expected to account for 68 per cent of all imports during the plan—that is, some ₦22 billion. Although there will be an overall balance of payments surplus during the plan, reserves will decline towards the end and be less in 1980 than earlier.

Whatever its other political commitments, Nigeria is firmly aligned with the West economically. When he launched the plan in April 1975 Gowon said:

> I hardly need to add that the foreign businessmen in our midst are as welcome as ever before in the fields which have been clearly defined by law. It is the hope of government that in the promotion of their business activities they will seek to involve competent and reputable Nigerians rather than front men who claim to have influence with governments and government functionaries.

If the plan's envisaged 9.5 per cent growth rate is achieved, it should raise the Nigerian GDP which stood at ₦14.411 billion in 1974–75 to ₦22.692 billion in 1979–80. It is also envisaged that per capita income should rise from ₦205 to ₦290 by the end of the plan. Of the GDP figure of ₦14.411 billion in 1975, ₦3372.7 million came from agriculture and ₦6 552.3 million from mining and quarrying (mainly oil).

Although finance is unlikely to be a problem for the plan, it could turn out over the five-year period to be more problematical than was thought at the start of 1975, for at that time the severe and continuing reductions in oil sales were not expected to last. Revenue for 1975 was then expected to reach ₦5 252 million and after the state allocation of ₦1 300 million it was assumed that the balance—some ₦4 000 million—would, with additional drawing upon accumulated surpluses, pay for the plan. Should the world depression and consequent low oil sales continue, the plan must face cutbacks. Even so, manpower rather than finances presents the biggest headache in implementation.

The size and scope of the plan is the direct outcome of the 1973 fourfold increase in the price of oil. Although oil over the period is expected to account for only 40 per cent of Nigeria's GDP, its contribution to government revenues and foreign exchange will be in the region of 85 per cent. When the OPEC states met in Vienna in September 1975 and split between the hawks and doves as to the amount they should increase the price of oil to counter Western inflation, Nigeria for the first time was firmly among the hawks. It may have more money than ever before but the commitments of the plan are on such a scale that effectively it must receive a median figure of $825 million from oil a month—and during 1975 it had dropped far below this.

The implementation of the plan required the establishment of six new ministries: Co-operatives and Supply; Civil Aviation; Social Development, Youth and Sport; Petroleum and Energy; Urban Development, Housing and Environment; Water and Resources.

In February 1972 the Nigerian Enterprises Promotion Decree was passed. Its aim was the indigenisation of the economy. It named 28 industrial and commercial types of enterprise reserved exclusively for Nigerian citizens and associates; it also named a further 25 activities in which Nigerians were to have equity participation of not less than 40 per cent. By 1974 530 companies had complied under Section I; a major objective during the Second Plan was Nigerian participation in mining—both of petroleum and solid minerals. The Third Plan should see this process carried a good deal further.

Agriculture and rural development is and must remain the most important single activity in the economy, for it provides the livelihood for the great majority of the population. The plan allocated ₦2.2 billion to agricultural projects and aims especially to make it possible for farmers to obtain fertilisers, pesticides and other agricultural inputs at heavily subsidised prices. It is establishing and encouraging tractor hire services while land development schemes are to be expanded. There are plans to increase storage facilities and build more farm-to-market roads; strategic grain reserves are to be built in all parts of the country, while the government has taken over responsibility for trunk 'B' roads from the state governments so as to release their resources for use upon 'C' roads and local authority roads—that is, the small highways most important to the farming communities. There is to be direct government investment in large-scale plantations and land development and irrigation schemes.

The problems facing any government contemplating an agricultural revolution are formidable. The land is underused; there is qualitative depreciation of the land that is used; the average output per farm worker is no more than ₦175 per annum; the land tenure system is highly complicated and leads to fragmentation of holdings. For some years—the whole of the 1970s in fact—agriculture was making a declining contribution to GDP even though it was increasing in abolute terms. There was poor agricultural performance during the years of the Second Plan. Demands for better staple foods and animal products are now expected to rise by 5 per cent and 7 per cent respectively. Agriculture must continue to meet most of the country's raw materials requirements for local industry and for export where it will continue to be an important earner of foreign exchange.

Of the total area of 98.3 million hectares, about 34 million or a third of the land is under cultivation and in this area almost all the tropical crops are grown. The total cultivable land in fact amounts to 71.2 million hectares so that less than half of that is at present cultivated. The country's livestock could be considerably increased with proper management and improvements. Thirty-nine per cent of the land is forest and 10 per cent is in the form of forest reserves. As with most other sectors of the economy, agriculture suffers from shortage of managerial and entrepreneurial skills which are virtually absent among the peasant farmers who often have very small and scattered holdings. The level of food production is barely keeping pace with population growth, due to low yields, decreasing soil fertility, limited use of fertiliser, unimproved crop varieties and breeds of livestock, lack of credit, inadequate extension services and the continuing use of only the simplest tools.

The plan aims to combat some of these major deficiencies. Opportunities for agricultural breakthroughs will depend upon three factors: the existence of growing markets for Nigeria's food products; an abundance of land and human resources; and the availability of improved technology. On the other hand the constraints to be overcome consist mainly of the following: shortage of skilled manpower; inadequate inputs; inadequate extension services; poor feeder-transport facilities; poor support services; land ownership problems derived from the complicated land tenure system; natural problems such as diseases and pests; labour shortages because of the continuing urban drift; lack of appropriate technology; the drudgery that leads to low returns. Constantly the problem comes back to the question of skills.

The government aim is to see that the minimum requirements of consumption are reached in the plan period, allocating funds as follows: crops—₦1646 million; livestock—₦344.046 million; forestry—₦109.727 million: fishery—₦101.554 million.

The country's livestock consists of cattle, pigs, goats, sheep, and poultry, and while nearly all the cattle are in the north the pigs are mainly in the south. The capital value of the livestock industry is somewhere between ₦1.5 billion and ₦2 billion and it is divided among 50 per cent cattle, 35 per cent goats and sheep, 7 per cent poultry and the remainder pigs, horses and other stock. The annual gross output at producer prices amounts to ₦170 million and at retail prices to ₦250 million. The livestock herds represent a major national investment as well as a way of life for large numbers of Nigerians. The national cattle herd stands at 8.5 million of which 90 per cent is in the north and belongs to the Fulani; there are 8 million sheep, 22 million goats, and 70 per cent of these are also in the north. Generally speaking, the keeping of livestock represents a backward agricultural industry and faces a number of problems: natural ones such as the tsetse fly; human and social ones—the traditions of the nomadic herdsmen; and organisational ones in that the industry has a poor infrastructure.

The total forest area of the country amounts to 360 000 square kilometres, or slightly over one third of the total land area, yet the present rate of consumption of usable timber could exhaust this in 25 to 30 years. Timber exports dropped from 514 000 cubic metres in 1966 to 211 000 in 1972. The biggest problem in this sector is that at present only 25 per cent of removals from the forest are regenerated. The plan aims to intensify the regeneration programme.

Nigerian fisheries are hardly an advanced sector of the economy. The total fish supply from all sources in 1972 was 710 000 tonnes of which 640 000 were produced locally and the balance imported. The existing total fish demand comes to 1 million tonnes—that is, there exists an unsatisfied market and by 1980 this could have increased to at least 1.5 million tonnes. It is the object of the plan to increase local fish production to 1.2 million tonnes by 1980. It is hoped to earn considerable foreign exchange by marketing shrimps. A total of ₦101.554 million has been allocated to fisheries during the plan period.

The transport sector has the largest single allocation of funds at ₦7.3 billion, of which ₦1 billion is allocated to the states while the balance goes to the federal programme. The aim is to achieve an efficient communications infrastructure by the end of the plan. The federal road mileage is to be increased from 7 000 to 30 000 kilometres as a result of the takeover of responsibility for 'B' roads. Major roads will be dualled. The railways, which are in deplorable condition and are 3′ 6″ gauge, are to have ₦885 million devoted to them, and standard gauge is to be introduced. The plan allocated ₦537 million to the airways and aviation programme; the aim here is to improve the domestic and West African routes and extend Nigerian Airways to cover all parts of the country. N322 million has been set aside for port development: 75 per cent of all cargoes go via Lagos, 16 per cent by Port Harcourt and 9 per cent use the other ports. The basic need is simply to expand all handling facilities. N47.5 million has been allocated to the improvement of inland waterways.

In the field of communications—telephones, telegraphs—Nigeria experiences huge bottlenecks and constant breakdowns. There is a lack of skilled technicians. N1 107.5 million has been allocated to all telecommunications projects. It is also intended to make the country's information services more efficient as well as using them to promote basic ideas of national unity and the country's image abroad. N380.225 million has been allocated to these services, including broadcasting, libraries and the federal government newspapers' corporation.

The plan aims to increase power production from the 1975 figure of electricity generation and consumption, which stood at 474 megawatts, by an additional 1 000 megawatts. State governments have been allocated N150 million for rural electrification programmes. Altogether N927.8 million has been set aside for this part of the programme.

Most developing countries, when attempting to implement development plans, face three restraints: savings, foreign exchange and manpower or executive capacity. As far as Nigeria is concerned neither savings nor foreign exchange will act as restraints; the bottleneck comes from manpower gaps. In manpower terms, therefore, the focus of the plan is upon an expansion of employment opportunities; the provision of industrial attachment programmes and occupational guidance to bridge the gap between school and work; and major efforts to strengthen educational and training facilities.

In 1975 the distribution in gainful employment of the country's manpower was as follows:

	%
Agriculture	64.0
Mining and quarrying	0.4
Manufacturing and Processing	16.8
Construction and Building	0.9
Electricity, Gas, Water	0.1
Distribution	12.2
Transport and Communications	0.6
Services	5.0

The public sector, including teaching, 'now accounts for 65 per cent of total modern sector employment which is placed at about 1 500 000.' The plan has vast manpower implications because of its size. By 1980 the labour force is projected at 32.74 million and it is expected that those in gainful employment will increase from 27.91 million in 1975 to

31.76 million in 1980. Of people employed in large and medium-sized establishments 6.1 per cent are in senior job categories, 16.8 per cent in intermediate, 29.1 per cent in the skilled and 48 per cent in the residual categories.

Plan manpower requirements have been estimated as follows: 49 210 senior level personnel will be required, of whom 43 550 can be supplied from various sources (these figures will depend upon training and upgrading). At the intermediate level 139 510 personnel are required, of whom an expected 126 290 can be found. It is estimated that 20 600 additional senior, intermediate and skilled workers will be required to implement the plan's agricultural projects, and these break down according to the three categories into 2 500, 7 200 and 10 900 respectively. In the health sector, for example, it is expected that manpower shortages will range from 50 per cent for doctors to 75 per cent for nurses. For full implementation the country needs to turn out yearly during the plan period 500 doctors, 200 pharmacists, 2 000 nurses, 1 500 midwives and 100 laboratory technicians, and to do so, of course, must expand all training facilities accordingly.

It is hoped that throughout the plan period unemployment can be kept at 5 per cent (it was 7.8 per cent in 1970). There is a major unemployment problem for school-leavers as the rapid expansion of education is not being matched by subsequent job opportunities. This is especially true among primary and secondary school-leavers. During recent years the level of expatriate employment has been increasing—there are currently 20 000 in the private sector alone, mainly in manufacturing and the construction industries. In terms of manpower the plan says: 'A crucial policy requirement is that university development and out-turn should be related to the requirements of the labour market for senior level manpower.'

Nigeria in the post-Udoji period can hardly be said to have a labour policy at all. There is need for both an incomes policy as opposed to the 1975 free-for-all and an employment policy. There is also need for Trade Union Education, Occupational Health Services and Youth Employment. The plan allocates ₦43.187 million to these fields and a key part of this small sector is that of National Youth Employment Programmes.

Education is the forerunner of manpower policies. At last Nigeria is approaching the achievement of providing universal education at all levels. The plan allocates ₦2.5 billion to education. There is to be Universal Primary Education (UPE) from September 1976, while the plan talks of equal educational opportunities for all Nigerians. Primary school enrolment is expected to rise from 5 million to 11.5 million by 1980. In the field of secondary education the aim is to treble the 1975 enrolment of half a million by 1980 and 800 new secondary schools will be opened throughout the country during this period. University enrolment is planned to double from 28 000 to 53 000 by

1980. There is also to be a general lowering of tuition and boarding fees for secondary education and special help provided for students in need.

In general terms the plan aims to expand facilities and so equalise individual access to education; reform the content and so make it more responsive to social and economic needs; consolidate higher education so that it more accurately responds to manpower needs; and streamline the machinery for educational development, rationalising the financing of education and tackling the question of providing adequate technical education. UPE will be free throughout the country from September 1976 and compulsory from 1979. In secondary education the aim is to encourage children to remain at school until the age of 15, while in technical education it is intended to build a system of five-year secondary technical colleges side by side with the secondary schools.

Altogether it is a formidable programme, but essential if the plan is to lay the manpower foundations for its successor due to start in 1980.

The largest allocations are for the development of the industrial sector so as to make Nigeria self-sufficient in petroleum products, petro-chemicals, pulp and paper, sugar and other strategic materials. Up to the period of the Third Plan manufacturing in Nigeria had been principally concerned with light consumer goods such as beer, soft drinks, cigarettes, shoes and textiles. The plan aims to ensure an industrial revolution so that Nigeria can start to produce its own trucks and cars (as opposed merely to assembling them), iron and steel and petro-chemicals. Thus, it is estimated that, despite setbacks to the iron and steel project during the course of the first two plans, this project will certainly go ahead, since it is expected that by 1980 demand will have reached 3.5 million tons of steel a year. N 350 million has been set aside for the two internal refineries at Kaduna and Warri as well as the expansion of the Port Harcourt refinery so that between them they should produce a total of 250 000 barrels a day. In addition, two export refineries are planned, each with a capacity of 300 000 bpd at a capital cost of N 780 million. This will be a guarantee against domestic shortages and allow Nigeria to participate in the lucrative world market for refined petroleum products. Also N 350 million is allocated to the Warri-Kaduna pipeline programme. If these major schemes are accomplished, then there will indeed begin to be a transformation in the economy.

The private sector is a vital part of the Nigerian economy and it is expected to provide some N 10 billion over the plan period. This will be especially welcomed in agriculture, manufacturing, building and construction. As the plan states, it is 'Government's hope that the new Nigerian businessman will seek to make his mark in the organisation of corporate businesses aimed at the creation of new productive assets.' It is a dynamic private sector and in terms of the new wealth now flowing in Nigeria the opportunities for developing it are virtually limitless.

The physical and human resources for industrial development exist and a dynamic entrepreneurial group is emerging. Yet in 1975—15 years after independence—manufacturing still only represented 8 per cent of GDP which compared unfavourably with many developing countries whose manufacturing sectors stood at between 15 and 20 per cent. Nigeria has virtually no engineering industry and few of the sub-sectors that go with such an industry: in 1975 the sector was dominated by assembly activities while its import content was high. There are a number of restraints upon this sector: inadequate infrastructure once more, shortage of industrial manpower and slow implementation of public sector manufacturing. The plan aims to give special encouragement to major industries such as engineering and chemicals, where 40 per cent and more of output is for export. What is clear from this section of the plan, however, is the real and apparently continuing dependence of Nigeria upon expatriate industrial investment and know-how. It may not be stated but it comes across.

The largest economic sector is mining. In 1962 mining provided 1.1 per cent of GDP; by 1972 this figure had reached 15.9 per cent; mining has replaced agriculture as the highest contributor to the GDP. The government has obtained a controlling interest in oil. During the Second Plan the Nigerian Coal Corporation was rehabilitated (it had been badly affected by the war) and two new corporations were set up: the Nigerian Mining Corporation and the Nigerian National Oil Corporation. The Mining Corporation (established in 1972) is to engage in commercial prospecting for all solid minerals except coal, while NNOC has basic responsibilities for the entire range of oil activities. Coal production is expected to grow during the plan period from 1 million tonnes to 2 460 000 tonnes in 1980 and exports of coal will increase from 600 000 tonnes to 1.5 million tonnes. The biggest problem here will be the transport of the coal from the mines to the ports. A total of ₦2.680 billion is allocated to mining and quarrying, while total public and private investment in oil is expected to reach ₦4.535 billion.

Basically the plan aimed to enlarge the country's superstructure and diversify the economy, particularly in the fields of mining and manufacturing, so that Nigeria would become—or start to become—a modern diversified economy. However, considerable attention has been given to social services and the idea of state responsibility for various types of social development. Thus ₦39.603 million has been allocated to Social Development and sport, including rehabilitation centres for the disabled, and youth camps. In urban development ₦1.8 billion, a very large sum indeed, has been allocated to a housing programme mainly aimed at the provision of low-cost housing for the low income groups. Health is allocated ₦700 million: the plan includes the extension of teaching hospitals, health manpower development and deployment, the development and expansion of hospital services, a comprehensive health coverage for the nation, disease control, planning and management

The vast sum of N2.827 billion is set aside for defence and a large amount of this is to be spent on capital equipment such as new barracks.

The Third Plan itself is ambitious and vast in concept; even if only threequarters to 80 per cent is actually implemented—as its optimistic proponents guess—an enormous amount will have been achieved. As the plan itself states:

> If implemented, the programmes and policies embodied in the Plan can lead to a complete transformation of the Nigerian economy and society. The announcement of the Plan is likely to raise the people's expectations, and it will be unfortunate if these are frustrated by lack of commitment to the goals, objectives and targets set in the Plan document.

Following the coup which brought it to power, the new government of Murtala Mohammed accepted the commitments of the Third Plan in principle. In 1976, however, the Obasanjo government carried out an extensive review of the plan, resulting in cutbacks on prestige projects and greater emphasis on health, housing and agriculture. The biggest change came with a fivefold increase in allocations over the period to health and health facilities from an original figure of N314 million expenditure at the federal level to N1 700 million. The target of 60 000 low-cost housing units in the Federal Government housing programme was increased to 200 000. Both these developments show a greater awareness of the need to pay more attention to the provision of social amenities, while any extra boost to the agricultural sector of the economy can be justified in view of its overall living standards of the majority of the people.

The budget for 1976–1977 showed a substantial revenue increase over the previous year: gross revenue at N5 756.2 million as opposed to N5 252.2 million for 1975–1976 was up 504 million or 9.6 per cent. When statutory and non-statutory allocations to the states had been deducted, the Federal Government was left with an estimated revenue of N4 330 million, but in the year that the country changed from 12 to 19 states (with all the special costs involved) and began the process of resiting the capital the government would need all the extra revenue it could raise. The country also needed, as the Head of State said, to practise financial restraint (despite its apparently huge oil revenues). General Obasanjo made this clear in his budget broadcast to the nation when he said: 'I wish to stress that although this country has a great potential, she is not yet a rich nation.' He called for an end to illusions of great oil wealth: 'With a population of some 72 million people and oil production of under 2 000 000 barrels a day, our resources from oil are not enough to satisfy the aspirations and general needs of our people for development and social services.' It was a soberly realistic approach to development and combined with the larger aims of the plan should ensure that the greater part of it is implemented on schedule.

Chapter eight

Development problems

Speaking as Chancellor of the University of Ife in 1973, Chief Awolowo said: 'Although the nation had achieved rapid economic growth, it had gained very little economic development.'[1] He was clearly making political points with an eye to the future return to civilian rule. Nigeria is an economic mixture of boom and backwardness. The papers carry success stories, American style, of men who have risen to the top—and there is much rising to do. In the pursuit of advancement young graduates take jobs to find themselves under old incompetents who know nothing and do nothing except cling to a position they are ill-equipped to hold. Consequently the graduates become disillusioned. In a society where education is thrusting forward a new generation with skills not previously, or at least not widely, available, this kind of situation is common enough. One senior man was reported to resort to one of ten Pavlovian reactions according to the nature of requests for a decision; he would send the file round for further comment, ask a particular member of his staff to research the question further and so on; the one thing he would not do was take a decision.

There is in Nigeria a gross imbalance of money and investment: thus 3 per cent of the population controls 66 per cent of investment and, clearly, where there is such disproportionate command of resources there must also follow grave difficulties in the development process in many other directions: 'too few will be doing too much and too many will be doing too little or nothing.'[2] The range of the problems is enormous. When, for example, the Federal Military Government instructed the government of the North West State to site teacher training colleges in towns which had water, electricity and proper roads—in other words, all modern facilities—it overlooked the fact that only four towns in the state answered that description—and it was a state of 65 000 square miles.

As elsewhere in Africa, there is in Nigeria great emphasis upon indigenisation of the economy. Yet the extent to which this is done, or possible, varies enormously from one area of development to another and from one area of sensitivity to another. Peugeot started a major assembly plant in Kaduna in 1974 and because of a convenient quota system to encourage expatriate business it may bring in a high proportion—relative to its total work force—of expatriates. Thus indigenisation in theory is often passed over for the time being in practice.

In the mid-1970s there were constant stories in Nigeria of every kind of hold-up—ports, railways, obtaining licences to operate—and everyone grumbled ceaselessly about them. Yet in terms of a vast country developing at great speed—even if lopsidedly—such delays are to be expected and are likely to continue into the foreseeable future. Were they not taking place there would be far more reason to complain, for then, indeed, something would be wrong. One Nigerian, Sam Aluko, has commented: 'Nigeria is less developed in terms of physical, human and even monetary resources than those countries (the USA and Canada) were in 1875.'[3] Not surprisingly, then, Nigeria is probing in many directions to find solutions to her development problems.

In political terms this means constant pulls between the states and the centre. Oil wealth is the key to the development of the economy now and for at least the next ten years, and here control of the purse strings has been firmly taken over by the Federal Government. In 1973 Gowon took from state governments the power of their marketing boards to fix producer prices in their areas. Since then the price fixing has been a federal prerogative, each commodity price being settled on a country wide basis. This was a calculated move both to get more fiscal power into the hands of the central government and to appeal to farmers by spreading some of the effects of the oil wealth, for export duties on marketing board produce were abolished and 'the only tax which the state governments impose on their export commodities will be the new produce tax at a maximum rate of 10 per cent.' Since this measure abolished an export duty of 18 per cent as well as the old produce tax, it represented a bonus for farmers.

Since 1975, however, a key to development (or its lack) lay in the small contribution of industry to the total economy. It stood that year at only 8 per cent, which it is hoped to raise to something like 40 per cent. To do so a large variety of problems must be overcome. It is fashionable among Nigerian civil servants to talk of transforming the economy; in many ways since independence Nigeria has enjoyed impressive growth. What as yet have hardly begun to emerge are home stimulants to self-generating growth. Between 1960 and 1975 the Gross Domestic Product (GDP) of the country has increased five times. Too much reliance, however, may be placed upon the oil money: producing a self-reliant economy is not simply a question of oil money being 'spread'. At least Nigeria need no longer rely upon foreign aid: in her First Plan she looked for 50 per cent of the investment expenditure to come from foreign sources, and in the Second Plan for 20 per cent. In the Third Plan she can produce all the finance herself—

and that alone is a source of political encouragement since it should free the national planners from those restraints which always come with substantial foreign aid. On 1975 estimates the total savings of the economy over the period of the Third Plan were expected to be N 49000 million, substantially more than the amount to be invested and, assuming an average annual reserve of N 5000 million from oil alone, there should be no problem about money to finance the plan.

Transforming an economy of the size and potential of that of Nigeria, however, does not depend upon money alone. The plan itself (see Chapter 7, above) has attempted to be comprehensive in its coverage of projects and the emphasis it gives to the various sectors of the economy. Yet the size of investments to be attempted are again less important than their type. The range of industrial projects—though no doubt it can be faulted in detail—is wide and reasonably comprehensive: petro-chemical industries, pulp and paper, sugar, salt, cement, refineries for both the home and the export markets. Especially important (see below, pp. 156–60) is the proposed iron and steel industry which has been germinating for more than twenty years and constantly delayed by the advice of foreign experts. Yet such an industry is crucial to the development of any economy in a self-sustaining sense and certainly to one the size of Nigeria.

Where in both relative and actual terms Nigeria's economy is weakest—and should be strongest—is in agriculture. This notoriously difficult development field merits a concentration of attention that it nowhere receives. The factors at work inhibiting agricultural advances are always more complicated and difficult to pin down than in the industrial sector: weather; land tenure problems; conservatism of farmers who even if helped with new teaching and supplied with fertilisers may simply not wish to put more land under cultivation—and so on. What—slowly—has emerged in the developing countries of Africa and elsewhere—where it is popular to encourage themes of back-to-the-land—is the fact that to attract people to stay on the land, let alone persuade those who have left to go back to it, there must be comprehensive plans for the development of rural amenities so that such rural areas can, in some fashion, compete as places in which to live with the glamour of the towns. This is an essential prerequisite that goes with producing new cash-crop farmers and persuading a peasant farming community that what up to the present has been solely a means of existence can in fact pay and might pay handsomely.

The country has a widely varied agricultural economy, ranging through cocoa, groundnuts, palm produce, timber, cotton, rubber, cattle products, which represent a source of basic strength. During the colonial period, however, Nigeria was trapped into a system of primary production of agricultural and mineral resources so that it developed into a series of export areas devoted to tin, cocoa, cotton, groundnuts. The marketing board system arose out of government monopoly buying of these major export crops in the period 1930–1946 from the small farmers. Since the changes of 1973 the boards have lost much of their power and the government is using at least some of the oil wealth to subsidise export crops. In recent years there has been a reversal in some of the old patterns of export crops—palm oil is a notable example—because growing local prosperity has led to greater home consumption, so cutting back the amount exported. Meanwhile a new form of agricultural development is to be found in the huge projects affecting wide areas: the Bakolari dam, for example, in the North West State will cost between ₦150 million and 200 million over 15 years and enable a wide area to be irrigated as well as producing a number of side developments.

Development problems in Nigeria are commensurate with the growth of its national income. GDP increased from £N1 315 million in 1962–63 to £N1 583 million in 1966–67, declined to £N1 506 million in 1967–68, then reached £N1 863 million in 1970–71. In the last year of civilian rule the total recurrent revenue was £N200 million, of which oil accounted for £N13 million; by 1973 total revenue had climbed to £N1 100 million, of which oil then represented £N600 million. In 1974 oil income alone reached £N3 500 million—that is, seventeen times what the independence government had to spend in 1960. This phenomenal expansion of revenue has not been matched by an equal capacity to spend.

The key to much of Nigeria's future development lies with current efforts at industrialisation. The aim of the Third Plan is to lay the foundations of a strong industrial base. At first Nigeria wants to supply its own industrial needs. In the long run, however, it aims to be a major industrial exporting country. The manufacturing industry in Nigeria has risen slowly from 5 per cent to 8 per cent (of the total economy) between 1960 and 1975 and Nigerian industry earns only about 2 per cent of foreign exchange. Half the sector is made up of light industry such as textiles, food products or tobacco; the engineering sector is very small with large gaps while as yet there are virtually no industrial chemicals, fertiliser or pesticide industries. The problems to overcome are substantial. Talented Nigerians tend to go into commerce rather than industry; since the sector is so small there has been a commensurately small build-up of infrastructure and there are few available skilled workers. There are also bureaucratic bottlenecks to new industrial developments.

The improvement of the infrastructure is vital to the development of heavy industry and an iron and steel industry will be the key to much of this. Despite 'indigenisation' the government wants to attract foreign investors to help establish engineering industries for export—with the proviso that in due course these will make part of their equity available locally. At the same time the country wants to encourage small-scale indigenous businesses. The question of how much true industrialisation is taking place arises in connection with the car industry. Both Volkswagen and Peugeot started assembly plants in Nigeria in 1974 and in 1975 Leyland went into partnership with the government to produce trucks. At first all three will produce for the home market; later they hope to tackle the export market. It is the aim, for example, that after three years at least 15 per cent of the 'completely knocked down' components of the Leyland trucks will consist of locally manufactured components. How soon Nigeria will have the capacity to produce and market her own car is another matter—but it is at that level of technology and that kind of industrial base that the country is aiming.

The manufacturing industry has remained remarkably small so far because industrialisation has consisted of topping up and finishing products that, substantially, were made elsewhere. The result has been a low Nigerian addition to their value so that they have made only a small contribution to the overall economy. The approach in the Third Plan is to establish the basic industries in Nigeria and despite the availability of money this will be far harder than the planners think. The problem lies in Nigeria's ability to purchase know-how without also having to bring in outside companies which merely exploit instead of making a sufficient contribution to the growth of the economy. The plan aims to break through the 'textiles first' strategy of industrialisation so much favoured by expatriate advisers and planners. At present, however, the industrial technology of the country relies upon foreign capital—and it appears that the plan expects Nigeria to continue doing so; this approach emphasises capital intensive projects which fail to raise or use the technical skills of the local people beyond the level of artisans. There can be no meaningful industrialisation in Nigeria without the creation of a basic structure of industries that produce machine tools, equipment, heavy machinery and chemicals. This brings the argument back in a circle to the absence of a steel industry and the urgent need, no matter what advice to the contrary, to create one.

Almost uniquely in a developing country, the problem is not one of a large number of possible projects seeking capital but of outside capital willing to come in and hopefully seeking projects in the knowledge that in Nigeria it is on to a good thing. A major difficulty to date, however, has been the neglect of the role of technological progress as a necessary attendant of capital formation for economic development.[4]

Despite the civil war foreign private investment in Nigeria continued to grow through that time from an already substantial base. In 1970–71 total investment stood at £N380 million compared with a plan estimate of £N354 million and a significant percentage of that was foreign. In 1971–72 this rose to £N465.4 million and of this about £N267 million—mainly foreign private—was the planned estimate for the oil industry over the period 1970–1974. A good deal of foreign investment—apart from oil—comes from the Commonwealth Development Corporation (CDC) which concentrates on agriculture; otherwise much comes through the longstanding companies such as UAC. The fact is that despite calls for indigenisation foreign private investment

> remains the lifeline of the Nigerian manufacturing industries. About 70 per cent of paid up capital is foreign private, while the remaining 30 per cent is about equally divided between Nigerian private and public capital subscriptions.[5]

All developing countries are concerned with the existing degree of foreign control of their economies. Nigeria is no exception. There is and has been a great deal of foreign control and despite the indigenisation programme recently carried out critics suggest that at most that was a superficial operation: that much foreign control remains and that a skilful foreign exploiter has little difficulty in coming into the country to exploit still more.

Two consistent critics of the present Nigerian economic set-up say: 'Imperialist domination of the Nigerian financial sector operates through foreign ownership and control of commercial banks, insurance companies, and allied institutions.'[6] This is true. So is the entrenched position of the big expatriate companies such as UAC and Holts (now part of LONRHO) who have become complacent about their business positions. The British, the West Germans, the Japanese and the French especially all have active and sizable operations within the economy. The commercial sector is dominated by foreign companies whose names have become Nigerian household words: UAC, UTC, John Holt, G. B. Olivant, SCOA, CFAO, Paterson Zochonis, Leventis, Bhojsons, K. Chellarams who between them control most of the wholesale trade in imported merchandise.

The process of indigenisation will no doubt change this grip; but it will take time. The Lebanese have been of major importance in the commercial sector in the country, but by the mid-1970s they were being squeezed out. Foreign concerns take money out of Nigeria in five ways: profits and dividends; interest on capital; contractor finance and suppliers' credit; service charges; and rent. The fact is that fifteen years after independence Nigeria had a long way to go before achieving national economic independence. To do so it will have to embark upon a far more ruthless policy of taking control of all foreign companies and assets.

The pattern of exports has been changing substantially in the 1970s. Between 1969 and 1970 there were increases of 39 per cent and 55 per cent in exports and imports. Exports increased from £N318 million to £N442 million and imports from £N248 million to £N378 million, a favourable balance of £N64.5 million. In the first half of 1971 imports and exports stood at £N259.9 million and £N280.8 million so there continued to be an overall trade surplus but it turned out to be a surplus of £N168.5 million in the oil trade and a deficit of £N145.6 million in the rest. By March 1975 Nigeria's principal exports were crude petroleum, cocoa beans, cocoa products, groundnuts, groundnut oil and cake, palm kernels, palm kernel oil, palm oil, rubber, cotton, timber and plywood and tin metal. At the same time her principal imports consisted of food and live animals; drink and tobacco; crude materials, mineral fuels, oils and fats, chemicals, manufactured goods, machinery and transport equipment and miscellaneous manufactured goods. What is now clear is that Nigeria has an excessive import bill and imports far more than is socially desirable. Many imports are 'ostentatious' or luxury goods. For the country as a whole the commercial sector, at 15 per cent of GDP, is still very small.

Nigeria's main trading partners, certainly for its traditional non-oil exports, are in Europe: Britain, West Germany, France, Belgium, the Netherlands, Switzerland. The largest proportion of Nigeria's non-oil exports still go to Britain: including oil the value of exports to Britain in 1974 totalled £368 million. The traditional trading pattern leads Nigerians to turn first to Britain for what they want: if they do not get satisfaction there they then go elsewhere. In the field of construction, especially large-scale works such as dams, the Italians come first. West Germany is a major source for machinery, Japan a source for an increasingly wide range of manufactured goods and electronics.

The market—the largest in Africa—is wide open. As a result there is an endless stream of would-be traders moving in hoping to obtain a slice of it. Nigeria wants to ensure that its own industry and commerce can compete with the outsiders in the expansion of demand that is taking place. This will not be easy, for few industries of any kind were established in Nigeria during the colonial period and those that were created are largely processing industries for raw materials—cotton ginning, palm oil crushing, plywood milling—while something like bicycle assembly was the apex of industrial achievement. To date industrial production has been biased in favour of consumer goods and most of those manufactured in Nigeria are of the semi-luxury kind.

Thus, as in so many other African countries, industrialisation in Nigeria has consisted of the familiar textiles first, beer, soft drinks approach; or the processing of raw materials for export. There has been a systematic neglect of capital goods that would be required for any significant industrial break-through.

Development is very lopsided: Lever Bros for example, have for long been in a monopoly position in Nigeria, where they operate under their own name and are also the parent company of UAC, but as a result of indigenisation they went public and 40 per cent of their shares are now owned by Nigerians—60 per cent remaining with the parent company, Unilever. The Nigerian business agglomerate is just beginning to emerge—Michael Ibru and Henry Stephens are the two best and so far virtually only known names in this direction—and they may swallow up some smaller businesses as a result of indigenisation. But as yet no very formidable class of Nigerian businessman has emerged, although there are plenty of entrepreneurs.

There has been substantial development in specific fields. Textiles is an obvious example: 45 per cent of the country's cotton is produced in the North Central State (Kaduna) and six major textile mills have been established in and around Kaduna; these are by British, Japanese, Taiwanese and Hong Kong companies. The Nigerian textile industry has the biggest potential in Africa. There are some 56 mills throughout the country and in 1975 another 50 were under construction or planning. The Nigerian demand is huge and has not yet been met by home production; when it has the country should become a major textile exporter. Textile production on 1975 stood at 500 million metres.

Building is almost totally dominated by foreign companies. In 1966, of 42 large building contracts 39 went to foreign firms and since that time the expatriate companies have, if anything, consolidated their hold on the construction industry. The enormous boom in construction that has come with oil has found the country simply unable to deal with the mushrooming construction demands: foreign firms have done so instead. The field is dominated by the Italians although there are major British companies such as Taylor Woodrow and Cubitts in the country and some German competition.

The Nigerian tin mining industry, of greater importance in the past than now, consists of Amalgamated Tin Mines of Nigeria and a number of relatively small companies, each guarding their own interests. Individually they do not possess the resources to develop the tin fields and make these really profitable. There has been a steady fall in production since 1968—between 1970 and 1973 production fell by 4.6 per cent per annum; there is a substantial problem of illegal surface mining; and there have been no big new finds. Nigeria's output is largely controlled by expatriate companies and as a result of their pressure the royalty payable was dropped from 17 to 11 per cent which represented N 100 a ton—a classic example of quiet neo-colonialism at work. The drop in royalties was not widely publicised as it might have produced a public outcry. Seven British-based companies such as Amalgamated Tin Mines of Nigeria account for 75 per cent of output at approximately 10 000 tons a year. Nigeria produces 5 per cent of the world's tin and is the fifth producing country; tin is her fourth most important export by value although it stands at only 7 per cent of the value of oil. In 1973 a National Mining Corporation was set up to seek equity participation in the larger companies—perhaps 80 per cent by 1980: that is, a slow process of nationalisation.

A major industrial bottleneck which provided an extraordinary story in August 1975 (for the new Mohammed government to deal with) concerns cement. The 1975 port congestion saga was largely a matter of endless cement ships waiting to unload, demurrage charges sending the price of cement soaring while the building developments resulting from the oil boom were being held up by the blockage. All this was compounded by the fact that Nigeria has not begun to develop an adequate cement business of its own. One reason why more cement production in Nigeria was not started earlier was that huge profits were to be made by the middlemen handling the import of cement. In the North West State Sokoto has a cement industry founded upon poor gravel and a political wish. In 1975 it was announced that the Nigerian Cement factory, Nkalagu, in the East Central State, was to spend ₦ 27 million in expansion to help meet the national demands so that its production will increase from 500 000 to 750 000 bags of cement a year by the end of 1976. The West African Portland Cement Company also announced plans to double its production to 1.5 million tons by 1977 and most of the additional output will come from the Shagamu Plant which will start at the end of 1977. In August 1975 157 ships, all carrying cement, were waiting in line at Lagos. In 1970 total cement supply was 1 062 000 tonnes and local production accounted for 596 000 tonnes. By 1973 demand had passed the 2 million tonne mark: local production had crept up to 1 222 000 tonnes; imports accounted for 855 000 tonnes. By 1974 Nigeria's consumption of cement had passed the 3 million tonne mark and a conservative estimate for the 1975–1980 plan period put consumption at 6 million tonnes a year. Despite plans for expansion local production is not expected to meet more than 60 per cent of demand over this period and the problem of importing large quantities will remain. The cement crisis of 1975 grew partly as a result of such reasons: the Ministry of Defence ordered far too much cement, whose carriers clogged the ports; the government could not free them and then was obliged to go to the Baltic Exchange and try to persuade foreign suppliers to cut back on contracts so that the backlog could be cleared.

The process of indigenising the economy started in the early 1970s. When fully completed it will make an enormous difference to industrial, commercial and economic development. The localisation of personnel will save huge sums in foreign exchange that currently go in salary remittances. Companies will save on expatriate labour, for the average cost to a company of expatriate personnel works out at £5 000 a year in excess of salary. Companies have been allocated quotas for expatriates according to their size and complexity: in 1972 the figure for such expatriates (including aid personnel) was 20 000. When the indigenisation proposals were originally announced they were welcomed; subsequently, the process turned somewhat sour for Nigerians because of the three long years the changeover took.

The indigenisation measures were announced in June 1971: 26 types of business—mainly those demanding relatively minor investments—were reserved exclusively for Nigerians, although they also included some relatively more important concerns such as assembly of radios and electrical equipment, newspaper printing and most service industries. Second came the List B concerns which were banned to foreign business unless the paid-up capital exceeded £N200 000 or turnover exceeded £N500 000; such a firm then had to have a 40 per cent Nigerian equity participation. This second list included manufacturing industries demanding a high level of industrial know-how such as chemicals, soap and detergents, textile and leather goods, distributing and servicing motor vehicles. On 21 October 1971, a Nigerian Ministry of Trade spokesman said there should be a three-year transition period for the complete take-over by Nigerians of certain categories of business. As critics were quick to point out, this gave ample time for foreign businessmen to get a fair price or do deals with Nigerian partners. In anticipation of these moves the banks went public; other companies took steps to raise their local shareholdings to 40 per cent—and often found difficulty in doing so. The smaller expatriate firms had to sell out completely.

The Nigerian Enterprises Promotion Decree aimed to bring large areas of the economy into Nigerian hands and those businesses under List A, totally banned to foreigners, had to be wound up by 31 March 1974. A board was set up to confiscate businesses after that date if they had not been correctly indigenised and heavy penalties were established for Nigerians acting as front men for foreigners. The programme was an open invitation to foreign firms to work out new ways to qualify them to stay rather than a means of obtaining greater Nigerian control. The bigger the operation the less likely that it would be affected; the people hardest hit tended to be the Lebanese population of small businessmen who were to find from 1974 onwards that their residence permits were not being renewed. The large foreign firms, meanwhile, showed willing by putting Nigerians on their boards and floating big share issues. Nigerian Breweries for instance offered 4 200 000 ordinary shares of 50 kobo at 40 kobo each; Bata Shoe Company also offered shares.

The big companies were also required by the decree to mount training schemes to speed up the localisation of the high level posts; committees were established to supervise the take-overs in the different states; and a Bank for Commerce and Industry was established. It was estimated that something like N 500 million of indigenous capital would be required to finance the take-overs.

The weakness of the indigenous sector—or rather of its members—to profit by Decree 52 can be seen in the following figures. In 1972 total foreign private investment was more than N 1 000 million of which mining (which was unaffected) accounted for half, and manufacturing for 30 per cent. Towards the end of the take-over deadline an estimated N 30 million had been spent on acquiring alien businesses, yet at that time less than 75 per cent of the businesses had been taken over while those not yet acquired had equity capital in excess of another N 30 million. Forty per cent of the shares offered by UAC and valued at N 10 million had not been taken up, and there was a similar outcome for other large companies that had attempted to sell their shares privately so that N 100 million was not an unreasonable figure for what was needed to complete the scheduled take-overs.[7]

The point was that the decree said foreigners had to sell, not that Nigerians had to buy, and much of the business on offer was in fact of low profitability and therefore unattractive. A good number of secret business deals were transacted. There exists the subsequent belief in Nigeria that a new class of *nouveaux riches* may have been created by the process of indigenisation: top Nigerian executives in the expatriate companies bought in secretly, not having to pay immediately; or close associates of the foreign businessmen did so, while some aliens remained undisclosed directors of the new companies. In some cases the state governments bought shares when companies went public; too few ordinary Nigerians became stockholders as the companies changed hands.

Indigenisation took off slowly and cautiously; the structure of the private sector changed little. There was no mass exodus of alien businessmen from Nigeria and no subsequent indication of one. Instead, doubts remain as to just how much of a take-over had occurred.

At the end of the indigenisation exercise, 40 per cent of share capital of all companies in Nigeria was in the hands of private Nigerian citizens, organisations or state governments. How much does this represent indigenisation? Indigenisation has been described as a device whereby the Nigerian bourgeoisie protects imperialist economic domination in the country. For example, only the Nigerian Coal Corporation breaks the total foreign monopoly of mining in Nigeria. As one critic put it, instead of the government acquiring all alien enterprises for the people, Nigeria adopted the elitist, selfish and discriminatory method of private acquisition through public loans:

> The worst example of this in Nigeria is the fraudulent indigenisation programme which has in effect utilised public loans to transfer numerous foreign enterprises to domestic capitalists.[8]

Nigeria is an economist's dream: a classic example of inflation as the result of too much money chasing too few goods, a situation made far worse by bottlenecks such as the port congestion at Lagos. No one knew or could have predicted the enormous boom that Nigeria was to enjoy in the post-1973 oil price-rise period.

Few developing countries face the problem of too much money: the result in Nigeria is that every conceivable thing is being imported and there are all the appearances of a get-rich-quick society evolving. Part of the trouble is that everything is required at once—more cement plants, more schools, more roads, better infrastructure for industrial and commercial growth. Yet apparent anomalies occur: apart from the shortages due to drought in 1975, more groundnuts are being consumed in Nigeria so that the crushing mills for the export trade stand idle while the trade itself has declined. Because the boom has passed the country's infrastructure there are not enough telephones; there are constant power cuts; there are water shortages for industry; and the entrepreneur who can find a way of importing spare parts—for almost anything—is liable to make his fortune, so desperate is the demand. A growing if still small-scale stock market—one of Africa's first—is as good an indication as any of the economic-capitalist state which Nigeria has now achieved, while another sign of the country's growing economic significance is the fact that merchant bankers from London and elsewhere are moving into Lagos to help finance development. (See Appendix 6.)

Despite indigenisation Nigeria is very keen to attract more foreign investors into the country. In some fields Nigerians have hardly begun to move: thus, the Bight of Biafra is one of the richest fishing areas in the world, swarming with Japanese, Russian, Norwegian and other fishing fleets and factory ships. One or two Nigerian companies have now entered this business in a small way, but the openings on the country's doorstep are potentially enormous: almost limitless business opportunities abound.

The political problems that accompany the boom are themselves formidable enough. How to spread the wealth to the people? How to ensure that agriculture keeps pace with the oil and industrial and commercial advances taking place? What do the rural people in the villages want as opposed to what the top military or political people say they want? The signs of boom are even to be found in the remotest rural areas. Where, twenty years ago, there might have been a single radio in a village, the herdsman now carries his portable set as he follows his cattle. Government policy has been to inflate prices so as to spread benefits to the rural areas; some cash crop prices paid in Nigeria are now above world prices.

These changes, expedients and problems signify a country on the move. What is not yet clear is where it wants to go.

Notes

1   Quoted in C. Legum, *Africa Contemporary Record 1973–1974*, p. B723.
2   *Africa Magazine*, June 1975
3   *Ibid.*

4   D. Babatunde Thomas, *Capital Accumulation, and Technology Transfer*, Praeger,
     1975, p. 4
5   *Ibid.*, p. 21
6   Oni and Onimode, *Economic Development of Nigeria*, p. 13
7   *Africa Magazine*, November 1974
8   *Economic Development of Nigeria, op. cit.*, p. 80

Chapter nine

Agriculture

Agriculture is the basis of life in Nigeria and despite oil the economy is and must remain founded upon it. The problems agriculture faces are formidable, yet 80 per cent of the people live, work or have livelihoods dependent on the land. Like the rest of Africa, Nigeria suffers from rural poverty and for years has experienced a steady drift away from the rural areas to the towns.

Agriculture employs about 70 per cent of the labour force; it suffers from low productivity and suffers from the vagaries of world prices while in purely Nigerian terms the civil war set it back. The Second Development Plan only allocated 12.9 per cent of total investment to agriculture while projecting a 2 per cent growth for the sector as a whole whereas a 6.6 per cent growth rate was projected for the entire economy. Agriculture divides into domestic and export. The system of marketing boards for the main commodities has ensured a long lag in the reaction of farmers and farm output to external influences. The share of agriculture as a percentage of the GDP has been dropping steadily: it was 63 per cent in 1960, 49 per cent in 1969 and down to 44 per cent in 1974. This change is not in itself a bad development since other sectors of the economy are growing fast and diversification will mean less absolute dependence on agriculture, which is a development to be welcomed, yet in absolute terms agricultural output declined seriously over the 1969–71 period and is now well below the 1960 level.[1]

Nigeria's agriculture was developed in response to colonial needs: that is, the export commodities such as cocoa, cotton, groundnuts, palm oil and kernel. Cash cropping for export assumes an international division of labour that would trap Nigeria in a primary production role while 'foreign exploiters rush mass-produced manufactures at exploitative prices on the country.'[2]

Nigeria's population is growing at a rate of nearly 3 per cent per annum to double in 25 years; agricultural output, however, is only growing at a rate of 2 per cent per annum. The current average food intake of Nigerians is 2 000 calories per head so that the people as a whole are grossly underfed. To raise the calorific intake from 2 000 to 4 000 over 15 years (taking account of the expanding population at the same time) would require a growth of 7.8 per cent. This is not an impossible target.[3]

Agricultural production reached a nadir in 1974 when the Central Bank reported that the index of output of export commodities for the first half of the year stood at only 52.8 as opposed to 100 in 1960. It was a year affected by drought, it is true, and the total groundnut crop was only 42 000 tonnes as opposed to an average of 500 000 tonnes; the cotton mills were forced to import, so bad was the cotton crop, and the foodstuffs position had markedly deteriorated. As the Third Plan was forced to admit, the supply of maize, millet, sorghum, wheat, yam, groundnuts, vegetables, fruit, palm oil, groundnut oil and melon seed oil would be short in 1975 and no better in 1980. The plan went on:

> The conclusion to be drawn is that at the present rate of growth of supplies, Nigeria will not be able to feed its people in the next decade unless there is a radical departure from existing attitudes to investment in agriculture.

The new plan will do much to change this (see Chapter 7), but it is far more than a question of pumping money into agriculture although the money at least is available. Farmers lack credit, there are far too few extension workers available to advise them, there are few efficient co-operatives and all too often marketing facilities and communications are poor. A key to a revival of agriculture, therefore, is that of improving the status of the farmer: in essence this means paying him more for his crops so that it becomes an attractive business to be a farmer and, as a consequence, encourages farmers' sons not to desert the land for the towns. Efforts have been made in this direction and in 1974 farm prices were sharply increased for certain commodities: cocoa, for example, at N450 a tonne obtains the highest available price in West Africa. Such prices are still not enough and the plan promised that prices would be fixed with 'no trading surpluses' in view. The nub of the problem, however, is not cash crops, which are relatively easy to encourage with artificially high government prices, but production of food for home consumption.

Nigeria is starting to look seriously at the major project approach to agriculture. The government is increasingly considering estate production of certain commodities while it is encouraging investment by the World Bank in major schemes. At Gombe in the North East, for example, there is a project to assist a total of 58 000 farmers working their own land while its wider benefits will assist more than 640 000 people in the state.[4] In this case the Bank is financing the building of roads, the provision of water, technical assistance, marketing and credit facilities for the production of 21 000 tonnes of cotton, groundnuts, sorghum and maize. There are other World Bank schemes such as that for cocoa in the West. The Third Plan is looking for growth rates in many crops of between 5 and 10 per cent. The potential for expansion exists; but in the mid-1970s agriculture had declined drastically.

Oil has replaced agriculture as the backbone of the Nigerian economy; the danger is that while oil lasts insufficient attention will be given to bringing agriculture back to pride of place. In 1960 agriculture was the country's major foreign currency earner. At the end of 1974 agricultural exports earned N-332.3 million and its share of total domestic exports then stood at only 6 per cent. In 1965 agricultural exports as a share of domestic exports were 62.8 per cent, in 1970 they had fallen to 37.8 per cent and in 1973 were down to 13.5 per cent. The Third Plan will inject N-2.2 billion into the agricultural sector between 1975 and 1980; more than just money will be needed.[5]

Nigeria is blessed with vast land resources. There are 91.2 million hectares of land of which three quarters are cultivable yet at present only a third of this is under cultivation. Much of the cultivable land, however, is in areas remote from the major centres of population and to open it up would entail large-scale movement of people and their resettlement—itself a difficult and highly political undertaking. The reason for low productivity in Nigeria is in part because many of the country's soils are—relatively speaking—infertile and require inputs of fertiliser, improved seed varieties and the use of pesticides which as yet the country has not begun to employ adequately. At the same time the population is increasing faster than food production. There is substantial soil erosion taking place in the southern humid rainforest areas. Erosion problems are exacerbated by the poverty and ignorance of many farmers and the lack, once more, of adequate extension workers to advise on the best methods of combatting erosion. Land poverty is coupled with the actual poverty of many of the rural areas where a pattern of subsistence farming remains unchanged after many generations. As the President of the Nigerian Co-operative Federation said in July 1975, the high cost of farm chemicals had constantly reduced Nigerian farmers to 'poverty-stricken citizens'. He was making a call to both the federal and state governments to review policies that allowed a continuing drift of the young away from the land to the urban areas.[6]

The utilisation of the land in Nigeria is just as wasteful as the burning off of natural gas: the country has vast tracts of uncultivated arable land, 'a storehouse for the agricultural revolution of this country'. Yet there is unemployment, shortages of food and so a huge food import bill.[7] This critic continues:

> Some 80 per cent of Nigeria's total arable land is still uncultivated. Yet the country is today suffering from acute food shortage. Our untilled and underutilised agricultural land is one of the huge sources of waste in the economy.[8]

This may be true in an overall sense yet much of the unused land is remote from population while there is little extra available land where the people live. There would therefore be formidable—though not insuperable—problems in bringing the unused land under cultivation. In this connection the Chairman of the Ibadan Chamber of Commerce, Alhaji Adebayo Adetunji, called upon the government in July 1975 to make grants to the states so that they could develop the unused hinterland.

As a starting point for any attack upon Nigeria's agricultural problems the position of the great majority of subsistence farmers should first be clearly understood. They get poor remuneration for their crops; they face major distribution problems; transport and storage facilities are poor; the drudgery of work on small plots has to be understood by those who speak glibly of 'back to the land' or the 'dignity' of work on the land; a majority are illiterate and there are few social or other amenities in the rural areas; extension services where they exist are bad or sparse; and most small farmers, in fact, are so poor that they cannot afford the technology—either fertilisers or machinery—needed for improvement. This formidable list of difficulties has to be overcome.

Nigeria is self-sufficient in food production—more or less—except for certain selected foods such as sugar and wheat which have to be imported: in the case of sugar there are major plans to produce large quantities in the North East and elsewhere. But while food production is only increasing at a rate of 2 per cent per annum demand is increasing at 4.5 per cent per annum (see Appendix 7). Currently 80 per cent of the total agricultural output is derived from the food sub-sector though it produces little foreign exchange.

Yet the country faces food shortages that should never occur. Thus, in the first six months of 1970 Nigeria's food import bill was £13 million; for the first six months of 1971 it had risen to £19 million so that a country which is 80 per cent agrarian is importing an increasing amount of food.[9] As a result of the cash crop syndrome Nigeria has come to face a serious food problem.

Delivering a presidential adress to the Nigerian Society for Animal Production in July, 1975, Professor A. V. Oyenuga said: 'The situation in the food front is so serious that it calls for the mobilisation of all available manpower and financial resources for its solution, if necessary under emergency situation.' The professor predicted impending famine for Nigeria by 1980 when the population would have reached the 90 million mark. He went on to say how low the average Nigerian diet had fallen and called for a reappraisal of the Third Plan as far as it concerned food production. The professor, an agronomist, was no doubt being deliberately pessimistic in order to make a particular point on behalf of the agricultural section of the community.

Nevertheless, there are unmistakable signs that Nigerian agriculture is far from able, on current form, to produce the food requirements

13 Despite oil, the Nigerian economy is founded upon agriculture, yet output has
declined. The Third Plan aims to reverse this decline. Pyramids of groundnuts
at Kaduna (above) and Kano (below) look plentiful but demand is increasing

14 There is a major
expansion scheme for
cocoa, long one of the
staples of the Nigerian
economy, while under
the Third Plan
production of maize will
be dramatically
increased

15 It is hoped to increase cotton output to 300 000 bales a year, all to be
retained for the home textile industry

16 Although 90 per cent of cattle in Nigeria belong to the Fulani who keep to traditional methods of farming, in other areas of agriculture modern mechanised methods are increasingly being adopted

of a rapidly growing population that will also expect—and should obtain—higher food standards. One billion six hundred thousand naira has been earmarked for accelerated food production in the Third Plan, and there are to be nation-wide integrated research and extension programmes designed to increase food output. Initially the programmes will concentrate upon such crops as sorghum, maize, rice, millet, wheat and cassava; 24 000 hectares will be cultivated during the plan period with the participation of 324 000 farmers throughout the country. It is hoped that this scheme will lead to an annual yield of 146 000 tonnes of rice; 97 400 tonnes of maize; 4 000 tonnes of sorghum; 93 000 tonnes of wheat; 3 000 tonnes of soya beans; and 10 700 tonnes of pigeon peas. All this is to the good but without far more sustained effort and thrust from the centre it still seems likely that Nigeria will fall behind in the production of essential foodstuffs for its population.

The poor showing of the rural sector in recent years has accentuated the drift to the towns. This in turn affects the urban area where large numbers vainly seek jobs while the rural areas have been depleted of their young people. Until the advent of oil, export crops were Nigeria's main source of foreign income, and as late as 1972 agriculture still accounted for 50 per cent of GDP. Yet it was no longer responding to the needs of a booming country and in that year every major agricultural export declined. Part of the explanation was in no sense damaging to the economy: that is, the farmers had been switching to growing food for home consumption in place of the traditional cash crops since, with a more wealthy population including a huge well paid army, they could get better prices at home. Despite this there were increasing indications that the farmers were not growing enough to feed the urban populations

The drift from the land, especially by the young, is an acute problem. To combat it will require the provision of rural facilities on a scale hitherto not attempted—proper water supply, electrification and so on. The key will be to make farming profitable—then the people will stay. There remain very small incomes for rural pursuits where the Udoji awards have had no place. And there are other influences at work. In the Rivers State, for example, it has become easier to obtain a job in 'oil' (which is also better paid) than to go on producing palm oil—once the staple product of the area—and this has declined in consequence. No talk of a return to the land and no measures to provide better rural amenities will in fact prevent a continuing drift to the towns if it is there that the money is to be made. As long as this situation exists, to the towns the people will go.

By the early 1970s the government had ceased to rely solely upon the peasant farmer to produce the foodstuffs required to feed an expanding population. It fixed prices centrally for the whole nation while making it possible for the peasant to get long-term, low-interest

loans from the Nigerian Agricultural Credit Bank. The policy has yet
to be fully developed.

In view of the size of Nigeria it has remarkably few large-scale
agricultural developments though some that are underway will make
significant impacts upon the economy as a whole. The Kainji
Development Corporation exists to develop agro-industries affecting
general agriculture, livestock and fisheries in an area of 300 000
hectares below the enormous dam as well as fisheries in the 1 300
square kilometre lake behind it.

Other large-scale projects are less advanced but urgently needed.
There is, for example, the Sokoto-Rima Valley Development Authority and the Chad Basin Authority. The latter aims to grow 24 000
tonnes of wheat, 30 000 tonnes of rice and 3 000 tonnes of long staple
cotton a year. In the North Central State (Kaduna) there is the
Funtua agricultural project which in 1975 had 160 extension staff: it
requires a total of 600. This is a tripartite scheme backed by the World
Bank, the Federal Military Government and the State Government.
Its aim is to determine the effects of widespread extension work. It will
cost N 39 million.

In mid-1975 a contract worth N 110 million was awarded to the
consulting and engineering company Impresit Bakolari Nigeria for a
dam and irrigation project. The reservoir will cover 30 350 hectares
and the project will provide year round agricultural activities in food
crops and the development of livestock and fisheries. Irrigation of the
first 60 000 reclaimed hectares is expected to start in 1977 although the
project will only be fully operational by the end of 1980. So heavy is the
cost of the scheme per settler, however, that its value may be
questioned in comparison with other ways of spending the money. The
then Federal Commissioner for Agriculture and Natural Resources
(Major-General E. O. Ekpo) said the government was giving priority
to the development of water resources to help agriculture. It was then
announced that four other River Basin Development Authorities
would be established: the River Niger Basin; the Benue; the Ogun-
Oshun; and the Hadejia-Jama'are.

The Federal Government has adopted a policy of engaging in direct
participation with state governments in a variety of ambitious
agricultural projects. These include large-scale ranching, irrigation,
grain storage and livestock disease eradication as well as the provision
of infrastructural support for the processing, evacuation, transport and
distribution of essential agricultural commodities all over the federation.

The Third Plan allocates N 2.2 billion to the agricultural sector. It
aims vastly to increase the production of food, tree crops, fruit and
vegetables; to establish 1.5 million hectares of cereals and 400 million
hectares of root crops such as yams and cassava; 117 000 hectares of
cocoa, 170 000 hectares of palm oil and 55 000 hectares of rubber. The

plan also emphasises the need for major irrigation projects, helping farmers with fertilisers and insecticides as well as better tools and equipment. All this makes good reading; the problem will lie in the implementation. The second plan with an allocation to agriculture of N225 million spent only N97 million of it. The money devoted to agriculture in the Third Plan is enough and probably more than the sector can absorb properly in five years. The basic problem will lie in available manpower resources to make sure that such money is absorbed efficiently and put to best use.

Nigeria has a number of agricultural institutions that will play a part in the implementation of the plan. For example, the Nigerian Agricultural Bank expects to lend N200 million during the plan period. It went into operation in December 1972 with financial assistance from the UNDP and the IBRD and up to the start of the Third Plan had made loans to the extent of 50 million. During 1975 Nigerians took over control of the bank from the expatriate experts who had been running it. Its policy is to assist those activities most likely to result in greater food supplies: such activities as the production of pork and eggs rather than longer-term ones such as cattle-raising. A need exists, however, for much stronger direction of agricultural development than so far has been given since independence. There is insufficient attention to agricultural education at the national level. Thus, most primary and secondary schools do not offer agricultural subjects; the new, much publicised, UPE programme pays little attention to agriculture.

Agricultural commodities suffered some severe setbacks in the 1970s. The coming years are likely to witness some interesting new developments in the Nigerian commodity field, for though production of many commodities may be substantially increased, this will not necessarily be followed by a comparable increase in exports since Nigerians will themselves be consuming them in quantity for the first time as a result of the new prosperity.

A good example of this is sugar. Nigerian annual sugar consumption stands at 170 000 tonnes but in 1975 the country's only sugar mill at Bacita produced no more than 40 000 tonnes of this requirement so that 130 000 tonnes had to be imported. Extensive plans are under way to turn Nigeria into a substantial sugar producer. There are three new sugar projects in the planning stage; the mill at Bacita is being expanded; and Tate and Lyle is to produce 70 000 tonnes at Sunti. By far the biggest scheme, however, is that of the Savannah Sugar Company development at Numan in the north east, a two thirds Federal and one third CDC scheme, the latter providing the technicians and management. The total cost of this project described by CDC's representative John Langton as 'the most exciting commercial development in Nigeria' will be N150 million; its plantations will extend over 25 kilometres; and in the end it will provide work for

30 000 people. It is expected to reach a production figure of 100 000 tonnes of sugar a year by 1982. If all these plans come to fruition Nigeria should be producing some 270 000 tonnes of sugar in 1984—more than her total needs in the mid 1970s—but by then it is probable that consumption will have expanded to absorb the extra output. At least the country should no longer have to import sugar.

The other major commodities are groundnuts, palm products, rubber, cocoa and cotton, and apart from cocoa none was doing well in the mid-1970s. Although the average marketed crop of groundnuts had for years been 500 000 tonnes, drought reduced the 1973–74 crop disastrously to 42 000 tonnes, and the expectations for 1974–75 were for only 250 000 tonnes. There has been a shift of emphasis in demand: public taste has been switching since the civil war from cheaper palm oil to the more expensive groundnut oil so that local prices for this have risen and in consequence less groundnuts have been sold to the marketing boards. This is part of the pattern whereby prosperity is adversely affecting the amount of cash crops available for export. Production of palm kernels has been falling for years, and although the world price reached a peak in May 1974 it declined again in 1975. The crushing capacity of Nigerian mills is 300 000 tonnes while production of palm kernels for 1975 was expected to reach 400 000 tonnes, so a number of new mills were being built. Palm oil consumption in Nigeria has increased so that production has been unable both to keep pace with it as well as the old export demands and as a result Nigeria no longer produces for export. Palm oil used to be produced mainly in the Rivers State and the East Central State but the industry ran down during the war and the palms went back to bush; the process of rehabilitation proceeds with Word Bank assistance. South-East State (now Cross River) is the major producer, though Mid-West (Bendel) and West (Ogun, Ondo and Oyo) are also important.

In the case of cocoa, long one of the staples of the Nigerian economy, crops average 220 000 tonnes a year and at N450 a tonne Nigerian farmers received as of 1974 the highest price for cocoa in West Africa so that smuggling has been discouraged. There is a major expansion programme for this crop in the plan. It is hoped to increase cotton output from 170 000 bales in 1973–74 to an annual crop figure of 300 000 to 350 000 bales (180 kg each); all cotton will be for home consumption to feed home mills. Even so, for the foreseeable future Nigeria will import large quantities of textiles.

Government policy on commodities in the 1970s was to pay farmers more and more money for their produce so as to stimulate higher output as well as keeping people on the land. In turn, however, the companies that rely upon these raw materials also have to pay increasingly higher prices so that sometimes Nigerian prices have outstripped world prices. In 1975, for example, the price of palm oil in Nigeria was above the world price. This raises awkward policy matters. The government wishes to pay higher prices to farmers, first, to ensure a spread of oil wealth to the rural communities, and second, to induce them to stay on the land and so stimulate production, including that of export crops. The policy may defeat itself if the price of export crops goes higher than the average world price. An alternative approach may have to be found with a system of subsidies to farmers so that the price of export commodities can be kept competitive.

Livestock present an altogether more complicated problem as far as modernisation of that sector of agriculture is concerned. In the north the Fulani run their herds over large areas and sell them for meat as and when they wish, automatically undercutting any specially produced beef so that such meat production cannot be a paying proposition. The country faces some cattle shortages—partly as a result of the drought which reduced the country's herd by two million head as well as reducing supply centres since it also slashed the herds in neighbouring countries such as Chad and Niger. Estimates for 1974 put the national herd at 8.5 million head; in addition some 287 000 herds of cattle were imported from neighbouring countries. The goat population was estimated at 22 million and sheep at 8 million. The poultry business was then booming, producing 45 million birds in 1974. But national population growth is outstripping livestock growth. Nigeria needs a livestock revolution: 90 per cent of the cattle population belong to the northern Fulani who raise their cattle by traditional methods and run them over extensive areas so that low productivity results; moreover, their sales are all too often for specific purposes such as the payment of school fees[10] rather than as part of a systematic livestock production process. There are major restraints upon changing the cattle approach in the north, though some are being removed with the construction of large-scale water conservation projects and the abolition of the jangali tax system. But certain problems remain: the tsetse fly, poor credit, a lack of qualified manpower and, generally, a poor marketing infrastructure. Long-term solutions, therefore, will require intensive work and education, a great assault upon cattle disease and, indeed, the farming way of life of the nomadic herdsmen—tasks that no government will be able to undertake lightly.

Marketing is still one of the greatest restraints upon an efficient agricultural sector. A recent study[11] showed that 44 per cent of food transportation was still by head; 35 per cent by lorry; 6 per cent by rail; 5 per cent by canoe; 5 per cent by pushcart; and 4 per cent by bicycle. There is an urgent need for new roads in the rural districts and secondary roads linking remote areas to the main highways and, generally, a need for better systems for marketing all cash crops. Processing and storage facilities are often insufficient, while proper rural marketing organisations are needed. There are problems of water wastage and the need for conservation measures in many parts of the country—as the drought brought home clearly and tragically enough in the north. It is not simply a question of dam-building. When a dam of particular capacity has been built to irrigate an area some distance away, other problems have to be solved: how much evaporates; who else taps the supply; how can the water be transported intact; and so on. Again, recent estimates suggest that as much as 40 per cent of gross agricultural output is lost through pests, weight loss and poor storage. Only about 120 000 tonnes of chemical aids are used per annum representing less than 1.3 tonnes a square kilometre of arable land. And in real terms extension services for much of the country are non-existent, with one extension worker for anything between 15 000 and 30 000 farmers. There are very few big farmers or plantations in Nigeria. The relatively big farmers consist mainly of civil servants or businessmen who may in their spare time farm 80 or so hectares. All these 'big' farms combined add up to no more than 1 per cent of farmed land.

At the root of any fundamental improvement of agricultural performance is the question of trained manpower. The crying need is for more and better extension workers. Under the Third Plan all the states are to have agricultural colleges which is a start. There are some major inhibiting factors in the agricultural sector: the first of these is the limited number of extension workers—the people simply do not exist to take new technology to the farmers. Generally there is a ratio of one to 3 000 and often it is very much worse than that. In 1975 in the North Central State (Kaduna)—a major agricultural area—there was a professional staff, with degrees, of 30. Senior technical staff with diplomas came to 62, intermediate staff with diplomas numbered 187, while junior technical staff with certificates numbered 229. There were also some juniors in training. Vocational staff at the village levels came to a further 289 with an additional 100 in training. To change the extension ratio from what in some places stands at one to 20 000 to one to 500 means up to 40 times as many extension workers as now exist in the whole country. Addressing the Nigeria Association for Agricultural Education in August 1975 the president, Dr Onazi, said that the additional manpower needs for the Third Plan were 20 600, of whom 2 500 should be senior staff category, while the rest would be junior and intermediate. Dr Onazi suggested that state schools of agriculture should be affiliated to existing and proposed universities while the state's Permanent Secretary in the Ministry of Agriculture observed that the UPE programme paid no attention to agricultural education.[12]

After manpower comes the question of fertilisers. One agricultural adviser has suggested that the quickest way for Nigerian farmers to improve productivity would be by stepping up the use of fertilisers. Farmers use no more than 2 kilograms a hectare, an astonishingly low quantity by any standards.[13] An easy way to increase productivity would be a heavy programme of fertiliser subsidies. But the correct use of fertilisers requires expert knowledge and here, once more, the problem comes back to the need for extension workers. Even so, most quite illiterate farmers have been converted to the need for fertilisers. The problem in recent years has been that of availability both in the absolute sense and in terms of price. It is little good teaching the use of fertilisers to farmers who then find either that none is available or that it is beyond their financial means. Oil now makes a Nigerian fertiliser industry feasible; it is much needed.

Agricultural possibilities in Nigeria are enormous; so far they have not come near to realisation. They exist in many spheres apart from the traditional fields of commodity production upon which the sector has long been based. There is poultry: a scraggy roadside hen sells in Nigeria for anything from N1.50 to N3.50 (in Calabar) and 12 eggs retail for 70 kobo to N1.20. The country ought to produce millions of properly fattened chickens on a ten-week cycle as a commercial venture. To do so would be relatively cheap, a business entirely confined to Nigerians and such activity should be embarked upon at speed during the period of the Third Plan. There is similar need and opportunity for piggeries; it is absurd that bacon and pork products are imported. Vegetable possibilities, especially market gardening, to supply the major urban centres also need new approaches: eight hectares of sewage waste outside Kano produce excellent vegetables (though hygiene considerations may cause concern). Vegetables fetch high prices in the markets and the demand is huge.

In the north, where the climate is comparable with that of California, there is great agricultural potential which as yet has been little realised. There are three possibilities: first, for Nigeria to become entirely self-sufficient and this would have to include expansion to take care of the rapidly growing population; second, for Nigeria to become a major exporter to its ECOWAS partners; and thirdly, to develop certain specialised fields—especially winter vegetables and fruit—for sale to the huge European market of the European Economic Community (EEC). Nigeria is capable of producing all types of grain. Often the biggest problem is that of harnessing water resources but at least this is now being tackled.

One valuable but vital exercise would be to identify new food development possibilities by examining the import figures for specific foods and asking what foods (such as wheat) could be produced entirely within the country. There are rather specialised economic considerations to bear in mind. For example, even were it to cost more to produce a particular crop than to import it, home production would nonetheless save foreign exchange as well as providing new development incentives. Such decisions are political as well as economic.

Everyone is aware of the need to transform the oil wealth, while it lasts, into other forms of development. The land is Nigeria's greatest abiding resource; it is woefully—in some cases pitiably—under-developed. Oil will make it possible over the next generation for Nigeria to put into agriculture resources of a kind that its neighbours—countries such as Chad, Niger and Cameroon—will not be able to afford. The result could be spectacular: the development of Nigeria, and especially the north, as the granary and food store of West Africa. This may sound like a pipe-dream, yet nowhere else has Nigeria such potential for development as it has on the land.

Notes

1   *African Development*, March 1974
2   *Economic Development of Nigeria, op. cit.*, p. 191
3   *African Development*, March 1974
4   *African Development*, March 1975
5   *Times International*, 28 July 1975
6   *Nigerian Tide*, 15 July 1975
7   *Economic Development of Nigeria*, p. 69
8   *Ibid.*, p. 141
9   Basil Davidson, *Can Africa Survive*, Heinemann, 1974, p. 22
10   *Daily Times*, 26 July 1975
11   *African Development*, March 1973
12   *Daily Times*, 13 August 1975
13   *African Development*, March 1975

Chapter ten

Education and manpower

Demands for more and better education have been a standard accompaniment of the development process in all post-colonial societies and in this respect Nigeria is certainly no exception. The magnitude of the task is different, however, as will be the demands upon its trained manpower. Striving for technological and economic breakthroughs like every other country on the continent and determined to break free of dependence upon imported expatriate manpower—to indigenise—Nigeria will snap up voraciously anyone with training, most especially at the middle and managerial levels. To turn out the people it needs Nigeria first has to create the solid foundations of an educational system at the primary and secondary levels and here it yet has a long way to go.

Successive Nigerian governments have paid lip-service to the concept of evolving an educational system uniquely suited to the country's needs. As far back as 1962 a delegation of educational administrators and teachers was sent on an extensive tour of Britain, the USA, European and South American countries to take into consideration the best aspects of education in those countries. Nothing followed. In 1968 a National Conference on Education was held in Lagos. Again nothing resulted. Today, faced with the pressing needs of an expanding economy and the urgent political demands that all the people should benefit from its oil wealth, Nigeria has still to find a coherent indigenous educational philosophy. Most of the existing educational pattern remains British-colonial, snob-dominated: the emphasis is on white-collar rather than technical aspirations while the need in a purely development sense is for more mathematics and the sciences, and above all, for technical colleges.

Certain facts are obvious enough in their results whatever the philosophy may be. First, that a society with a literacy rate of only 20 per cent out of 70 million and more people is wasting a vast amount of its potential skills. Second, that there can be no real breakthrough unless educational opportunities exist for all. Third, that the dropout rate is very high and, for example, the unemployment rate is highest among primary school leavers who far too often simply have not attained enough education to qualify them to do anything. Nigeria is still a country of educational contrasts. At one end of the scale are large numbers of people with no formal education at all; at the other there are private schools modelled on a nineteenth-century British pattern rather than geared to Nigerian needs in the last quarter of the twentieth century.

One of the problems in Nigeria has been educational diversity from state to state. Different policies and varying standards result from lack of funds leading to poor staffing, inadequate equipment, sub-standard libraries and so on. Finances now are less of a problem. Equipment alone is not enough to provide a good education; staff take years to train and for a long time still Nigeria must remain partly dependent upon expatriate teachers.

Perhaps the beginnings of a single approach to education can be a seminar whose 'Report of the seminar on a national policy on education' was published in June 1973.[1] This suggested:

> Nigeria's national philosophy on education must be based on equal opportunities for all citizens of the nation at the primary, secondary and tertiary levels, both inside and outside the formal school system. Such a philosophy must have as its central base, the physical, intellectual, spiritual, emotional and ethical integration of the individual into a complete man.

This sounds magnificent, but what does it mean in practical terms when despite the money there do not exist the teachers even at the lowest primary level to see that all Nigerians start off on this splendid egalitarian path? The report advocated free universal basic education in a variety of forms suited to the needs and potential of students depending upon their situation and opportunities. In most of southern Nigeria the current educational approach is based upon a 6–5–2–3 year plan: that is, six years' primary education, five years' secondary, two years' higher school certificate course and three years' degree course.[2] This is fundamentally the old British pattern. In some states primary education is free, in others not, though by 1979 it should be free throughout the country.

Secondary education is neither free nor compulsory. The 1973 report suggested a new approach with a 6–3–3–4 system substituted. In this case there would still be six years' primary education followed by three years' secondary education that would include pre-vocational subjects (metalwork, woodwork, typing) so that those who wanted to seek employment at an early stage would already have some training for it. The next three years, however, would be a continuation of secondary general education that also included some marketable skills so that school leavers after the sixth year could obtain employment; the last four years would be for university or higher educational training.

Secondary education in Nigeria still expects to cater for only a fraction of the potential school-going population. With the coming of UPE, however, the states are beginning to expand their secondary school building programmes. Manpower is the greatest restraint: there are not enough teachers. Now that all universities have been federalised students should be encouraged to feel free to train in any part of the country at the institute of their choice. Such a move would also promote a sense of national unity and encourage mobility among academic staff. Nigerian secondary pupils still sit the West African School Certificate; Nigeria may have its own Examination Council and set its own examinations. In many ways Nigeria remains within a British colonial straitjacket. Much of the heritage is sound enough but it was conceived in circumstances and at a time totally different from the mid-1970s. To answer the urgent needs and aspirations of its people as it emerges both politically and economically as the first nation of Africa, Nigeria needs to create a system more suited to its own needs. Nigerian society is currently changing at great speed; its educational system should catch up with the changes.

There are special political problems connected with education and the most important of these centres on the question: how does the north catch up? Ahmadu Bello University, now the largest in the country, turns out graduates (some of them southerners) as fast as possible, but the educational imbalance between north and south has always been one of the key political problems of the country. Because of the small number of graduates in the north as opposed to those in the south at independence, demands have grown up for a quota system for places in universities. The gap between north and south—however many efforts to catch up are being made—is still so wide that it will be many years before there can be any sort of educational uniformity of opportunity across the country. In 1972, for example, the Federal Commissioner for Education said that

> so wide is the gap that roughly speaking, for every child in a primary school in the Northern States there are four in the Southern States; for every boy or girl in a Secondary School in the North, there are five in the South. And for every student in a post-secondary school in the North, there are six in the South.[3]

This assessment shows the extent to which the north lags behind; while it 'catches up', the south will continue to forge ahead.

The introduction of Universal Primary Education in Nigeria—between 1976 and 1979, it is hoped—will cost many millions (the least of the problems) and require tens of thousands of primary teachers. Even if these numbers of would-be teachers can be found, many are unlikely to reach the quality required. Statistically the problem is formidable. There were approximately 4.5 million children in primary school in 1975. By 1981 this figure will have rocketed to an incredible 18 million (all children between the ages of six and 11) who will qualify for primary education when full-scale UPE is in operation across the country. Provisional estimates of the costs of the UPE programme give an annual figure of N-208 million for the first six years and then when full attendance has been reached a new figure of N-600 million a year. These figures are tentative estimates based upon the 1963 census details. The 1973 census was cancelled; the possibility is that the number of children qualifying for primary education could be significantly greater than these figures suggest. Phase one of UPE, planned to start in September 1976, requires the admittance of all six-year-olds to school; thereafter schools are to admit all eligible children each year. For the first year alone an additional 40 000 primary school teachers will be needed. By the time the six-year programme has been completed in 1981 (when in theory all eligible children automatically go to primary school), an additional 450 000 teachers should have been added to the 1975 figure of 150 000 primary teachers. The capital costs of such a programme will be vast, and here again the north starts at a disadvantage, for primary education has been sadly neglected there and schools too often have been allowed to run down.

It is one of the ironies of the Nigerian educational story that the gigantic UPE exercise started casually when Gowon was on tour of the north in 1974: in response to a question from a small girl the General announced the intention to launch Universal Primary Education in 1976.[4] Thereafter the government and state departments battled to get the scheme off to a reasonable start. The figure of N-600 million a year in 1981 (see above) will be the teacher salary bill. There will also be vast capital costs. Pupil enrolment over the six-year period 1975–81 is expected to quadruple. Nigeria is obtaining loans from the World Bank as well as UNESCO technical assistance for the programme. But the main problem will be that of recruiting enough teachers. With strains upon every level of manpower as the Third Plan gets into high gear the chances of finding all the teachers the programme requires are not good. And in the north the problems are far worse. Thus, of the 4.5 million pupils attending primary school in 1975 only 15 per cent were from the four far northern states, although these contain half the country's total population. With 3.5 million children at primary school the southern states are not far off having achieved UPE. Although the resilience of Islamic culture in the north must not be underestimated, UPE will bring within measurable distance, for the first time, the possibility of the north's catching up educationally with the south.

One difficulty is that even though it is easy enough to find candidates for the teachers' training colleges, up to a fifth of those who pass through them do not subsequently go into teaching. Further, at a time of unprecedented expansion in all aspects of the economic, social and political life of the country everyone attracted into teaching will be someone taken away from other fields. Nigerians set great store by education and there is much enthusiasm for the attainment of UPE, but in view of the myriad problems attached to the programme it seems unlikely that the proposed 1976 intake of 2.5 million children into the primary system will be achieved. And what Nigeria still has to face is the fact that even when UPE is implemented in full, primary education will be for years to come the terminal point for a majority of children. It will be many years before a primary school leaver automatically goes on to secondary school; a secondary school child automatically completes six years if it wishes; and before a place of higher education is automatically open to a secondary school leaver.

Secondary education has to be paid for: the next educational target should be to make that universal, free and compulsory—an even more daunting task than the 1970s UPE target. There is a great deal of educational waste in Nigeria with high drop-out and failure rates. In primary schools the drop-out rate varies between 40 and 60 per cent and thereafter there are high failure rates throughout the system. In the mid-1970s the annual drop-out rate from primary schools was 400 000, while of the 240 000 qualified to go on to secondary school education there would be available for them no more than 70 000 places.

There is a long way to go in technical education, too, although an upsurge of attention to this branch of training took place in the mid-1970s. One of the last educational decisions of the Gowon regime in July 1975 was to establish a national board for technical education. The board was to operate on the lines of the National Universities Commission and be solely responsible for development and disbursement of funds for the growing technical education programme. The government then approved a grant of N100 million to the states to aid their technical education development programmes. Meanwhile the Third Plan proposed the establishment of a centre for the development and co-ordination of adult education. Nigeria's famous—only—technical college, Yaba College of Technology, is to be joined by three more such colleges in other parts of the country and these, especially, are designed to help meet the increasing demand for middle-level manpower.

At independence Nigeria enjoyed a better established university tradition than most African countries which at that point in their histories were only just creating universities of their own. Nigeria's leading universities are of a high standard, and Ibadan at least enjoys an international reputation. They are—and rightly—the centres of many storms, discussions and political upheavals and play a vital part in the intellectual life of the country. Yet they, too, faced the need for radical surgery and change in the mid-1970s as Nigeria's educational needs not only exploded quantitatively, in terms of demand for places, but changed quite fundamentally in terms of the requirements of a vast country just about to embark upon a mammoth industrial and technological revolution. In 1975 Nigeria had six universities: Ahmadu Bello; Nsukka; Ife; Lagos; Benin; Ibadan (with a campus at Jos). Since then four new universities—at Calabar, Jos, Maidugari and Sokoto—and two new university colleges—at Ilorin and Port Harcourt—have opened, or are in the process of doing so.

The Third Plan's university programme concentrates upon consolidating and expanding the six existing universities so as to ensure the maximum use of their facilities, and getting the four new universities and two new campuses into full operation. In combination these developments should enable the student population—about 27 000 in 1975—to be doubled to about 53 000 in 1980. In particular, greater emphasis will be placed upon the distribution of students among the various disciplines, especially the study of medicine, pure sciences and technology. The aim is to achieve a 60 to 40 science to humanities ratio.

The plan sets aside N370 million for higher education. This is broken down under the following headings: undergraduate bursaries N60 million; postgraduate bursaries, N24 million; student loans scheme, N40 million; while N246 million has been set aside for the development of new universities, provision of student and staff amenities and improving and adding to facilities of the existing universities. There is to be an expansion and liberalisation of the policy regulating the grant of scholarships, bursaries and loans, and scholarship will be used deliberately as an instrument in the manpower development strategy.

A recent innovation in the Nigerian educational field has been the establishment of the National Youth Service Corps, which takes university graduates for a year's service in a variety of ways, mainly as teachers. It is a useful means of supplementing scarce teaching manpower. From 1975 all Nigerians graduating overseas have been liable for national service and Nigerian employers throughout the country have to ensure that graduates either have a certificate of exemption or a certificate to show they have completed their service before they can be employed.

Teachers remain at the core of all the educational problems and future plans. By pursuing a 'liberal' policy with regard to the recruitment of teachers from abroad, Nigeria is not doing enough to enhance the professional prestige of her own teachers. Further, a good many of those recruited overseas are not of sufficiently high calibre. Professor Adamu Baikie has argued that untrained Nigerian teachers were being penalised by the recruitment of teachers from overseas who were equally untrained, and called for the 'professionalisation' of teaching.[5] The problems he touched upon can be understood by examining some of the desperate straits certain states have got into in their efforts to find teachers for their rapidly expanding programmes.

The North West State (Niger, Sokoto) is vast in size, remote in terms of its sparse communications and has only four towns possessing all the major facilities and amenities. The general manpower needs of the state are so great that anyone produced by the educational system at virtually any level of learning-competence is immediately employed. Scholarships of all kinds and at all levels overseas are automatically taken up; in mid-1975, for example, the state, with a total population of approximately 8.5 million, had just one physics graduate. When a College of Technology was opened the state had no students qualified to take advantage of it. In 1968 it had 60 000 children in primary school; by 1974 the figure had risen to 170 000. UPE in 1976 could mean a total intake of 250 000 children of whom 100 000 would be new pupils. Possibly the state could just handle such numbers if all available teachers are utilised and buildings are also available. To take all 250 000 children who qualify for primary education the state has to find an additional 3 700 teachers. To cope with the coming educational expansion the state has turned over half the secondary school system to teacher-training. Thus, in September 1975 some 22 000 students were expected to be in post-primary training of whom 60 per cent would be in teachers' training colleges and 40 per cent in secondary schools. Teacher-training for primary teachers in this state consists of a five-year course after primary education, in colleges which are the equivalent of secondary schools. At the end of this period the children are turned out as teachers. The state also has specialist UPE centres: 14 training colleges for 4 700 students.

The state is heavily dependent upon teachers sent by the Federal Government; its teachers' training colleges are extremely remotely placed. In 1975 of 800 secondary school teachers in the state between 250 and 300 of them were expatriates: a mixture of British volunteers or contract teachers, Canadian volunteers and contract teachers recruited from India, Pakistan and Egypt. The standards of some of these teachers were known to be extremely low and one story freely circulating in Sokoto (before the July coup of 1975) was that a teaching contract could be purchased for N 300 at the Nigerian High Commission in India by someone with virtually no qualifications at all. The fact that such a story, whether true or false, could be told is indication enough of the dependence of the state upon manpower resources other than its own.

The pattern is similar for the North Central State (Kaduna), where every aspect of education is urgently in need of manpower, especially at the teacher-training level. In theory the state introduced comprehensive education in 1972 but had not got the schools three years later, when only 30 per cent of primary school-leavers went on to secondary school. The state is trying to expand the 27 existing secondary schools and under the Third Plan hopes to gain some 16 new secondary schools. It has also—a recent and novel departure in Nigeria—one school for the blind and one for the deaf and dumb. The state's primary enrolment in 1974 was 160 000 children; by 1979 it will be 539 000 while the figure is expected to reach a staggering 1 108 000 in 1984–85. It will require more than 10 000 new classrooms alone by the end of the plan period and the capital costs for the five years will be in the region of N175 million. In the words of the North Central State's own educational plan:

> Clearly the process of attaining UPE will entail a radical social and economic transformation of society, and not simply an educational one. In many sparsely populated areas of the state a resettlement programme for farmers will be essential if education is to be brought within reach of their children.

The state also faces special educational problems in relation to the nomadic Fulani; and it is just coming to realise that their education has to be co-ordinated with such things as the supply of water services.

Once more the problems come back to the question of adequate teacher-training. During the plan period the state aims to increase the numbers of its primary teachers by 11 000 and then by a further 27 000 by 1985. To meet these requirements the state's existing nine teachers' training colleges are to be expanded under the plan to have 30 classes each and deal with 1 100 students each, while a further ten new institutions of the same size are to be started. Finally there is the wastage—an expected 10 per cent—to be faced.

Such statistics for this one state over the 1975–80 plan period indicate the size of Nigeria's overall educational problem as it tries to meet its manpower requirements. During the current plan period the North Central State must provide an additional 10 242 primary classrooms, an additional 10 828 teachers and an additional 13 324 staff houses at a capital cost of N175 112 947. Thereafter the recurrent cost of its educational programme will be N92 393 994. And this was only one (admittedly one of the most educationally backward) of twelve states, all of which are striving to alter the basis of their educational systems.

The story in the North East State (Bauchi, Borno, Gongola) is similar. At least money is no longer a bar to educational development. In 1975 the state established 10 new teachers' training colleges which, added to 27 existing ones, were all to produce primary teachers.

The biggest problem concerns secondary school teachers. The sciences are reasonably easy to cover, teachers for such subjects being recruited abroad from India and Pakistan. The most difficult teachers to recruit are for English and mathematics. As with the other northern states the North East relies heavily upon expatriates and it also expects the Federal Government to supply between 80 and 100 National Youth Service Corps one-year volunteer teachers a year. Of its 800 secondary school teachers some 350 to 400 are expatriate, mainly on contract. They include Britons, Indians, Pakistanis, Canadians,

Americans and Irish, volunteers, and perhaps fifty teachers recruited from other parts of the country. More secondary teachers were coming on stream in 1975, however, and increasing numbers were being sent for three-year 'in-service' training degree courses at Ahmadu Bello University.

Of its primary school leavers 15 per cent (on a quota basis) could continue into secondary education in 1975; this situation will continue in the state after the full introduction of UPE. A further 10 per cent of primary school leavers go on to teacher-training. In 1975 the state had 40 per cent of the eligible children in primary school; it expected to take in 25 per cent of those eligible in September 1975 and 50 per cent of those eligible a year later in September 1976. Even the new crash courses to produce primary teachers will only turn them out in quantity by 1979.

The problems these states face are formidable enough: the rapidly growing demand for education and the determination to see that it is met, luckily, are as great. But just a cursory examination of the figures relating to UPE in these northern states brings out the huge manpower problems faced by Nigeria as a whole.

The Third Plan must cope with major manpower shortages; lack of the right skills will continue to slow down and hamper the process of development for years. Though the country possesses much entrepreneurial skill, it also has many gaps to be filled. Almost certainly the Third Plan will fall down in those areas where the manpower skills are in shortest supply. State after state can report its own particular manpower problems. They may vary from one part of the country to another but the pattern is much the same: a lack of engineering technicians, secondary school teachers, craftsmen, industrial supervisors. In the Cross River State, to take just one example, the ratio of doctors to the population stands at 1 to 55 000.

High-level managerial manpower is the key to the successful implementation of the plan. It has been estimated that 49 210 extra people in the higher level ranges will be needed during the plan period. Yet to meet this, university enrolment is only being doubled which means that only by 1980—the end of the plan period—will a total of 28 000 graduates actually have been turned out. In addition it is hoped a further 4 600 graduates trained overseas will return to augment the high-level manpower requirements. Even so, and despite other expedients—4 000 people to be turned out by non-university institutions and 6 000 to be upgraded from intermediate to high-level categories—a shortfall of 6 340 over the period is expected. Either this figure will not be met at all, with consequent damage to the actual implementation of various parts of the plan, or it will be met in whole or in part by the importation of expatriate skills on the usual temporary basis—and that present dangers of a different kind.

There are a number of ways in which these shortfalls may be

overcome. They consist mainly of upgrading exercises: the Centre for Management Development will step up its various training programmes to accelerate management education and training; the Industrial Training Fund is to increase the scope of its activities; while both the federal and state governments are to increase and intensify on-the-job training. Similarly, all educational bodies are likely substantially to expand their activities. Yet again, restraints upon these expansion plans will themselves be a matter of manpower. One crucial question, therefore, must concern those aspects of the economy that will be permitted to continue with a high level of expatriate management: construction and manufacturing; the medical profession; and the upper levels of teaching. One result is likely to be a further liberalisation of the expatriate quota allowances.

Then come the shortfalls at the intermediate levels and these are estimated to run at 13 200 for the plan period. The worst areas are again the building and construction industries, technicians and technologists in most branches of industry, some aspects of the medical profession such as nurses, assistants in accounting and maintenance technicians in just about every branch of activity.

The Third Plan has massive schemes for manpower training at most of the appropriate levels and admits the grave restraints upon the whole that manpower shortages are liable to impose. A sober recognition of the problem represents a long step towards solving it. At the top in Nigeria there are not enough people for the jobs; at the bottom there are too many people after the jobs. There is also a growing awareness that some training is increasingly inappropriate: that is, many sectors of the economy are still preparing for breakthroughs of a kind that more modern technology has now bypassed. Public debate during 1975 about manpower needs and shortages showed how the plan had made the country at large aware of how much people with the necessary skills (whether managerial or technical) were in short supply.

Manpower resources have also to be related to problems of job distribution. Despite oil, the Nigerian economy is still largely a subsistence one. Only 40 per cent of the available labour force is employed and 70 per cent of this remains in agriculture. Manufacturing still uses little more than 10 per cent while 12 per cent is in commerce. Service industries are grossly under-developed using only 4 per cent of available labour while transport and communications (unsurprisingly, perhaps, to Nigerians) employ a minimal one per cent. In particular there is a high unemployment rate among young people, greatest for those aged between 18 and 23, then those from 15 to 17 and thirdly for those from 24 to 29. Sixty per cent of Nigerians who do work do so in the subsistence sector—that is, in farming, petty trading, crafts.[6]

These statistics, however, should be viewed with extreme caution:

not that they are necessarily wrong in theory but that the practice is often quite different. Thus it is quite easy to talk of high and intermediate level manpower without looking at the practical application of personnel in the field. It has been well argued[7] that many highly trained Nigerians are in the wrong jobs which do not employ their skills at all. Others are demonstrably under-used as, for example, engineers doing little more than supervising labour. The gaps seem far more acute in the middle-level 'maintenance' fields—the constant breakdowns of electricity supply in Lagos illustrate this point well enough. Many newspapers have campaigned as Nigerians have complained that skilled people are simply inadequately employed; few things can be more discouraging for the new graduate than to find that his hard-won skills (of whatever kind) are insufficiently appreciated or used.

Nigerian educational snobbery is also biased against the middle-level skilled man: the system tends to produce too many intellectuals and too few technicians. A survey in 1972 showed that 7 per cent of advertised vacancies for doctors went unfilled; 20 per cent for pharmacists; 5 per cent for all categories of engineers; 9 per cent for schoolteachers. For accountants, architects, town planners, surveyors, research and production chemists the figure was 14 per cent and at the intermediate level for general research assistants it stood at 23 per cent.[8] Dr Chris S. Abashiya, the director of the Staff Development Centre at Kaduna, has pointed out that while in other countries there exists a ratio of six technicians to every one professional, in Nigeria the ratio stands at one to one. He attacked snobbish attitudes in education and the fact that the country's cultural heritage made people 'look down on those at the lower rungs of the ladder.'[9]

Lack of executive capacity explains many of the bottlenecks to development. In a scathing attack upon management the *New Nigerian*[10] in August 1975 suggested that blaming semi-skilled workers for inefficiency was no answer and that most of the defects in performance were directly traceable to managerial and organisational defects. As the plan got under way Nigerians were acutely aware of the shortcomings in training and management generally and the public debate carried on through 1975 divided neatly into two: those who argued statistically that the country simply did not have enough of the various categories of manpower to answer its needs; and those who argued that much manpower was wasted, or misplaced and that given more sensitive approaches to workers by management and greater care in attracting graduates (including the large numbers thought to be resident overseas) the country could fill a far greater proportion of its manpower needs than a preliminary examination of the figures would suggest.

The overseas argument was an important one: the *Sunday Punch* estimated in July 1975 that 8 000 qualified Nigerians were in the USA, over 15 000 in Europe and 3 000 in the Far East, Australia and New Zealand. It suggested they were unwilling to come home because of the environmental and job uncertainties that awaited them in Nigeria. Most such fears, the paper said, were unfounded while it was up to Nigerians to help develop their country: the implication, however, was that insufficient care was taken in allaying whatever fears existed. Shortly afterwards the *New Nigerian*[12] estimated that 12 000 Nigerians would leave for the USA in 1975, of whom half would be students. Such figures give an idea of the numbers of potentially highly qualified people who leave Nigeria and of the possible numbers who ought soon to return to fill the gaps and so reduce dependence upon expatriates.

While this debate went on in Nigeria its High Commissioner in London announced that many of the students then completing their education in Britain were apparently unwilling to return home. He said the High Commission was taking special steps to encourage such students to return to Nigeria: registration centres were to be established to recruit qualified Nigerians for jobs at home. Later that month it was announced that 200 Nigerians abroad had been offered appointments by the federal and state public service commissions. The Federal Public Service Commission then said that these were part of a total of 350 Nigerians abroad found suitable for appointment during the last joint overseas recruitment tour by the commissions. The breakdown of the areas from which those who accepted these jobs were returning made interesting reading: 136 were returning from the USA, seven from Canada, 14 from West Berlin, seven from East Berlin, seven from Bonn, 28 from the USSR, nine from England and two from France.

One Nigerian businessman suggested[13] the best way to attract Nigerians home and then keep them would be to give them responsibilities and opportunities early so that they could progress by self-reliance. There is certainly something depressing and distressing about a country developing as fast as Nigeria with such a great potential which regularly has to send its public service commissions abroad to recruit its own citizens.

The message conveyed by the statistics of manpower shortages is clear. There is also a need for imagination: in recruiting to the right jobs; in using skills at all levels to the full; in ensuring that the trained people now resident abroad are enticed home because they see an exciting future for themselves in developing their own country.

Notes

1   *Daily Times*, 19 August 1975
2   *Ibid.*
3   *Africa Magazine*, November 1974
4   *African Development*, March 1975
5   *New Nigerian*, 7 August 1975
6   *African Development*, March 1972
7   *Sunday Punch*, 13 July 1975
8   *African Development*, March 1972
9   *New Nigerian*, 6 August 1975
10 *New Nigerian*, 8 August 1975
11 *Sunday Punch*, 13 July 1975
12 *New Nigerian*, 9 August 1975
13 *Sunday Punch*, 13 July 1975

Chapter eleven

Labour and Udoji

With the rapid expansion of industrialisation envisaged under the Third Plan as well as development in other directions resulting from the spread of Nigeria's oil wealth, the power of unions—organised or not and the government's policy towards those unions are bound to become increasingly important. Similarly, the government's policy towards salaries must take on even greater importance, as the whole salaried sector expands, than the spate of Udoji-inspired awards have already given to it. (The Udoji Report and its consequences will be discussed later in this chapter.)

Nigerian unions have had a chequered history. Under military rule their position has been curiously anomalous: on the one hand, forbidden by decree to use their powers and strike; on the other hand, increasingly using the threat of their power to obtain what they want. As the biggest employer of labour the government has a vested interest in controlling the unions and is deprived of much of the power it might otherwise wield as an impartial arbitrator. For example, in the Posts and Telecommunications strike in 1973, the government gave way. The Posts and Telecommunications workers represented one fifth of the entire federal civil service. Other key sections of organised labour, such as the banks, are in a position to cripple the economy—if they choose. The possibilities of trouble were very close to the surface just before the 1975 coup for the simple reason that some of the states were not paying wages and salaries because they had no money; chaos threatened essential services such as health, transport and water supply. During that July, for example, the Ibadan City Council's 3 000 employees threatened to disrupt essential services in the city unless their salaries and wages for June were paid. They had not been paid because the state had not received the monthly subvention it normally got from the central government. This could have been described as a local difficulty; the point, however, is that federal and state civil servants and municipal workers are becoming increasingly organised. Representing a very large proportion of the total work force, they can effectively bring things to a standstill if they choose to do so.

Militant unions are on the increase in Nigeria. One such is the National Union of Nigerian Bank Employees (NUNBE) whose

General-Secretary, Alhaji Babs Animashaun, called in 1975 for a 200 per cent increase of salaries and wages because of the banks' wealth and 'rich hidden assets'. The Central Bank of Nigeria in the meantime had stopped union organising—a demonstration of its strength. There was a wave of industrial action in mid-1975 which was put down by some observers and critics to the inability of trade unions to engage in more meaningful discussions with employers and management so as to strengthen their bargaining power. There was also a considerable element of a 'wildcat' approach to bargaining among the unions and no very evident sense of the direction in which they hoped to move.

The unions' position in Nigeria is by no means strong. The Secretary-General of the Nigerian Trades Union Congress (NTUC), Sam Bassey, said in 1973 that 'conditions for labour unity do not exist in this country'. The existing labour laws are designed to discourage strong union activity. At .the same time another unionist, the Secretary-General of United Labour Congress (ULC), Emmanuel Odeyemi, said that 'the present labour law which was drafted to create weak unions should now be changed to facilitate the stronger unions'. The Trade Dispute Emergency Provisions Amendment Decree 53 of 1969 made lockouts or strikes an offence. It was also an offence to organise a lockout or strike; to act, purport to act on behalf of workers, to threaten to take part in or organise a strike, to publish in the media anything likely to cause public alarm or industrial unrest. As a result of this last provision very little on the labour front tends to be reported, a major advantage for the government. Most government and many other leaders in Nigeria appear to think that labour relations should be government-controlled.

Despite such legislation and a government that has set its face firmly against union activity, the unions are becoming increasingly organised; they are prepared to use other tactics than the strike—the go-slow, for example—to achieve their ends. A decree of November 1973 (Decree 31) stipulated that trade union funds could not be used to further political purposes and laid down conditions for federating unions or amalgamating central labour organisations. The decree conferred on the Commissioner powers to ban trade unionism 'in such other establishments as the commissioner may from time to time by order specify'.[1] As the *Daily Times* commented, this 'is tantamount to a suspended death sentence on practically every trade union organisation in Nigeria. . . . It is frightening.' Decree 53 (of 1969) worked—more or less—until 1972 but then was met with increasing labour unrest.

By mid-1975, however, the unions were becoming a force to be reckoned with that was causing increasing anxiety to the Gowon government. The unions—certainly as long as political parties are banned—have perhaps the only organised potential that is remotely on a par with that of the army. What gave rise to a new sense of union power was the government acceptance of the main recommendations of the Udoji Report (see pp. 120–123) and its decision (contrary to Udoji's advice) to backdate the claims nine months. The awards may have been justified for the civil service and they may have followed two years' freeze; the fact is, they unleashed far more than was ever intended. The white paper did not cover the private sector; there was also discontent about differentials under the awards anyway. There followed a wave of go-slows, lockouts, strikes and working to rule so that whatever the original intentions of either Udoji or the government in implementing the report there developed a national salary and pay rise scramble by any group that could organise—and many that could not—all seeking their 'udojis'.

Within weeks of the report's publication taxi drivers, dockworkers, doctors, nurses, engineers, bankworkers, bus drivers, truck drivers, shop workers, customs officials, railway workers, construction workers, electricity engineers and water engineers were all to strike. Most people in the public sector got the awards they were after—more or less—while the government put pressure upon the private sector also to make awards of 30 per cent and more, as well as back payments. This especially incensed the private sector since it had not had a pay freeze during the previous two years which was the justification for the back payments in the public sector.

The Udoji award certainly had a spectacular effect upon the labour situation throughout the country. In some cases wages were virtually doubled; in many the unions demonstrated their strength and got their demands with ease in face of a government that was clearly frightened at what it had unleashed. The effect upon inflation was catastrophic, perhaps increasing it to as much as 40 per cent.

The Udoji scramble effectively killed Decree 53 of 1969 and immensely strengthened the union movement, since the unions simply ignored the prohibition on striking and when it came to the point the government did not try to enforce it. Then both sides played a cat and mouse game with each other: the unions not openly flaunting their disobedience; the government trying to use conciliators when the unions threatened—discreetly—to take industrial action. It is doubtful whether the Udoji awards solved anything: all they did was contribute in a major way to inflation and that is likely to spur on the unions to future demands. As long as the oil wealth continues to flow, and can be seen to do so, it will be difficult for the government to resist such claims effectively.

It is possible that for a time the unions will concentrate upon improving other aspects of work—fringe benefits, better holidays, industrial compensation—and try to use their power to force the government to take measures against inflation. Sooner or later, however, they will reach the point when they go for another major round of wage increases and then—depending upon the state of the economy and inflation—may well come the real crunch between unions and government. The strength of the unions in relation to the government may well be an early test for a future civilian government.

Organisation of unions has got a long way to go. Union registration laws have allowed a group as small as five to form a union and by mid-1975, for example, there were 1 870 registered unions, many of them minute, while in a number of industries several unions were operating. Most unions are linked to one of the four major union groups—and there are plenty of divisions among these. The biggest of these groups is the ULC (United Labour Congress) with 400 000 members which is affiliated to the ICFTU in Brussels. Second comes the Nigerian Trades Union Congress with about 300 000 members. This is affiliated to the Moscow-based WFTU so that the two main world union federations are represented—approximately on a par with one another. Two smaller groups are the Nigerian Workers' Council and the Labour Unity Front. In December, 1975, however, the Mohammed government decreed that foreign trades union organisations and secretariats—except for the ILO and the Organisation of African Trade Union Unity—were banned from activities in Nigeria. The wage-earning labour force of the country stands at approximately 3 million and about one million of these are union members. One of the great weaknesses of the Nigerian unions has been the quarrelling on ideological issues between these different groups. In 1975 there were moves towards greater unity of action: the basis for this was laid in October 1974 with the Apena Declaration which aimed, hopefully, at a Nigerian Labour Congress. In mid-December 1975 the Nigerian Labour Congress was launched.[2]

There has been plenty of legislation—or decree-making—in the 1970s about union activities. Decree 31 of 1973 provided for the merger of unions, their federation or the amalgamation of central labour organisations; the Labour Decree of 1974 covered working conditions; the Amendments to the Banking Decree of 1975 included provisions to ban bank unions from undertaking action that could endanger the national economy. Much more important, however, is the need for a sense of co-operation between government and unions instead of entrenched and total suspicion. Only then will industrial peace become a likelihood. The possibilities for this stem from the Nigerian Labour Congress. It has a 50-man steering committee representing all the central organisations and the neutral unions, but its 'genesis owes more to government pressure than to any real consensus of opinion among Nigeria's four main union groups. . . .[3] If the NLC can become effective it will wield considerable potential and actual power: it could end mushroom trade unionism and reduce the main unions for the industrial sector to 25 or so. But of course it is not simply a question of efficient trade union organisation—either at the centre or on a union-by-union basis. The question of union attitudes and ideology must also be considered.

What seems likely to happen in Nigeria is a series of pressures to force a change of approach: militant labour is beginning to feel its strength; management equally is gearing itself for a new era of labour relations. One suggestion put forward by the then chairman and managing director of the *Daily Times* in 1975, Alhaji Babatunde Jose, was for worker participation in ownership of industry and in the decision-making process.[4] There is nothing especially new in this, although it may not have been tried as yet in Nigeria. What is important is the belief that new approaches are essential in a situation which might otherwise get out of hand.

There are many anomalies to be tackled. In 1973, for example, a labourer was paid a wage of only 5 per cent of a middle-rank civil servant's salary. The reason for such a huge gap was in part a leftover of colonialism: the civil servant bases his claims upon international standards; the labourer is paid according to African conditions. Increasingly, too, as the country industrialises and modernises in other ways, unemployment and how to overcome it will become a major political preoccupation. A socialist observer suggests that

> Unemployment in Nigeria is not inevitable; it can be completely and totally wiped out by a socialist reconstruction of the economy under the government of the working people.[5]

Maybe: many would not agree with such an assessment or if they did agree would prefer not to court the other consequences of becoming a totally socialist society. But again the changes brought by rapid developments demand ideological as well as pragmatic solutions.

Periodically a major wage award has been used as a device in Nigeria (as elsewhere) to quieten the labour front. The Adebo award of 1971 was largely designed to help workers to meet the rises resulting from inflation. It was a precursor of Udoji. The Udoji Report—to the chagrin of its chief author—was not accepted in its entirety by the Nigerian Government. It was, however, the occasion—something certainly not intended though it should have been foreseen—for a spiralling avalanche of salary and wage demands. In a sense the report became a disaster since the only part of it to be taken seriously was the awards section, which was instantly seized upon by a public increasingly suspicious that the oil wealth was not going to be fairly spread across the country, and used as the basis for huge wage demands. The name Udoji entered the language: people thereafter talked increasingly of parities and relativity—and they had a government-established criterion upon which to base their claims.

The Udoji Commission was set up as a result of a recommendation in the Adebo Commission of 1971 and took two years to accomplish its work. It established eight special task forces with a total membership of 105 and many taking part were expatriates: principally British and Canadian, with one Ghanaian, apart from the Nigerian members. The commission consulted a wide range of individuals and organisations who included government, civil service, specialists, administrators, academics, in Nigeria, Australia, Canada, Britain, the USA and Tanzania. Special studies of the Nigerian economy were commissioned, as was the relevance of the French administrative system to administrative reform in Nigeria. The commission received a total of 545 memoranda and took oral evidence from 192 persons and organisations. The result was one of the most painstaking and comprehensive reports ever produced in Nigeria.

The Udoji Report[6] was presented to the government in September 1974. It dealt at length with the whole structure of the civil service: it examined the cultural and environmental factors that affect the service; it looked at a new style of service, at manpower problems, at the structure and organisation, personnel management, financial management, planning and statistics. It devoted chapters to the different branches of the civil service—the judiciary, police, prisons, public enterprises, local government service, the teaching service, universities. The commission had tried to establish a new approach to the whole tradition of the civil service; but the only section of the report immediately, and with great interest, noted by the public at large was Chapter 15 (Grading and Pay). From a national point of view it could well be argued that it was a mistake to set out a salary scale that everyone could afterwards relate to.

A key statement in the report concerned public service salaries:

> Public service salaries, if they are to have any economic base, must be generally related to salaries for comparable work in the private sector, which reflect the economics of the market. These comparisons must be based on comprehensive analyses of posts in the two sectors.[7]

This was justified at the time the report was prepared, for then the civil service had fallen behind the private sector. Ironically, in the end, the report partly reversed this situation so that what civil servants were scheduled to receive became the criterion against which claims would be made. Another clause of the report, whose key word—differentials—was at once seized upon by the public, read:

> Differentials between salaries for one grade as compared to the next grade should be substantial enough to reflect the differing levels of responsibility and to provide for appreciable salary increases upon promotion.[8]

The salary awards the commission recommended were so huge that they raised some awkward questions of intent. Minimum salaries of established staff in the public services were to be increased by 130 per cent; federal permanent secretaries' salaries by a possible 110 per cent; that of the Chief Justice from N9 000 to N16 200 and other top posts such as the Inspector-General of Police or Vice-Chancellors on a comparable scale; and most generous provisions were to be made for retirement and pensions. The arrears paid following the award amounted to N-500 million to about 700 000 Nigerians out of 70 or so million in a country where the average annual per capita income is N-200.

Not surprisingly, chaos followed: quite simply—whatever the government and the commission may have expected—what Nigerians in effect said was that if civil servants were going to receive such munificent rewards from the oil boom, then so should everyone else. And everyone else with great rapidity staked their claims and the spiral of demands rapidly gathered momentum. Other anomalies also produced complications: by compressing some 75 salary grades into 10 the report ensured that many differentials disappeared, so that within the range of a grade seniority no longer counted, which caused discontent among the more junior ranges of the civil service.

The upsets within the civil service were, no doubt, bad enough but they concerned a relatively small though important group of people. The real impact of the report was upon the economy at large. Its most amazing aspect is that no one—apparently—foresaw what publication would spark off. The result was that the government was forced to make concession after concession as one group after another demanded their increases. Thus, shortly after the award, the government granted doctors a 40 per cent increase over their pre-Udoji salaries and then had to concede that the minimum salary addition could be from 8 to 30 per cent, so that the Udoji scales simply became a rather loose general guide as to how much a group might demand.

It was not simply inflation but an open invitation to future industrial unrest: 94.5 per cent of the economically active population of Nigeria did not benefit from the awards or the subsequent spiral at all.[9] These consisted mainly of poor farmers or the self-employed— petty traders and artisans—whose annual income is less than a third of the minimum wage award of N-720 that now went to workers in the public sector. Thus, in effect, the award started a scramble among little more than five per cent of Nigeria's total population for a larger share of the wealth resulting from the oil boom. If nothing is done to spread some of the national wealth to the great majority unaffected by the award—and in most cases unable to organise themselves to demand their share—the word differential could take on a different and more sinister meaning than it has at present.

The long-term results of Udoji may be incalculable—in labour relations; in promoting the gap between those able to obtain such awards for themselves and those not so able; and in terms of a policy for the equitable distribution of the oil wealth. So far this has been inequitable, not least as a result of the report and its immediate repercussions. It may also give greater power to organised labour.

When at the beginning of 1975 the dockers demanded wage rises in line with the Udoji recommendations their demand was ignored. They waited seven days, then they struck for three days; and then the employers called them back and promised to pay what they had asked.

Unfortunately the Udoji Report came at a time when in any case something would have triggered off a round of salary and wage demands. Ordinary Nigerians saw the huge increase in national revenue from oil and they wanted their share of it. Udoji helped them to get it. The award gave an immense stimulus to inflation, although it is difficult to arrive at a clear figure. The deputy governor of the Central Bank of Nigeria claimed that inflation had been held at 12 per cent for the first half of 1974. Once the Udoji payments got moving in the first half of 1975, however, inflation increased markedly, partly as a result of the vast increases in top salaries, but also because of the arrear payments which released a large lump sum onto the market and led to a huge spending spree that cleared shops and again added to the inflation spiral.[10]

Perhaps the Udoji Report, with all its consequences, did no more than highlight a process which in any case was being brought about by development, the oil boom and industrialisation. The issue is not that everyone claims more and more and uses Udoji as their yardstick for doing so, but that Nigeria has created for itself—or allowed to grow—the kind of economy in which this can happen. There was little evidence of either control or restraint in the post-Udoji award scramble. The Udoji Report—unhappily—may have sparked off a pattern of economic behaviour that will dominate the development boom of the following decade.

Notes

1	*African Development*, March 1974
2	*West Africa*, 5 January 1976
3	*Ibid.*
4	*Daily Times*, 31 July 1975
5	*Economic Development of Nigeria, op. cit.* p. 61
6	Public service Review Commission, Main Report, September 1974, Federal Ministry of Information, Printing Division, Lagos (Chairman—J. O. Udoji)
7	*Ibid*, p. 165
8	*Ibid*, p. 165
9	*Africa Magazine*, March 1975
10	*African Development*, March 1975

Chapter twelve

Transport and communications

At the commencement of the Third Plan Nigeria was woefully ill-served by almost every form of communications: appalling traffic jams in Lagos and other major towns were the rule; the railway system was so old and creaking as to be regarded as a national joke; the telephones were so few and those so unreliable as to make it simpler to call in person rather than try first to make an appointment by telephone; an air service whose public relations give an entirely inaccurate picture of its actual performance; and a level of port congestion that existed nowhere else in the world. These inadequacies were admitted by General Gowon when he outlined the Third Development Plan and they are the reason why transport and communications are to receive more than ₦7 billion in the Plan. As a result it is hoped that by 1980 Nigeria will have the beginnings of a modern infrastructure of communications. She certainly needs it. Many current problems—the poor distribution of petrol to the interior of the country in 1975, for example—are (in part) the result of depending upon a system of communications that was simply not designed to handle the economic expansion that is now taking place.

Road construction is far in advance of other sectors of the communications infrastructure: more than 3 000 kilometres of new roads were built throughout Nigeria in the four years covered by the Second Plan while work was in progress on 2 570 kilometres of roads at the time the Third Plan was launched. On the other hand the railways have been plagued with labour troubles; in many respects they are little changed from the narrow gauge jerry-built construction hastily laid in 1898 during the colonial 'opening up' of the interior. Nigeria Airways have been plagued with management problems, lack of modern aircraft and ground equipment, while the airports need bringing up to international standards.

Under the Third Plan the government is to concentrate especially upon the roads so as to open up the vast hinterland of the country and stimulate economic activity. To do this the Federal Government took over the responsibility for 16 000 kilometres of secondary roads which so far had been that of the state governments; the latter will therefore be able to concentrate their resources upon rural link and feeder roads. The plan devotes ₦400 million to the modernisation of the railways: they are to be changed to standard gauge, heavier tracks are to be laid and as many curves and gradients as possible eliminated. The plan aims to improve the domestic and West African air services and devotes ₦390 million to the airways. Shipping is tackled in two ways: 19 new vessels are to be added to the Nigerian National Shipping Line to enable it to carry some 30 per cent of the nation's seaborne traffic; and improvements at the lesser ports of Warri, Calabar, and Port Harcourt are designed to take some of the pressure off Lagos.

The plan devotes ₦770 million to telecommunications and postal services and aims to create an additional 10 000 postal establishments by 1980. Major efforts will be made to see that this sector can cope with the rapidly growing demands being made upon it.

Inevitably the ports draw attention for they are the gateway to Nigeria for the bulk of her imports and their inefficiency, the slow turnround, the incredible waits in the line-up at Lagos (sometimes as much as three months) have become internationally notorious and so a direct reflection upon the government of the country. They also tell the world another story: that of the enormous economic boom Nigeria is enjoying which is the direct explanation for most of the port congestion.

From the end of the civil war until late in 1974 imports ran at a regular 200 000 tonnes a month; then, suddenly, they shot up to 300 000 tonnes a month. In development terms these figures are far more important than the static one of export tonnage at 810 000 tonnes. The increase in imports has shot ahead of any capacity to handle it. Lagos was designed as a railway port, yet so bad are the railways that sometimes only two or three trucks a day are available at the port and 80 per cent of off-loaded cargo goes out by road.[1] The plan sets forth major port expansion schemes especially for the handling capacity of the other ports—Warri, Port Harcourt and Calabar—so as to take some of the strain off Lagos. Yet the problem will remain at Lagos where traffic will continue to grow fast as a result of the economic boom, so that it is doubtful whether new berths will be ready quickly enough to keep pace with the expanding demand.

New developments are taking place at Calabar where one berth exists and two new ones are under construction; Port Harcourt, which has twelve berths, is to get two or three more. But most ships want to use Lagos: it is the first port of call from Europe; it serves the most industrialised and populous commercial hinterland; and it is still the starting point for the best communications to the north. Other inefficiencies do nothing to make the port problems easier. Offloading of ships stops in the rain. The line-up of ships waiting to offload can claim demurrage—another inflationary strain upon the economy. Yet despite all the criticisms that can be levelled against the Nigerian Ports Authority (NPA), statistics also tell a story of remarkable accomplishments: the tonnage discharge figure at Nigeria's ports for May 1974 was 188 437; a year later in May 1975 it had risen to 301 098 tonnes—an increase of 59 per cent and a tonnage increase of 112 661—and the fact is that the increase was handled. The Third Plan allocates N-322 million to ports development; it is not enough.

In 1964 imports entering Nigeria through Lagos totalled .99 million tonnes; ten years later in 1974 they came to 2.29 million tonnes. This is the crux of the ports crisis: handling capacity. Some of the high inflationary costs in the Nigeria of the mid-1970s were the result, in part, of demurrage fees for ships that had waited in the line-up for as long as three months. Further, when the official figures gave 230 ships waiting at Lagos, unofficial estimates put the total as much as 100 ships higher. Part of the crisis, however, appeared to be an absolute reluctance on the part of the Nigerian Government to develop ports other than Lagos; were that to be done effectively half the problem could be cleared at once. Failure to develop Port Harcourt—perhaps in part a legacy of the civil war—and indecisiveness over the ports of Warri, Koko and Calabar also contributed to the congestion at Lagos. Early in 1975 there were no more than 90 ships waiting at any one time to berth in Lagos and in April, when General Gowon visited the port, 67. By mid-July there were 230 (the number was steadily increasing) and by October when the new regime was taking major steps aimed at decongestion the number had risen to 400.

Port Harcourt has long been the traditional gateway to northern and eastern Nigeria. From the outside world it takes mixed cargoes while its main exports consist of palm oil and kernels, rubber and cocoa, tin from Jos and groundnuts from Kano in the north. The port also handles traffic from Niger. The war brought the port to a standstill. The railway deficiencies made matters worse so that in mid-1975, for example, when the railway should have been supplying five goods trains daily to help clear the port, it rarely provided more than two. Various political factors delayed redevelopment after the war: the Ibos preferred to use Lagos since relations with the Rivers people remained extremely poor. In 1975 Port Harcourt had not yet been restored to its 1965 handling capacity. The port can take only 14 ships at a time.[2] Before the war positive steps were being taken to expand Port Harcourt; these included the construction of more berths and the building of more warehouses.

The country's third port is the old one of Calabar: the problem there is the low draught. Calabar itself serves only a small hinterland but also offers another route to the north. As Nigeria's congestion worsened in the weeks before the July 1975 coup, the then Federal Commissioner for Transport, Captain O. I. Olumide, said: 'Bureaucratic processing which normally entails unnecessary delay would be brushed aside to enable construction work on the new port complex to take off the ground soon.'³ The river is to be dredged so as to allow large ships to use the berths; this has not been possible to date because of the shallow draught at the entrance to the Calabar river as well as in the navigable channel. The port is to have an additional 860 metres of wharfage for the simultaneous berthing of four large or six moderate sized vessels, three new transit sheds and two warehouses of 7 000 square metres each.

The general port situation was chaotic and adversely affecting development when in July 1975 the new government of Brigadier Mohammed took over. It treated port congestion as a top priority. In mid-August, only three weeks after it had assumed power, the new regime took over 60 privately owned jetties in Lagos for exclusive use by the federal authorities between 6 pm and 5 am daily as it, too, came to grips with the country's most choking bottleneck. Government intervention of one kind or another will, no doubt, lead to greater efficiency at the ports; it will not solve the question of insufficient resources and facilities to handle all incoming traffic.

Because of this Nigeria began to look for help to her neighbours, a not inappropriate gesture in the year that ECOWAS was born. An agreement was reached in July 1975 between Nigeria and Ghana whereby Nigeria-bound vessels with government consignments could discharge their cargoes at Ghanaian ports for these to be sent on by road. When the two Commissioners for Transport signed the agreement in Lagos that August, the Ghanaian, Colonel Peter Adekun, described it as his country's step towards the realisation of the objective of ECOWAS. Apart from waiving customs dues on the goods passing through Ghana, the latter agreed to make available to Nigeria the services of its transport commission. Ghana indicated that the implementation of the agreement would mean increased Ghanaian consumption of petrol and this Nigeria agreed to supply. All officials and workers involved in the operation were to be issued with special travel certificates by both parties to the agreement.

Thus, interestingly, an attempt to decongest Lagos port by sending goods through Ghana had ripple effects which encouraged greater co-operation between the two countries and would, in a practical way, forward the delicate political growth of ECOWAS. Comparable arrangements had to be made with neighbouring Dahomey (now Benin—the name was changed to the People's Republic of Benin on 30 November 1975) and Togo through whose territory the overland consignments of goods had to pass. Investigations were also started during 1975 to see whether Nigerian-bound goods could be imported through Cotonou in Benin.

In a further move to get control of the ports situation the new government issued fresh regulations in August 1975 requiring all shipping agents to register with the Nigerian Ports Authority before undertaking activities in the country; in addition, agents had to furnish the NPA with information as to port or ports of sailing and estimated time of departure of vessels and port or ports of discharge in Nigeria at least two months before departure from loading ports so that the NPA would be able to co-ordinate all sailings as well as regulate the arrival of vessels in Nigerian ports.

These and other moves were expedients to deal with congestion. In the long run, as her economy continues to grow, Nigeria needs more port facilities and there are several restraints upon this requirement. First, for so large a country Nigeria has a small sea coast, and there are serious limits to the size of vessel that her lesser ports such as Calabar can handle because of bars and shallow draughts in the river mouths and channels. Second, there must be an absolute limit to the total of goods that Lagos can handle not only in port terms but also in terms of road and railway transport to the interior. Third, there is the question of logistics: the faster the Nigerian economy moves the more imports it will require and, therefore, the greater port facilities to handle them. It is doubtful whether in the oil boom years ahead a situation will ever arise in which there is not at least a measure of port congestion.

During almost daily references in the Nigerian press to the chaotic situation in the ports in 1975 a headline appeared in the *Sunday Observer*[4] 'Goods Now To Be Imported By Road' followed by the story of a British transport company that was to take goods overland to Nigeria across the Sahara. The firm, Terminal Transport Services, was to use 12 metre trailers and expected these to make the trip in two weeks: each truck and trailer with two drivers would cost £13 000 for the full journey including ferry charges and, as the firm said, this compared very favourably with sea freight rates. It also gave a boost to the Trans-Sahara Highway and focused attention upon road transport into Nigeria. After Europe and the ferry to Algiers the route south was to be through Tamanrasset and Agades in Niger to Kano in the north of Nigeria and finally Lagos. Shortly after this announcement another British freight company said that it, too, would initiate an overland service to Nigeria. Thus port congestion stimulated the development of road transport into Nigeria and may well bring in its wake growing and welcome co-operation with the country's land neighbours.

In their turn these moves focused attention upon Nigeria's roads— on the whole the best part of the country's communications infra-structure. There had been little planning in the years since inde-pendence although there had been a huge increase in the volume of road traffic. By the mid-1970s the roads were sustaining enormous strain and consequent damage. The urban centres, especially Lagos and Ibadan, suffered from appalling traffic chaos for the same reasons. By the time the Third Plan was launched Nigeria had 96 500 kilometres of roads of various grades of which about a quarter were tarred: some were substandard and dangerous after the rains when

17 A time-honoured scene in a typically crowded lorry park. Trading is vigorously
pursued among the parked vehicles, each bearing the customary maxim

18 Princess Alexandra was Britain's official representative at Nigeria's
Independence celebrations in 1960. Accompanied by the late Sardauna of
Sokoto, she toured a specially staged exhibition in Lagos, and (below)
watched an Ekpo masquerade at Enugu

19 Lagos has been the scene of some exciting new building in recent years.
Above: the gates of the football stadium; below: the National Theatre under
construction, in readiness for the Second Black Arts Festival

20 Nigeria has come a long way since independence. Ibadan University (above) is now one of ten universities in a country determined to make Universal Primary Education a top priority. New skyscraper buildings form a background to cheering schoolchildren celebrating the anniversary of Independence (below)

they would become full of potholes. The major trunk roads are on the whole very good, especially those to the north, but the quality varies greatly across the country. From a development point of view the most important roads are the rural feeder roads which are vital for integrating isolated districts into the mainstream of economic and social activity. These need much attention: since the plan deliberately relieved the states of responsibility for 'B' trunk roads they in turn can use their resources to develop their rural networks. Good rural roads linking agricultural areas to the main highways could make an enormous difference to the impact of the plan upon the rural populations.

In Lagos itself traffic chaos became an accepted part of the life of the capital city. The papers constantly tell of traffic jams, urge various solutions and bemoan the fact that little changes. Yet here, too, is a problem of inherited infrastructure: Lagos was not designed to cope with the volume of traffic that it had to deal with by the middle of the 1970s; the city and island form a natural bottleneck anyway; and however efficient policing of the roads might be, when a country doubles the number of drivers on the road each year something has to give way. It is not simply a question of more roads or bridges out of Lagos; there is also the need for effective traffic management. Within days of assuming power the Mohammed regime took certain measures: it banned all vehicles over five tonnes from using the Lagos roads except between the hours of 11 pm and 5.30 am; it instituted rigid checks of vehicles for road worthiness; and it employed the military to reinforce the police in far more concentrated traffic control measures than had formerly been the fashion. There were some immediate improvements in the general flow but such measures could not alter the volume of traffic to be handled by an inadequate road system. Lagos now faces the same problems that major cities such as New York in the industialised world have long had to cope with (and they are notorious for their traffic chaos as well). In an economically conscious nation it is, perhaps, some consolation for hours spent fruitlessly in a traffic jam to know that Nigeria has joined the ranks of the other industrialised countries as the free and easy flow of traffic into its capital city breaks down.

Nigeria Railways (Nigeria Railway Corporation—NRC) are the least efficient sector of the transport infrastructure. They have steadily lost traffic to the roads ever since independence and the growth of airfreight has also adversely affected them. The track needs to be modernised, freighting to be containerised and the whole system to be fundamentally overhauled.

The country has 3 505 route kilometres of railways and little has been done to them for years. Up to the early 1960s the railways were the chief means of evacuating northern produce such as groundnuts. Soon after independence, however, private road hauliers moved into this lucrative market and the railways entered a period of spectacular decline. The railways possess—in theory—unique advantages for transporting people and goods north and south but this activity has been progressively discouraged by a history of derailments, a growing inability to keep to schedules and generally poor facilities. At one time 70 per cent of the NRC's revenue came from transporting groundnuts from north to south: apart from fierce competition from road haulage the drought in the early 1970s led to a major decline in groundnut production which made the situation worse.[5] Further complications for the railways will follow the government's decision to change the tracks to standard gauge (at present they are 3′ 6″) since this announcement halted repair construction work because it no longer seemed worthwhile to spend money on a system that was in any case about to be altered.

NRC has an unenviable reputation in Nigeria for poor labour relations and frequent strikes. After the 1975 coup there were newspaper demands that the new Commissioner for Transport should give full support to the general manager of NRC, particularly over the question of strikes, arguing that no one should be allowed to sabotage the economy by calling the workers out on unnecessary strikes as had frequently been the case. But no one factor can be blamed for the condition of the railways and certainly not the workers themselves whose strikes, at least in part, reflect the poor conditions and discontents that go with a declining system.

It was one of the paradoxes of the Nigerian communications system in 1975 that while the ports, cities and airports could all be described as congested the railways were basically underused. For the fifteen years following independence the NRC ran at a deficit and the tonnage transported declined. In 1958–59 agricultural tonnage carried came to 850 000 tonnes; by 1970–71 this had dropped to 350 000 tonnes. In 1961–62 11 000 people used trains as passengers; by 1973–74 the figure had dropped to the lowest recorded at 4 670. In 1972–73 its operational losses were ₦21.8 million; the following year, 1973–74, they were up to ₦33.1 million.

The railways are outdated in equipment, state of repair, and their ability to handle traffic: there are too many extensive track curvatures, the bridges are weak, the rails are too light, grades are very steep and the signalling system is old. As a result trains average no more than 55 kilometres an hour, there are frequent stoppages and a high accident rate. There is a total of 3 505 kilometres of single track route serving the two major ports—Lagos and Port Harcourt—heading north separately from those points to railheads at Kaura, Namoda, Nguru, Jos and Maiduguri in the northern states. Large areas of the centre of the country have not been penetrated by the railway and many of the newly developing cities and towns of flourishing commerce are not served by a railway. For a country the size of Nigeria—913 072 square kilometres—3 505 kilometres of rail is hopelessly inadequate. The question facing the government in 1975 was one of railway development priorities. On the one hand it was possible for a military regime to insist that long distance cargoes be shifted by rail and as one paper argued[6] this would have had a number of advantages: congestion on the roads in the Apapa dock area of Lagos would be eased; the railway would be revitalised and its goods carrying capacity updated; the NRC might then begin to pay its way. On the other hand such action could be counter-productive if, because of poor performance, the long-term result was simply to drive transport back to the roads again.

The government budgeted ₦885 million for the entire railway system during the period of the Third Plan. Of this ₦171.1 million is to keep the system running while ₦713.9 million is for re-equipment and construction of the new standard gauge. In 1975 NRC's 28 000 workers were underemployed; and the railway was wasted. Once the tracks have been relaid at standard gauge NRC ought to become a major instrument of national development. There is also a need for new extensions of the railway, most especially for an east-west line which would not only link towns and population centres across the country but also link the Nigerian railway system to those of its neighbours in the Economic Community of West Africa (ECOWAS). For it is not only Nigeria that is still dependent upon an old colonial rail system; comparable problems affect its neighbours.

The two other forms of internal transport are the airways and the inland waterways. Both Lagos and Kano international airports need much updating and improvement to keep them level with international requirements. This is especially true of the northern airport, while the country as a whole is vast enough to justify modern internal air transport: 18 internal airports are scheduled for redevelopment.

As for the country's internal waterways—the giant Niger and Benue rivers—these have hardly been developed at all. Admittedly they present a number of difficult problems to overcome as highways—shallow draught, narrow and dangerous channels for navigation, the northern rivers drying up between the rains—yet none of these reasons explains the extent of the neglect that has been their fate when they do have great potential as a means of transporting heavy goods—one of the cheapest forms of transport there is. At least this was coming to be realised and the rivers were used increasingly during the 1970s by landlocked Niger.

Telecommunications is the other major field deserving urgent attention. International telephone calls from Lagos to Europe are still easier much of the time than internal calls to Jos or Maiduguri. And for a country that is booming there are so few telephones available in the towns that business firms have their own WT systems as the only sure way of conducting their affairs efficiently. The greatest drawback here is one of manpower. There are not enough technicians or repair men to keep even the inadequate existing system going properly. If the Third Plan brings about a vast telecommunications expansion it should also give top priority to ensuring that enough skilled electricians and other engineers are produced to make the system work once it has been expanded.

Nigeria urgently needs an efficient and updated infrastructure of communications, and this the Third Plan aims to develop. Even so, it will be surprising if at least some of the bottlenecks do not remain for a considerable time to come. They represent the inevitable price to be paid for economic expansion on the scale and at the rate that Nigeria is enjoying during the 1970s and should continue to enjoy as long as the oil boom lasts.

Notes

1   *African Development*, March 1975
2   *Daily Times*, 15 August 1975
3   *Daily Times*, 8 July 1975
4   *Sunday Observer*, 20 July 1975
5   *New Nigerian*, 25 July 1975
6   *Times International*, 12 August 1975

Chapter thirteen

Foreign affairs

Nigeria's foreign impact is not commensurate with its size or potential. In Africa Egypt and South Africa at opposite ends of the continent make far more impression, though for very different reasons: of the Arab states both Algeria and Libya are consistently and often dramatically in the news; in East Africa Kenya, Uganda and Tanzania make a persistent impact in their own particular ways; so, too, do Zambia and Zaïre; and sometimes in West Africa it might be supposed that Ghana or the Ivory Coast are commensurate in power terms with Nigeria when their foreign policy pronouncements are taken into account. None of this is necessarily a bad thing: a low-profile foreign policy often means that when a country does exert itself over a particular matter it is all the more effective. Nigerians, who are often accused of being brash, loud and pushing, are—on the world scene—almost subdued, and few would imagine in assessing its performance that Nigeria is the largest country on the African continent with 70 million or more people; that it is the seventh largest oil producer in the world; and that its vast potential may well one day put it in the top dozen countries of the world.

Nigeria's immediate and most obvious influence is in its own region of the continent—the West African bulge—and there, following the signing of the ECOWAS Treaty in 1975, it may be expected to expand its influence considerably over the next decade. It is a leading member of the OAU and especially in those matters that most consistently affect that body—the affairs of southern Africa—it has adopted an increasingly radical line. It is a member of the Commonwealth in which despite or perhaps because of suspicions of Britain (arising out of the latter's role in the civil war and also because of its ambivalent attitudes towards southern Africa questions) Nigeria has become an increasingly effective performer, carrying great weight in its councils and able to influence substantially its deliberations. As a member of the UN it has followed the normal Africa bloc lines over general issues but has hardly made an impact of the kind some other African states have achieved. And as a member of that new and immensely important body—OPEC—it has taken a back seat, though moving increasingly into the camp of the price hawks. It played a leading role in terms of Africa's relations with the EEC; it has— inevitably—a special relationship with Britain; and with the other great powers it has managed to make clear a non-aligned stand despite the fact that in commercial matters its interests and sympathies are overwhelmingly pro-western and capitalist.

The international involvement in the civil war—especially that of Britain, Russia and France of the great powers but of many others besides—was a major factor helping to shape the subsequent Nigerian view of what its foreign policy should be. Indeed, in the five years that followed the end of the civil war Gowon showed a marked preference for foreign affairs—some of his critics would say, to the neglect of home affairs—and though throughout that period Nigerian world impact was considerably less than it might have been, the country also came to feel its strength and realise the extent of the influence it might wield.

At the Commonwealth conference in Singapore in January 1971, for example, it was probably far more Nigerian pressures (which included the threat to switch arms purchases from Britain) than the rhetoric and appeals of Tanzania and Zambia that helped hold Heath back from what otherwise might have been a headlong rush into selling arms to South Africa. During that year, with the civil war memories receding, Nigeria became more confident and so more involved in the questions relating to arms for South Africa, dialogue, the proposed British-Rhodesia deal, and the question of an OAU High Command. It also emerged as a militant champion of the southern Africa liberation movements.

During 1971 Gowon was to visit a number of West African states— Gambia, Mauritania, Niger, Senegal, Cameroon; he also visited Ethiopia and Kenya in East Africa. Nigeria early recognised Amin in Uganda and formal relations with both Tanzania and Zambia were resumed (they had been broken because the two had recognised Biafra during the war). In theory at least, a radical foreign policy towards southern African affairs was emerging but there was something of a gap between the rhetoric and the performance. Nigeria came out firmly at this time against any association with the EEC. Consistently from 1971 onwards Nigeria worked hard to improve relations with its West African neighbours.

Part of Nigeria's problem in international relations—certainly as far as the rest of Africa is concerned—is, ironically, its great size in comparison with its neighbours. With between 70 and 80 million people it represents a fifth of the total population of the continent. It is, therefore, a giant in Africa. With its oil wealth it is also an economic power, although in fact it needs to channel all its wealth into its own development. Its possession of wealth does, however, provide some useful leverage for external relations—Nigeria has become an actual if modest aid disburser in recent years while its large potential market makes it a commercial partner of great value to the major trading countries from outside the continent.

Speaking of the country's wealth and size in 1974 Dr Okoi Arikpo, then the External Affairs Commissioner, said that Nigeria feels it is in 'a frightening position' in relation to other smaller African countries. Nigeria's great size is understandably a cause of concern to its neighbours: it explains French support for Biafra since for its own reasons of *realpolitik* France wished to see the dismemberment of Africa's giant as did Nigeria's immediate neighbours if only, in their case, to make them feel more comfortable. And this suspicion by the small for the large—a perennial problem in foreign relations—is the main reason why Nigeria, with real sensitivity to its neighbours' susceptibilities, has adopted a low-profile foreign policy.

While supporting the liberation movements and endorsing their claims at the OAU Nigeria has itself been circumspect: it refused, for example, to allow the PLO to set up offices in Nigeria and Dr Arikpo, in a clear reference to the countries like Botswana that have borders with Rhodesia and South Africa, said:

> We do everything possible to use our resources to keep the Organisation of African Unity going. We contribute to the freedom fighters and we do try to show the smaller but independent countries that we are not telling them what to do.[1]

Under Gowon (leaving aside the interregnum of the civil war) Nigeria's foreign policy in the period 1970–75 emerged as far more radical than during the period from independence in 1960 to 1966 and the break-up of the old Nigeria: until that date Nigeria had also maintained a low profile but its image then was as a moderate, almost a conservative, in foreign affairs, although it did abrogate the defence treaty with Britain in 1962 and oppose the French Saharan nuclear tests. With the civil war Nigeria's foreign policy came of age. The harsh realities of big-power politics and would-be intervention in its affairs taught it the most practical lesson of all as far as foreign policy is concerned: that other nations will only help in order to reap advantages for themselves; otherwise they oppose (in the hope of obtaining advantages elsewhere) or remain neutral. From the end of the war Nigerian essays into foreign affairs have shown a marked lack of rhetoric and a sensible understanding of the basis of power. It is Nigerian economic strength (the market it offers and its oil) which provides its major weapon in foreign affairs.

Relations with Britain were slow in recovering following the civil war. They began to look up in 1972 when Lord Carrington (Britain's Minister of Defence) visited Lagos and issued the invitation to Gowon to visit Britain. Another year was to pass, however, before this took place and then—despite hard work by the British Foreign Office— only after Nigeria had obtained certain commitments as to what

Britain would not do with regard to developments in Rhodesia and southern Africa. For Britain Nigeria had been the greatest of its African colonies, and despite ups and downs in relations, including potentially disastrous British fence-sitting during the early stages of the civil war, the two-way relationship was never marred by the racial overtones that affected Britain's dealings with those territories complicated by sizable white settler minorities. The obvious close connections relate to trade, army traditions, language, law and a number of other affinities that exist as a direct leftover of the imperial age. In London Gowon certainly showed that he knew how to play up to his audience as he quoted Shakespeare at the banquet in his honour. Better relations were materially helped by the fact that in 1973 10 per cent of Britain's oil came from Nigeria while, after South Africa, by far the largest British investment stakes on the continent were in Nigeria. Soon after his London visit Gowon went on a state visit to Russia. He was criticised in Nigeria for having gone to London first: Russia, after all, had provided far more military assistance (in terms of value) to the Federal Government during the war including aircraft which Britain had refused and had done so more promptly than Britain. And Russia by 1974 was supplying substantial technical assistance to Nigeria as well as providing her with several thousand scholarships a year. Later in 1974 Gowon visited China, completing a round of the big powers (with the significant exception of the USA) to demonstrate Nigeria's essential non-aligned stand in world affairs. The result of his visit to China in September 1974 was an increase in Chinese agricultural, technical and cultural assistance and exchanges.

Relations with the USA have never been especially warm: partly, perhaps, stemming from the unfortunately gauche remark of Dean Rusk at the outbreak of the civil war when he said 'We regard Nigeria as part of Britain's sphere of influence',[2] partly because of a genuine remoteness of the USA from Nigerian affairs, even though black Americans have endeavoured to identify closely with Nigeria; and partly because of more than one awkwardness in American dealings with Nigeria and the failure to arrange a Nixon–Gowon meeting when the latter attended the UN, or (a typical example occurring in July 1975) when the American diplomatic corps refused to vacate a building in Lagos after being requested to do so by the government until the Nigerians actually surrounded it with troops. However, as the *American Post Despatch* said in August 1975, following the coup in Nigeria, 'In as much as Nigeria supplies five per cent of America's oil, there may be some diplomatic response in the US to the coup in black Africa's richest nation.'[3] Although potentially there are enormous cultural ties between the two countries the relationship between Nigeria and the USA is mainly a commercial one.

At the end of 1975 and early in 1976 Nigeria and Russia came closer together over the question of Angola. In October 1975 Nigeria took delivery of the first batch of Soviet-built supersonic MiG 21 fighters as a first phase in modernising her air force: the air force already had both MiG 17 fighters and Ilyushin 28 bombers as part of its fleet from the days of the civil war. As the war in Angola worsened and the Russians and Cubans as well as the South Africans became involved, Nigeria became one of the first African states to recognise the MPLA as the government of the country. At the emergency session of the OAU held in Addis Ababa at the beginning of 1976, Nigeria took a strong line in support of the MPLA when a deadlocked position ensued—22 for MPLA and 22 against.

Over Angola the government adopted one of the most positive leads that Nigeria has taken over any African issue for a long time. Having recognised the MPLA government itself, Nigeria then proceeded to canvas other African states to persuade them to follow its lead; in the event its diplomacy may well have been a deciding factor in achieving majority recognition for the MPLA. The Commissioner for Youth and Sports, General Olufemi Olutoye (who also plays a diplomatic role), went to a number of African capitals to persuade their governments of the need for a stand over the Angola issue; the Commissioner for Foreign Affairs, Colonel Joseph Garba, as well as the then Chief of Staff Supreme Headquarters, General Olusegun Obasanjo, threw their weight behind a campaign to obtain majority African re-cognition for the MPLA. Both Olutoye and Obasanjo visited Ghana's Acheampong within a week of each other and then, following a visit by the MPLA Prime Minister, Lopo do Nascimento, Ghana recognised the MPLA. Other countries such as Libya, Niger and Chad were also influenced by Nigerian pressures.

During the Angolian crisis President Ford circulated African heads of state with his views on the question. The Nigerian reaction was to publish his letter in full—and the reply—in which the President was accused of 'arm-twisting' and 'insulting the intelligence' of African leaders. President Ford was told in no uncertain terms that Africa was not prepared to bow to the dictates of a super-power.

The reasons for the strong stand taken by the Mohammed government over Angola were important and indicated a new line in foreign policy. First, and very clearly at the time, there was a vacuum in African leadership over Angola and other issues; Nigeria is the African state most able to fill such a vacuum and give a lead, and here it showed itself prepared to do so in forthright terms. Second, it was determined to come out in opposition to South Africa whose defiance of Africa over apartheid and Namibia was now blatantly reinforced by its intervention in Angola. Nigeria argued correctly that the Republic had to be stopped and shown that it could not pursue its aims in black Africa by arms with impunity. Even a limited South African success in Angola would have set back by years the revolutionary changes at last taking place in that part of the continent.

Third, Nigeria brushed aside American and western arguments about Russia in Angola: the Russians had helped Nigeria in the civil war without ending up running the state; but in any case Nigeria saw it as racist neocolonialism for the West to instruct Africa about the dangers of accepting Russian assistance. This new and tough approach to an African problem—an approach it was prepared to back by precise diplomatic initiatives—foreshadowed a more active and dynamic continental role for Nigeria.

The Commonwealth, although often decried by the Nigerian press, has played an important role in Nigerian foreign policy. Nigerian accession to it in 1960 ensured that South Africa would be forced out a year later; almost literally the last action of the Prime Minister, Abubakar Tafawa Balewa, before he was killed in what were the beginnings of the civil war, was to chair the Lagos Commonwealth Conference of January 1966 on Rhodesia; while the Federal Government was prepared to turn to the Commonwealth for possible help with mediation before the civil war actually got moving. Unobtrusive Nigerian diplomacy at Singapore probably did more than anything else to temper the intention of both Heath and Home to resume the sale of arms to South Africa; at the Ottawa meeting of August 1973 Gowon played a central role over the main issues of arms to South Africa, Rhodesia and support for Namibia, as he was to do again at the Kingston meeting 18 months later. The Commonwealth provides Nigeria (as it does its other members) with an extremely useful forum for effective diplomacy as well as a special means of exerting pressures upon Britain.

Nigeria, which had concluded an earlier agreement with the EEC in 1966 that was never ratified, approached the EEC in the 1970s with caution; then in forthright terms it condemned the idea of Yaounde-style association with the European Common Market for itself or other Commonwealth African countries, preferring for a straight trade agreement. Subsequent Nigerian championship of the 'Associables and Associates' was a key factor in winning reasonable terms for the African countries in the battle that led to the Lome Convention of January 1975. At that convention it was agreed to abandon reverse preferences and to adopt export stabilisation schemes, and both these achievements were due mainly to Nigerian leadership. Nigeria in fact could have stayed clear of the negotiations since its oil gave it the leeway to do so. It did not, and the success of the negotiations—from the African point of view—resulted from Nigeria's correct use of its diplomatic strengths in relation to Europe: it had the bargaining power in both its products and the market it offered, making it a most attractive potential partner for the EEC. It knew this and used it significantly in the bargaining that took place.

The southern Africa issue dominates much of the continent's diplomacy and in the case of Nigeria also profoundly affects relations with Britain. During the first five years of the 1970s Nigerian leads on southern Africa had a substantial modifying effect upon British policies while over this period it shifted steadily into the radical camp. Nigeria quarrelled with Britain over the November 1971 Home-Smith proposals for Rhodesia; it gradually increased its backing for the various liberation movements; it applied sanctions to Rhodesia; it turned down the tempting South African offer of a deal (gold for oil); it gave qualified support to the Kaunda-Nyerere détente exercise that started late in 1974 though making plain it was ready for a switch back to guerrilla tactics if it failed; and its recognition of MPLA at the end of 1975 was probably decisive in influencing the course of events that followed.

Since 1970 oil wealth has enabled Nigeria to become an aid donor: only a modest one (which is as it should be considering the size of its own development problems) but nevertheless a donor. At the end of 1974, for example, arrangements were completed for the IMF in Washington to borrow $120 million from Nigeria to help finance oil credits for other countries; then the World Bank borrowed $240 million at 8 per cent interest. In the Commonwealth which has a number of specialised agencies for technical assistance Nigeria is the only developing country to have increased substantially its aid contributions. It has done this for the Commonwealth Fund for Technical Co-operation (CFTC) which supplies technical assistance to promote economic and social development in the developing countries of the Commonwealth. Nigeria raised its contribution for 1974–75 to £430 000 and agreed to maintain it at that level for a further two years provided the advanced economies such as those of Britain and Australia also kept their contributions at comparable levels.

On a bilateral basis Nigeria disbursed an estimated £2 million in relief to the Sahel countries following the drought and these included Ethiopia and Somalia outside West Africa. It provided Mali with two gifts of £25 000 each in 1973; it has made available to Botswana technical assistance in the form of legal and police personnel; it gave the newly independent Guine Bissau ₦500 000; it provided aid for Zambia after Smith closed the border in January 1973 and Zambia was faced with a mammoth rerouting exercise for her copper; and at the Kingston Commonwealth Conference it promised aid to Mozambique in the event of the latter closing its borders to Rhodesia and so losing its revenue from the transit of Rhodesian goods.

Indeed, by 1975 Nigeria was in the position of receiving suppliants for its assistance. In July of that year, on his way to Monrovia to attend Liberia's 128th anniversary of independence, King Moshoeshoe II of Lesotho stopped off in Lagos for talks with Gowon. The King sought technical assistance from Nigeria to help Lesotho's development programme; he also explored the possibility of training 'young nationalists of Lesotho' in Nigeria.

Nigeria is becoming a power in Africa; sometimes, as over the EEC issue, acting as its effective spokesman. Important enough strategically and economically to carry growing weight with the great powers, Nigeria plays an expanding role in the councils of the OAU, the Commonwealth and OPEC. All these activities make up its general foreign policy. Of most immediate concern to Nigeria, however, must be its relations with its neighbours of West Africa and here it faces the greatest difficulties and the biggest challenges. It does so quite simply because of its size in relation to all the other countries of the region: the population of the 15 members of ECOWAS comes to 125 million and nearly two thirds of this number are Nigerians. As a result the others fear its economic and political domination; if, therefore, it is to lead West Africa effectively it must do so with circumspection.

Nigeria has cultivated relations with its West African neighbours since 1970 and Gowon believed in sharing Nigerian economic prosperity as a means of drawing the countries of the region closer together, showing a passionate determination to bring English- and French-speaking states of the region into closer relations and harmony. Perhaps in the long run the creation of ECOWAS may go down as Gowon's greatest achievement. Money power is always a most effective instrument of policy though, if mishandled or overused, it may backfire upon its user. Between 1970 and 1975 Nigeria made some substantial grants to Togo, Dahomey, and Niger to help balance their budgets and reduce their dependence upon France. Most of Nigeria's Sahel relief funds went to Niger, Chad, Upper Volta and Mali. Gowon worked on the assumption that half the divisions in West Africa were the artificial leftovers of the colonial age and that what the countries shared in common of past background, culture, commercial ties and interests could more than compensate for the differences of language, law and political approach that marked off Anglophone from Francophone countries. In this his judgment was clearly right.

There was never any question of ECOWAS being incompatible with the various existing organisations in the region (most of them between two or three countries) such as the Chad Basin Commission, the Organisation of Senegal River States, the River Niger Commission, the Nigeria-Niger Joint Commission, the Liberia-Sierra Leone or the Ghana-Togo Commissions. Nothing in the projected West African Economic Community need be at cross-purposes with these various commissions which were developed to answer specific purposes. Part of the difficulty in forming a West African regional association undoubtedly lay in the patterns of relations left behind by the colonial division of the area; with states divided as between Britain and France; and many of them looking outside Africa rather than to their neighbours. The Nigerian approach under Gowon was pragmatic and realistic: a stage-by-stage advance that never attempted to be too ambitious too quickly. The fact that Gowon won the support of

Houphouët-Boigny to the idea of a trans-cultural regional grouping for economic purposes perhaps ensured that the treaty would come into being, for traditionally the Ivory Coast leader had been against such groupings as unrealistic.

Nigeria has a major vested interest in improving the overland communications facilities of the region, for its own chronic port congestion difficulties led in 1975 to an exploration of the possibilities of imports coming into Ghana or Benin and then cross land to Nigeria. In any case Nigeria is the starting—or finishing—point for two of Africa's planned major new highways: the Trans-Saharan Highway and the Trans-African Highway and both these will have an important impact upon ECOWAS. In economic terms Nigeria could become the factory for western Africa with a series of new or improved highways (both road and rail) radiating outwards from it. The easing of border requirements (to cut down smuggling), the adoption of common road, rail and coastal shipping practices as well as legal and other requirements (all envisaged in the ECOWAS Treaty) are essential steps towards greater regional co-operation. They are also a prerequisite for any growth of Nigeria's economic impact upon the area for at present the bulk of its trade—and certainly more than need or should be the case—is outside the continent to Europe rather than with its neighbours. During the 1970s Nigeria did undertake some development deals with its neighbours of potentially great significance. In February 1973, for example, it agreed to export crude oil to Sierra Leone's refineries and to import Sierra Leone high-grade iron ore for its proposed steel industry (still to be started). In fact the ore proved so low-grade that this Sierra Leone mine has ceased production. Sierra Leone also agreed to import Nigerian coal and Nigeria took Sierra Leone's scrap rails for use in its coalmines. Also that year Nigeria invested ₦65 800 in Guinea's iron ore mines, acquiring a 5 per cent holding in the Guinea company.

As Nigeria has felt itself becoming an economic giant so, more and more, it has wished to pursue policies commensurate with its power. The development of ECOWAS was its major contribution to African unity in the period 1970–75. The Commissioner for Foreign Affairs over this period, Dr Okoi Arikpo, was constrained to say, however, that it was 'a false and pernicious idea that Nigeria's economic and political weight would be a threat to its smaller neighbours.'[4] Maybe; the statement needed saying as it will need reiterating for the fear of the giant remains. Nigeria is the key to any West African regional grouping: it has tried hard to co-operate with its smaller neighbours and help them without appearing to dragoon them into a pattern of its devising; it is by no means an easy political exercise.

In January 1975 Gowon visited Dahomey (Benin) and Togo and in the former country it was agreed to establish jointly owned sugar- and cement-producing complexes which will only be 160 kilometres from major Nigerian markets. Thus Nigeria pursued its policy of establishing factories in neighbouring countries. In Togo a £15 million oil refinery is being constructed; it will be commissioned in 1977. When that happens Nigeria will import phosphates from Togo in exchange for crude oil. Nigeria is also involved in a joint project for an oil refinery in the Ivory Coast.

Nigeria's problem of too much cash and too many projects to implement is complemented by the general poverty of its smaller neighbours. There can and should develop, therefore, a working partnership between them, but always provided that the smaller countries do not become too worried about Nigerian economic dominance and provided Nigeria constantly watches and understands their suspicions and sensitivities. As the result of patient diplomacy fifteen West African states met in Lagos on 28 May 1975, and signed the ECOWAS Treaty (to establish the Economic Community of West African States) and a month later ten of the fifteen had ratified the treaty. Three years of hard bargaining and complex negotiations produced the treaty which represents a major advance for Africa as a whole as well as for West Africa in particular. The community should be in a position to obtain far better conditions in trade deals with the advanced economies of the EEC and North America, especially for its raw materials, than previously. Far more difficult and long-term will be the process of social and economic integration as between the member states. The treaty provides for free movement of goods and people, the abolition of visas, the right to reside anywhere in the community, to work, or to undertake commercial or industrial activities without residence permits. As with the EEC the realisation of any or all these aims will be hard and there will be many setbacks. At least a start has been made and just as the greatest effort in bringing the treaty into being was Nigeria's, so the successful growth of the community in the future will depend more upon its good judgment and reactions to its smaller partners than upon the actions of any other member.

In other matters Nigeria has consistently tried a conciliatory approach and, wherever possible, avoided appearing to throw its weight about. Even where it has exerted very considerable pressure—as upon Britain over the sale of arms to South Africa—it has done so diplomatically, behind the scenes, rather than in too obvious and overt a fashion. Many African countries adopt the reverse approach but then they have so little real power to back up their policies. Nigeria has the power and prefers the soft approach. In the councils of OPEC, for example, although it has moved steadily into the hardline camp that demands higher oil prices, Nigeria also decided in October 1974 to sell crude at cut prices to those African countries which have refineries—a move seen as a rebuke to OPEC Arab states. Nigeria, however, might also consider the plight of the African states—

just as hard-hit by high oil prices—that do not have refineries.

Nigeria's foreign policy can be divided into two areas: relations with her immediate neighbours in West Africa; and relations with the rest of Africa and the world. In the former it goes softly and its primary aim must be one of reassurance; in the latter it is beginning to feel that it has a good deal more room for manoeuvre and can afford to adopt tougher lines and approaches where its interests are involved.

One of the criticisms levelled at Gowon after the coup—as at Abubakar after his death—was that he concentrated upon foreign to the neglect of home affairs. There is some truth in this, but no country of Nigeria's size and potential can afford to neglect foreign affairs, and by and large the international image that Nigeria achieved in the Gowon years was one of which it could be proud. There is the counter-danger that in the period of the Third Plan when Nigerian attention will be concentrated upon making major economic, commercial and industrial breakthroughs, it may neglect foreign affairs and become too inward-looking. It would be easy enough to do; it should be avoided. It is a measure of Nigeria's standing in Africa that when the news of the coup came through to Kampala on 29 July 1975, and it was realised that Africa's most powerful black leader had been toppled, this effectively took the punch out of the remainder of the conference. At least four leaders hurried home early; whatever their ostensible reasons, it was fear of comparable coups that drove them to abandon the Kampala OAU Summit in mid-session. It may not have been the most auspicious event for the OAU but the partial collapse of the conference on the news of Gowon's fall was certainly a unique form of tribute to the growing power and influence of Nigeria.

Notes

1   Quoted in *African Development*, March 1975
2   *West Africa*, 22 July 1967
3   Quoted in *Evening Times*, 4 August 1975
4   *African Development*, March 1974

Chapter fourteen

Corruption

When people discuss corruption in Nigeria, no one denies its existence or attempts to cover up the extent to which it is to be found in public life. It is there—all too obviously—admitted and deplored. Thereafter the problem is how to tackle this social ill and control it. The media constantly examine it. The malaise goes deep. It is easy to criticise those caught blatantly involved in some act of corruption; it is equally easy to blame those in authority for not taking action. Some would ask for the most drastic penalties; others argue that corruption in one form or another is endemic to the society, that 'dash' or a ten per cent rake-off or payment to some middle man is so automatic that it should be regarded as part of the country's way of life. Many firms—it is rumoured—simply write into their budgets appropriate sums of money to be used for bribery.

It is no answer to say that corruption exists in all societies, although indeed this is true. Corruption takes different forms from country to country, whether it is of the most open kind from which Nigeria too obviously suffers—demands for a cut for arranging a contract, for example, or whether it is the more subtle kind such as the operation of the old boy network in Britain which is designed to ensure that a member of the group rather than the most able contender for a post qualifies. But when corruption reaches and passes a certain level in the life of a society it takes a heavy toll: from the credibility of the leadership; of faith in the possibility of improving society; of any desire to work according to honest practices. In such an atmosphere it becomes difficult and sometimes impossible to persuade the young as they come onto the public scene for the first time that there are standards of morality to which they should adhere. Indeed, it becomes increasingly hard to create any ethical norm of behaviour acceptable to society as a whole. The recognition of a problem, however, is the first and easiest step towards a solution; the difficulty comes in finding the cure.

Sometimes it is a question of asking where the line should be drawn. In 1975 there were housing scandals, such as a house costing N̶13 000 being rented out for N̶5 000 a year. Part of the problem stems from the enormous acquisition of wealth from oil: some people have been able to get their hands on some of the new wealth; others have not—and feel left out. The national problem is how to share out the wealth; the individual problem is how to get one's share. The wave of strikes and wage demands that followed the Udoji award at the end of 1974 gave a taste of the general public's determination not to be left out: in such a situation it is easy to envisage the growth of a 'dog eat dog' society.

Corruption and ethics are twins. When on 1 October 1974, the military regime of Gowon reneged on its promise to return to civilian rule in 1976 this, too, was a form of corruption: it represented the inability of government to keep to its word. The reasons given in support of the decision were unconvincing. The public interpreted the move quite simply as the determination of the army to hold onto power because it enjoyed its fruits too much to relinquish them. And if that is the public's understanding of its rulers it becomes a short enough step before the individual adopts the philosophy which assumes power is legitimately his to keep for as long as he can hold it regardless of any obligation that in theory goes with it.

The Third Plan itself is worth scrutiny in terms of the priorities it sets and the opportunities it provides. The most obvious politician's complaint was that it aimed to spend more on defence than on agriculture or education—and that, certainly, could be represented as a form of corruption on behalf of the forces in power. It has been argued by politicians again that the soldiers squandered their nine years in power under Gowon and did not produce a constitution for the country. The problem here, as so often, is the efficacy of any policy that depends upon those in charge of it working themselves out of a job.

As one newspaper put it in mid-1975: 'Meanwhile too, public anger has focussed on the corruption which it is conceded on all sides is a major corrosive force in the national life.'[1] As long as great affluence is apparent alongside extravagant public spending it is unsurprising if the poor of urban or rural Nigeria look with cynicism at their rulers and at the system they uphold. Brigadier Emanuel Abisoye, the Adjutant-General of the Nigerian Army in 1975 commented that 'All Nigerians are corrupt' apparently meaning that society encouraged the belief that everyone was on his own and should struggle by whatever means for whatever he could get. The press often quotes examples of corruption so wide-ranging as to embrace all aspects of the national life: petty racketeering during shortages of commodities; the payment of large sums to secure government contracts; payment, for example, of N-50 (instead of the official N-2) for driving licences when the purchasers wished to evade taking the test; charges at Lagos airport of N-10 to ensure a smooth passage through customs.

The fact is that the Gowon government not only did nothing to implement the promise in its nine-point programme to clean up corruption but allowed corruption to grow worse. Shortly before the July 1975 coup, for example, various ministries, the police, the armed forces and government corporations were given powers to award contracts without the approval of the Federal Tenders Board—so that controls against corruption were being eased and not strengthened. The weakest explanation of the failure to investigate corruption was Gowon's contention that too much exposure would erode public confidence in the government. This is one of the oldest political justifications for inaction: that it is better to let things lie than upset public confidence in the system. It doesn't work: in the long run, if the people see a system defending itself in such terms, they begin to dream of destroying it altogether.

There are self-generating problems connected with corruption: after the civil war the Nigerian army numbered some 250 000 men. It might have been thought that this army would soon be drastically reduced but it was not (until measures to halve if were announced by the Mohammed regime at the end of 1975). The trouble in the years after the war was that the 250 000 soldiers found themselves among the best paid people in the country and for them a continuing army career ensured a reasonable life that otherwise might disappear. The consequence has been tremendous rank-and-file pressure for the army to remain at such a formidable size whatever the country's true military needs. Was the failure of the top military men (some of whom would themselves be axed in any cutback) to prune the army a form of corruption? And if it was, what of the trade union that threatens industrial action to prevent redundancies since, it argues, part of its job is to protect the livelihood of its members (an argument and situation well known in Britain in the 1970s)? Is that corruption? Part of the difficulty over questions of corruption has always been one of definitions.

Attacks upon the press when it asks too many and too awkward questions on the grounds that it is breaking emergency laws or somehow disturbing the peace but in fact because it is making life awkward for those in control is another form of corruption. In the declining period of the Gowon regime the two famous cases of Tarka and Gomwalk focused attention upon abuse of high office. The Minister of Communications was forced to resign after a businessman had sworn an affidavit accusing him of misusing his office for private gain; yet when another businessman swore a similar affidavit naming the Governor of the Benue Plateau State he was arrested and imprisoned for three months without any trial until public outcry forced his release.

In a sense Nigeria is suffering from a surfeit: of oil; money; development; expatriates; new businesses; and it is expanding faster than its ability to absorb some of the effects of all the activity that is taking place. In consequence it is a society that is wide open to a range of abuses that are exceptionally difficult to curb. The condemnations and constant articles upon the subject show an awareness that verges on the masochistic, but again and again one returns to the same starting point: what to do; how, by whom; when. Appointments have their own price and bribes are too often treated as though part of a legitimate transaction. Corruption is most usually taken to mean the receiving or offering of money or other clear advantages in return for contracts, not being obliged to discharge an obligation, obtaining a job for which one is not qualified, sidestepping justice, leaping ahead of a queue and so on. In many of these activities the exercise of corruption is blatant. There is also a permissive acceptance of bribery and corruption in Nigeria most often expressed by such phrases as 'everyone does it', it 'is an accepted part of life' or that 'dash' is normal. When people cease to justify corruption as normal and therefore as acceptable there will be a chance of eradicating it, but not before. The question that needs to be answered is: why should it prevail?

Poverty in juxtaposition to great wealth is one of the easiest lures to corrupt practices, especially in a fast-moving economic climate when the poor of one day are seen to be the rich of the next. Then the question becomes: how did they get there when others stand still in their poverty? The attractive norms of the consumer society and the great pressures upon any moderately well-off Nigerian by his many relatives put him in the position where the demands upon his total income exceed the income. At that point he faces temptations to corruption. Whether or not he succumbs in part at least depends upon whether he has the opportunity. This is when abuse of official position is most likely to start. Such temptations exist in all societies; they are especially likely to flourish in one such as Nigeria where a lot of wealth has started to flow suddenly, where quick and sometimes spectacular fortunes are being made, where a man who does well is instantly expected to take on all sorts of burdens connected with his relatives who besiege him for money or jobs or both, and where in any case the society's norm appears to be material possessions more than anything else and, finally, where many of these material possessions are being enjoyed for the first time. When social values are too obviously related to wealth, corruption tends to have a field day.

The evidence of corruption is too overwhelming to invite denials. Attacks upon it, however, are more in the form of statements of condemnation rather than government action. Few seem to know where a war against corruption can be successfully started. There have to be both legal and social sanctions against corruption: legal ones exist, but these alone are not much good if everyone pays lip-service to them while essentially taking no notice.

Social sanctions against corruption must be difficult to activate in a society where year after year scandals occur as copies of examination papers are sold to students in advance to enable them to pass. There are leakages of questions and falsification of results as well as admission malpractices at the start of school years when pupils either enter secondary school for the first time or prepare to go on elsewhere. Certificates rackets have been uncovered in the WAEC and at the University of Lagos. It is difficult to imagine how new generations of Nigerians can be instilled with ethical values against corruption when such activities are a normal annual occurrence.

When the new regime took over in 1975 there inevitably followed many official probings as governors were changed and malpractices came to light. The extent of fraud and malpractices in one administration—that of Ukpabi Asika in East Central State—was on a major scale: the state government had only published one set of audited accounts in five years and these showed that N11.9 million had been spent in excess of authorised expenditure; the government could not produce 346 payment vouchers covering N747 403 and nearly another N1 million was unaccounted for altogether. These particular abuses came to light quickly; it was an open secret that comparable abuses could be discovered in most other states. All too often, it appeared, auditing was deemed to be an unnecessary occupation. At the purely legal governmental level strict standards of public auditing are one obvious starting point for any corruption clean-up.

Public accountability is a *sine qua non* for any regime that would cut out corruption. All too often state governors, while from time to time ritualistically condemning corruption, continued to live at a pace and in a style that they could not possibly have sustained on their salaries. Top people were rarely if ever investigated for malpractices. Sometimes, however, examples were made of those lower down the scale, presumably to show that those at the top were doing their job. As the 1975 changeover took place demands were made for investigations into the affairs of the retired governors while it was suggested that others in public office should declare their assets so that what they could not account for became forfeit to the state. The time to initiate changes was when the new government came to power, and a massive investigation and purge did follow (see above pp. 32–33), though it will be some time before its effects can be truly judged.

There is plenty of exhortation from the top: people are urged to be honest or civil servants on courses are told to show devotion to duty, yet there is little enough evidence that those who exhort practise what they so readily preach. Three days before the 1975 coup the Grand Khadi of the northern states, Alhaji Abubakar Gummi, said that tyranny and oppression had become the order of the day, that detention was the reward of anyone who tried openly to criticise the way things were run. He went on: 'I do not think there is anybody who is trying to put the house in order.' And he added: 'Those who are expected to set good precedents for their subjects have become victims of excessive ambition and materialism.'

Nigeria's free-ranging press faced many attempts to silence it during the Gowon regime. As the *Daily Times* said in an editorial of September 1974:

> At any time when the Press is engaged in a crusade that embarrasses any government, it is not uncommon for highly placed men in government to warn the Press that it was going beyond its bounds.[3]

A free and fearless press is a prerequisite for any real attempt to clear up corrupt practices of whatever kind. The press in Nigeria has usually shown itself willing enough. Governments have not been so forward.

There is a growing anti-corruption lobby in Nigeria. There are calls to investigate, to punish the guilty, to force public men to declare their assets. There are plenty of people willing to write to the papers and complain of corruption. Through all the talk not much evidence has emerged that people of influence and power are convinced that a change is either possible or essential. Too many of those who condemn corruption also assume that responsibility for its cure lies with someone else. And this leads to the core of the corruption problem: it is only likely to be eradicated when enough people want it to be eradicated; when the climate, both moral and ethical, leads a sufficient number of people to want to oppose corruption in all its forms and at all levels. Such people, moreover, must be prepared to go to great and inconvenient lengths that may endanger their own positions so as to combat it. Thus it becomes a question of education. And so another question has to be faced: how many Nigerians positively oppose corruption and are unwilling to succumb to it in any shape or form? Allied to that is the larger question: how many Nigerians must feel like that before there are enough of them to influence general opinion and so effect changes in the accepted practice? The possibility of such a group successfully emerging must depend upon the extent to which the *laissez-faire*, galloping economy does not beguile with its riches and corrupt with its opportunities. Precept is the most difficult of all things to teach. Fundamentally a change of attitude towards money is required and that, perhaps, more than anything else is the first prerequisite for a change.

Between 1970 and 1975 there was no attempt by the Federal Government to eradicate corruption. And during that period the subject certainly got an airing. Writing in the *New Nigerian* in 1972 one observer said:

> Most demands for pay rise in the federation are more or less sectional demands for an adjustment of the imbalance in remuneration for service or place in the society. And this calculation continues.[4]

In a sense this is a key to the whole process. Looking hard at the question Professor Aluko said:

If the society is corrupt, tribalistic, nepotic, extravagant and ridden with violence, it is because its aristocrats—its leaders, rulers and the middle class—are corrupt, sectionalistic, violent and roguish. The day that leadership destroys the canker-worm within itself, the rank and file of the society will be frightened to indulge in questionable and sharp practices. Therefore, if we want to reform society we must first reform the calibre of the aristocracy.[5]

The Nigerian debate over corruption is not only concerned with the taking of bribes—that is, the cash side of corrupt practices although, of course, that is important enough—but also with the search for a national standard of behaviour and so the need for exemplary conduct from the leadership of the country.

Corruption can also be traced—certainly in socialist terms—to what has been called the national squandermania of luxury: one of the baneful effects of capitalism.[6] Luxury leads to high-level corruption, a tendency to accumulate wealth by hook or by crook in order to live big. Materialism can have the effect of reducing people's worth to a computation of the size of their car or house. Can sanctions against corruption be applied when no one will take any notice? Furthermore, can they be applied in a society that is still intensely tribalistic so that people will not apply them against their own? There are exceptionally difficult problems in tackling corruption in a society where ties of kinship are very strong and play so important a part in everyone's daily life.

When the new government came to power in 1975 it denounced corruption. This is standard practice, but admittedly it did more than talk in the months that followed. With the aim of uncovering corruption and corrupt practices, a purge of the public services and the military was set in motion. This could hardly have been avoided in view of the widespread charges of corruption that the new men had levelled at their predecessors. By the November some 10 000 officials had been compulsorily retired because of corruption or inefficiency. Yet at that stage it had to be noted that a good many of those retired were reported as reappearing in other jobs shortly afterwards. This threw considerable doubt upon the real purpose of the purge. Was it genuinely to eliminate corruption? Or was it to make a show of doing so, itself a corrupt activity?

It is one thing to launch an assault upon corruption. More important, however, is the long-term perspective: the measures to prevent its recurrence or at least its worst excesses; and the promotion of a way of life that would eschew corruption anyway.

Nigeria is in no sense unique. No societies can claim to be free of corruption: in some it is more discrete; in others it is less a question of money and more one of privilege. It so happens, however, that at this particular juncture in her history Nigeria suffers from some of the more obvious and blatant forms of this social disease and that many Nigerians, prominent and humble alike, are aware of it, discuss it, deplore it and search for a way to combat it. Such a way has yet to be found. What is certain is that corruption will not be eradicated by decrees or purges. If it is to be combated successfully this requires a process of education which will persuade the leadership of the society to condemn it and demonstrate by their own lives that they will not tolerate it.

Notes

1   *Nigerian Tribune*, 9 July 1975
2   *Daily Times*, 21 July 1975
3   *Daily Times*, 11 September 1974
4   *New Nigerian*, 21 September 1972
5   Quoted in *African Contemporary Record* 1972–73, ed. C. Legun, Rex Collings, 1973
6   *Economic Development of Nigeria, op. cit.*, pp. 72 73

Chapter fifteen

Neocolonialism

Nigeria has problems of identity: as an ex-colony whose culture and economy have been distorted by the British; as an African state that is an entity in relation to the rest of the continent; and as a single nation made up of several major parts—again a result of its colonial past. Despite the wealth, size and great potential of their country and a certain characteristic self-assertiveness, Nigerians sometimes demonstrate an extreme sensitivity to what outsiders, and most of all what the British, say or think about them. There are in Nigeria many evidences of British past influence and presence: in political and social ritual and behaviour; in the major trading companies (such as UAC); in education and the universities; in the courts; in the language; in the army; in the press. In many respects the country remains a colonially oriented society and much of the structure, certainly at official and formal decision-making levels, is Western rather than African. Part of the social and political problem which can produce anti-British outbursts when things go wrong results from a continuing search for a balance between what Nigerians want for their country as Africans and what they have inherited and would like to keep from the colonial experience.

Dealing with neocolonialism is far from easy. To retain anything from the colonial era brings the accusion of being a colonial lackey, yet to reject can bring the even more difficult accusation that the rejection is a gesture when perhaps there is nothing better to go in its place. The fact that arguments about Nigerian identity are couched in terms of whether or not British-inherited practices are suitable to the Nigerian scene is evidence enough of the problem and the sensitivities that go with it.

Sensitivity to the international (western) press is a characteristic not confined to Nigeria but prevalent throughout Africa. There is, nonetheless, substantial Nigerian reaction to the western press and most especially to that of Britain. There is a readiness to over-react to British press criticisms; a fear of what foreign journalists might say; a desire to impress; a diffidence at being connected with a foreign critic. A classic example of this attitude was the leader of the *Nigerian Herald* of 1 August 1975, which began:

When in the early morning of July 29, an announcement was made that a change was effected in the leadership of the Federal Military Government, our foreign detractors felt we would shed blood.

Later the editorial went on:

With the new government's superb handling of the situation and General Gowon's matured re-action, Nigeria has shamed our detractors especially and particularly the British Press, which is already propagating inciting speculations and comments. . . . Their comments were meant to incite us against ourselves; they were meant to divide and destroy us. . . . But that is understandable. . . . Populous, rich and powerful Nigeria is a force to reckon with. . . . We, however, hope that the so-called civilised people of the Euro-American world would have a lot to learn from our maturity.[1]

The editorial veers between two extremes. On the one hand it holds out the power change in Nigeria as something that was handled with maturity and of which the country could be proud, indeed, as an exercise from which the West should take a lesson. On the other hand it accuses the British press of propagating and inciting speculations with the intention of dividing and destroying. The British press is not noted for its sensitivity to or understanding of the African scene; even so, this accusion is possibly a little harsh. Expecting trouble and writing editorials as though Nigeria was bound to collapse into chaos (the British as well as their press specialise in prophecies of doom) is not the same as wanting that to happen. The real point is that Nigerians really need not bother—one way or the other. British neocolonialist influences will finally peter out when it becomes possible for Nigerians to shrug their shoulders and carry on with whatever they are doing regardless of what the British press may say.

Many remainders and reminders of imperialism contribute to neocolonialism either as continuing influences or by creating an anti-colonial backlash which itself is part of the neocolonialist syndrome. There is anti-British feeling in the north because the British did not interfere enough to provide more educational opportunities which would have made northerners better equipped to compete with southerners in the post-independence era. Yet the Ahmadu Bello University in Zaria positively swarms with expatriates—900 out of a total of 1 800 university staff in 1975. There is the easy tendency to blame the colonial past for current ills. There is over-readiness to accept Western (British) standards or pontificating as the norm when they are nothing of the sort. And these exercises are often helped by a large continuing expatriate presence—very small in terms of the country's total population but large enough in those areas where the expatriates might expect to exert an influence.

It is one of the curiosities of history that the main British empire started when British merchants and adventurers went to India to make their fortunes. It was the lure of money that took them there as indeed in the great days of imperial growth it was always money that acted as the spur. Today, in the twilight of whatever empire is left, Britons are to be found in Nigeria—for money. It is a booming, bustling country and people from all the sophisticated economies of the West are in Nigeria, if at all, because they think they can make a quick fortune there. A visit to a club or restaurant in Lagos that caters for expensive and often brash white tastes should convince Nigerians of that fact.

Expatriate indoctrination also goes on. There are many expatriates in the universities, some of whom can be described as 'liberals' or even 'radicals'. In some respects they are dangerous; in others they should be encouraged. They are dangerous because their very radicalism gives them an acceptable cachet under which they put across views that constitute a form of brainwashing. An example of this was highlighted in the *Nigerian Standard* in August 1975 when a political scientist (anonymous) was attacked for indoctrinating his students with the notion that 'present instability in African states is inevitable'—the title of his lectures was 'Inevitability and Instability'. His lectures were attacked for brainwashing the students against the country's efforts at nation-building since, the newspaper writer claimed, they led to psychological defeat before they gave nation-building a trial. Maybe; perhaps this represents the summit, as it were, of neocolonialist brain-washing techniques. On the other hand if what he teaches is demonstrably nonsense, then teaching it surely does no harm: one of the purposes of a university is to enable students to detect and expose fallacies.[2]

Much more crucial perhaps is the realm of industry where far too many decisions are taken by expatriates. These decision are more likely to be neocolonial in intent. Thus:

> Imperialists now essentially make most decisions about what lines of industry to develop, the pricing of industrial output as well as the overall direction of industrial growth. As a result of all these, industrial surplus gets appropriated by imperialists for overseas development. Fraudulent indigenisation is no solution to this neocolonial domination.[3]

Closely aligned to the industrial interference is the field of aid. As a result of her oil wealth Nigeria is now in a position to dispense with financial aid and in fact will soon cease to qualify for aid of all kinds. It will continue to seek technical assistance from abroad though able to pay the full costs for it. Thus, although still a developing country, it should be able to call the tune with regard to technical assistance personnel. But neocolonialism is a field in which such personnel excel, half the time merely by being themselves rather than as a result of directives, training or even intent. The issue at stake is the purpose of aid. For the donors it is a matter of safeguarding their Nigerian interests; in consequence Nigeria ought to dispense with all aid as soon as possible so that its development is in its own hands. Now it has the financial means to do this; its educational system ought before too long to ensure that it has the personnel to do it as well.

That neocolonialist attitudes all too readily prevail is apparent enough. In the negotiations for Nigerian participation in the oil industry, for example, the government 'went it alone', without a single expatriate adviser or official in either the Ministry or NNOC. Instead, Nigeria's 'whizz kid', Philip Asiodu, acted alone and an oil man said, admiringly: 'He could get a job on a European Board any day of the week—and be the Chairman by the weekend.'4 It would be hard to better so patronising a neocolonial attitude as that.

Nigerian education is still far too exclusively based upon the British pattern. There may be nothing wrong with British education (though many would dispute that); there is likely to be a great deal wrong with it in Nigeria simply because, at the lowest level, it represents a transference of one thought process and approach (which is imposed from above anyway) upon a different people with a different background: 'On the intellectual level, bourgeois scholasticism aimed at preserving colonial mental dependence and narrow empirical habits of thought shall be liquidated.'5 So say two critics; the question, of course, is how?

The depredations of white culture in Nigeria have been increasingly combated in recent years by such writers as Wole Soyinka, Chinua Achebe or Kofi Awoonor, who with others have interpreted the conscience of Africans and their philosophy, religion, social life and politics in counteraction to former white interpretations. So many areas of African life were interfered with by the whites: religion; the marriage system; while many Nigerians argue that the breakdown of relations between parents and children is one of the direct ill-effects of Western influence. Clothing and the importation of Western 'swinging' ideas may be an inevitable result of widespread contact with the West especially for business reasons and in the search for material growth. Such importations, regretted by many Nigerians, are nonetheless an inevitable result of contact. If this is a form of neocolonialism it is one that regrets will not alter and education is unlikely to eradicate. One Nigerian, trying to assess the value of white impact upon the country, wrote:

> Before I conclude this piece I wish to say briefly that the coming of the whites brought us some goods especially in the field of education. Through them, myriads of doctors, engineers, lawyers, technicians, writers, scientists etc. have been produced. For this we are grateful to the whites. Despite the contribution of their

educational system to our own advancement, the overall effect of their so-called civilisation on our society has been largely negative.[6]

It is sad that when members of that somewhat brash but well meaning American organisation 'Crossroads Africa' arrived in Nigeria for a summer's activity—metaphorically and literally—building bridges, a traditional ruler in the former East Central State, Igwe Isaac Iweka II, claimed when the 13-man team visited him that Christian activities had been among the greatest obstacles to the survival of certain aspects of Nigerian culture which, he said, Nigerians were anxious to preserve:

> A conscious effort is now being made to reconcile the incompatible contents of our cultures with progressive institutions, by modific-ations which can be made without our cultures losing their essence.[7]

This preoccupation with culture, and especially such a reaction to visiting foreigners, is an indication of the scars left by whites and the felt need to reassert something indigenous.

In quite a different sense the extraordinarily long drawn out saga of steel is also part of the neocolonialist scene. Currently Nigeria relies almost exclusively for its capital goods such as machinery, spare parts and equipment upon imports. No major country can seriously begin to alter such dependence unless it first establishes its own iron and steel industry. With 70 million people and vast economic potential Nigeria has yet to do this; until it has got its own industry it will remain dependent and lack control over the most essential aspects of its economic development.

The fact that it has not yet got an iron and steel complex of its own is not for lack of trying. Indeed, over two decades there has been talk, investigation, planning, a flow of international consultants—and still nothing at the end. Planning for a Nigerian industry started originally in 1958 when the Federal Government showed interest in the idea. Various studies were carried out to ascertain the feasibility of rolling mills; then, as the availability of iron ore at various places such as Agbaja became known, the emphasis of the planning shifted towards the creation of an integrated plant. The country has coal. With the creation of the Kainji dam to provide hydro-electric power and the emergence of new techniques that meant it was not necessary to have a large market or use coking coal, the whole project appeared feasible. Between 1961 and 1967 a variety of proposals were put up to the government by different international bodies. First came Westing-house and Koppers; then in 1963 came proposals from Demag of Germany, Ferrostall-Wellman, Mckee of the USA and David Ash-more of Britain for production that would range between 100 000 and 300 000 tonnes a year. In 1965 Nigeria formed United Nigerian Iron and Steel Company (UNISCO), a consortium of American, German and British interests which proposed to use the direct reduction process and electric smelting. The Swiss firm Interconsulting became the consultants. Large-scale tests were then carried out in Canada and as a result it was decided that Nigerian ore was too poor quality for the process and the development lagged. A UNIDO consultant then carried out a study of steel demand in Nigeria and this led to renewed optimism for the future. Ten years of Western companies' involvement, however, had only produced hopes to be dashed. Nothing concrete remained.

Then in 1967 came the Russians. They recommended a return to blast furnace production. Their report, however, suggested that the iron ore deposits in the country were of poor quality and they too suggested further studies and surveys. In 1970 the government agreed a contract with the Russians who were to provide specialists and equipment to prospect for mineral resources in the five years to 1975. In 1971 a Nigerian Steel Development Authority was established. The Russians carried out aero-magnetic surveys. In September 1970 drilling was started on deposits at Birnin Gwari in North Central State, but a year later the drilling was discontinued because of the poor quality of the ore.

Meanwhile drilling had started in Kwara State where some more promising ores had been discovered. By 1975 drilling operations and further surveys were being concentrated at Itakpe and indications early in the year were that the first iron ore mines for the steel complex would be there. Coal exploration, meanwhile, paralleled the search for iron ore. The Russians investigated port sites—Port Harcourt, Warri, and the inland ports of Lokoja, Ajaokuta and Agenebode to find the best site for a steel mill: they suggested Warri, Agenebode and Ajaokuta. Ajaokuta seems most suited since it is only 40 kilometres from the Itakpe ore deposits. Up to the launching of the Third Plan in 1975 progress was exceptionally slow and complicated. No matter who did the investigations they always found obstacles to the actual establishment of the steel industry that Nigeria wanted. A steel complex had been promised in both the first and second plans; by 1975 it was a joke that the Third Plan might really produce one.

In July 1975 the steel project received yet another shock when the annual report of the Nigerian Steel Development Authority was published, revealing that the iron ore deposits and some of the coal upon which the industry was to be based were of too low quality. It was one more setback in a story of endless delays and Nigerians who had hoped that an iron and steel industry would form the take-off point for industrialisation were disappointed yet again. Steel production has long played a more important role in any modern economy than have primary raw materials; only countries with their own industries can hope to dictate the pace of their development. By this time, however, Nigerians were beginning to suspect that international politics rather than just poor raw materials were playing a part in the story. As the *Nigerian Tide* said:

> Like other Nigerians, the *Nigerian Tide* has begun to suspect that our iron and steel project has been caught in a web of powerful international intrigue. After heavy investments and expenditure on the establishment of the industry, it is difficult for ordinary Nigerians to accept that after 17 years of efforts the iron and steel project has failed to make any satisfactory headway.[8]

It was a major point. For even if all the stocks found in Nigeria are of poor quality that alone is insufficient reason for not starting an industry. Nigeria could import the raw materials for such an industry and since the oil boom it has the money to do so. Therefore, it was asked, why such continuing delay? *Nigerian Tide* went on to query whether the industrialised countries of Europe were not deliberately discouraging the establishment of a Nigerian industry.

The key question posed by a long article in *Times International*[9] of July 1975 was whether foreign speculators were poised to sabotage the appearance of such an industry because it would adversely affect their interests. Obviously the Nigerian demand for steel products from abroad will fall as soon as its own industry goes into production; equally, with its fast development plans it represents a most lucrative potential market for steel products of virtually every description. There must, therefore, be plenty of inducements for an industrialised country such as Britain to prefer to continue selling products rather than helping establish a successful industry that would rival its export business. Further, should a Nigerian industry develop and in its early days not be used to capacity in Nigeria itself, in theory it would then become the natural supplier to its West African neighbours. The proposed plant at Ajaokuta is expected to produce 1.5 million tonnes of steel and iron a year which would meet the country's immediate domestic needs.

Whether foreign interests tried to kill the project or not must be almost impossible to prove. The suspicion remains strong that they have done so. Had it not been for the increasing oil revenue the Federal Government itself would have killed the project a long time ago: in 1960 when first estimated the cost stood at N240 million; by 1970 when the Russians became involved it had soared to N800 million; by 1975 with an uncertain future experts were predicting that it would cost N1 500 million by 1980. In 1975 government circles were arguing that the Russians were far more interested in trading with Nigeria, and that Russia, as the second largest world producer of steel, wished to increase its share of the Nigerian market. It was reported that the Russian Technoexport Company deliberately refused co-operation over certain policy matters so that when an annual target for Ajaokuta of 3.5 million tonnes was suggested they turned it down. It was also suggested that the Russians were far more interested in building the infrastructure round the site at Ajaokuta than in beginning the actual plant. At such a rate—or non-rate—of development it was clear the plant would not be in operation at the end of the Third Plan period.

But where can Nigeria turn next? The story helps illustrate the helplessness of a country that is dependent upon outside expertise to launch a major development project: if, for whatever reasons, the foreign consultants hold back, the development is in trouble. This clearly seems to have been the case with Nigeria's iron and steel plans. Despite the Russian claim that the ore available at Lafia and Itakpe is too low-grade, the Nigerian Government maintains that these ores are of sufficiently high quality and will do as the basis of the industry. Much of the Third Development Plan is geared to depend upon iron and steel output from the plant at Ajaokuta. If this does not materialise and as a result the plan suffers and Nigeria has to prolong its dependence upon outside sources for steel, considerable bitterness will follow while far more precise accusations of neocolonialist blocking are liable to be made.

The story, which is nearly twenty years old, is a classic one of conflicting interests: some purely economic arguments; others that are political. The combined effect, however, is that a country which in theory is on the verge of economic take-off remains in practice totally dependent upon outside sources for this crucial development material. Further, those outside sources are great powers whose interests in Nigeria's development are one-sided and unlikely to coincide with Nigerian aspirations. Consequently Nigeria must look with scepticism upon the advice they produce; yet advice in purely technical terms it requires and seeks.

Some classic economic arguments have also been advanced—by expatriates in Nigeria itself—to the effect that the economy is not yet at the stage to justify an iron and steel industry. Such arguments are irrelevant to a country that wants such an industry—and especially a country of the size, potential and wealth of Nigeria. They are advanced despite the fact that to make sense a modern industrialised state must produce its own iron and steel. To argue that conditions do not warrant such an industry is tantamount to saying that it is not necessary to become a modern industrialised society.

This economic arguments runs as follows: the money needed to establish a steel industry could better be utilised in a multiplicity of small schemes that would spread wealth and development to more people than a single large industrial plant in one place. The argument can be reversed. To argue against such a development is to ask in effect that the Nigerian economy should be held back in a crucial area so that it should be dependent for a longer time upon outside forces. The immediate establishment of a steel industry will itself have multiple effects; even if more expensive than imported steel products Nigerian-made ones will nonetheless release foreign exchange for other purposes that should more than compensate for the higher price of domestically produced steel. Further, by starting to make Nigeria feel that it is becoming independent of foreign expertise such a development will bring it closer to true independence than a welter of small and immediately more obviously justifiable schemes.

The truth is far from easy to ascertain. What does seem clear, however, is: First, that powerful outside interests would prefer Nigeria to depend upon them for iron and steel rather than produce its own; second, that investigations over so long a period — 1958–75 — which have included half the major western powers and then the Russians and still not produced an industry on the spot must make even the most open-minded observer highly dubious as to their value and intentions; third, Nigeria now has the wealth to start such an industry at once and, if necessary, to import raw materials until it finds enough of its own of the required quality; fourth, only when it does have its own industry will it begin to feel economically independent and able to make economic advances under its own control. For all these reasons Nigeria ought to go ahead, no matter what the cost, and ignore advice to the contrary.

Until the coup 1975 was to have been the year of FESTAC (World Black and African Festival of Arts and Culture) and that mammoth cultural jamboree itself raised many neocolonialist questions about culture and Nigerian identity. As the *Nigerian Herald* said:

> No self-respecting nation ever advertises its culture. We never hear of 'White Culture' or 'White Festival'. We never hear of 'Yellow Culture' or 'Yellow Festival'. The culture of Japan is beamed to the rest of the world in what that country contributes to human progress.[10]

In the months before the coup and Mohammed's subsequent postponement of the Festival, arguments of all kinds, although always centring upon Nigerian culture and its projection to the world, raged round the Festival preparations. Defending the government for pressing ahead with the Festival despite adverse criticisms, Chief Anthony Enahoro said that there were some Nigerians who would not see 'anything good in the promotion of culture.'[11] Nigeria had attached such importance to the Festival that it had appointed Chief Enahoro with ministerial rank to manage it. The Festival was partly a question of culture; and partly — as a result of hosting it — a question of Nigerian international prestige.

The Festival was in part a search:

> All these activities (relating to the Festival) form a part of the Blackman's effort to redefine his identity and re-establish a good image for his race. In Nigeria, the governments and the people have

been showing increasing interest in culture by the staging of traditional dances and musical performances as well as by public discussion. Indeed, concern for the revival of African culture is now heard more frequently than ever before in the public statements of socially and politically prominent Nigerians.[12]

Many Nigerians were doubtful: they were suspicious of a process which artificially created a cultural climate. Scathingly, for example, the *Nigerian Tribune* talked of 'the parade of semi-nudity which passes for traditional dances' and other articles asked what the philosophical basis for a cultural revival might be. Nigeria was both seeking an international image and trying to find a degree of cultural unity for a vast and widely diverse society. The second objective had far more point than the first.

The difficulty lay in highlighting a culture without too obviously creating an artificial one which no one would accept. Had there been no colonial white period there would equally certainly not have been this search for cultural identity. The trouble lies in the fact that the white man's culture captured and eclipsed the black man's. Often enough the Nigerian media examine the impact of Western culture and regret what it has produced. Failure of trust; sexual licence; behaviour of the young towards the old are constantly cited as the adverse results of white impact. This may be true; it is doubtful that it can now be altered. More important is the extent to which a black cultural reawakening is an attempt to return to old values discarded or overlain as a result of white impact. An awareness of changes resulting from white contact is one thing; a conscious programme to turn the clock back is something rather different. There appeared to be an element of the latter in the culture fever of 1975. A genuine attempt to rediscover the past is to be commended; the Elejigbo of Ejigbo, Oba Omowonuola Oyeyode Oyesosin, for example, urged Nigerians to show the world that 'we are a people with a past in culture and theatre.'[13] It should go without saying; the fact that it needs to be said is the key to what is happening and has happened in the recent past.

A theatre workshop in Port Harcourt in July 1975 included a symposium entitled: 'Is a truly Nigerian theatre possible?' The panel urged that Nigerian playwrights and theatre practitioners should endeavour to root their writings and theatrical manifestations in the moods and aspirations of the people. Such talk and hustle about culture is basically good for any society: it is the constant looking outwards to see what the rest of the world thinks about it which reminds, again and again, that it is also part of a process of breaking free of colonialism—an over-emphasis upon being Nigerian that can be unhealthy.

During all this debate one little cultural event of great importance was recorded: at the Welsh International Eisteddfod Nigeria won first prize for the international folk dance competition and second prize in the folk song contest. The Nigerian group performed a Yoruba wedding dance and the Efik maiden's dance; in the folksong contest they sang one song in Hausa and another in Etsakhon. Here was Nigerian traditional culture being recognised for what it was at an international gathering and winning high prizes.

Nigerian culture goes back far enough; it is diverse; and like all major cultures it has imbibed from others, including, of course, that of the recent imperialists. Preoccupation with it may be politically understandable at the present time; the important thing, however, is an acceptance of its validity in its own right rather than the constant comparisons with other cultures to see how they take it. What counts is whether Nigerians want and accept their own.

Notes

1   *Nigerian Herald*, 1 August 1975
2   *Nigeria Standard*, 7 August 1975
3   *Economic Development of Nigeria, op. cit.*, p. 174
4   *African Development*, March 1974
5   *Economic Development of Nigeria, op. cit.*, p. 126
6   *Daily Sketch*, 15 August 1975
7   *Daily Times*, 8 August 1975
8   *Nigerian Tide*, 16 July 1975
9   *Times International*, 21 July 1975
10   *Nigerian Herald*, 17 August 1975
11   *Nigerian Herald*, 9 July 1975
12   *Nigerian Tribune*, 10 July 1975
13   *Nigerian Herald*, 8 July 1975

Chapter sixteen

The press

The Nigerian press is the most outspoken, volatile, witty and free in black Africa. Its criticisms of government and establishment are far-ranging and pointed; its pursuit of the pompous and incompetent can be very funny as well as relentless; its coverage can be exceptionally wide and also, sometimes, quite parochially narrow. There never seems to be any lack of space for Nigerian writers who in consequence go on at length. Its 'in memoriam' pages provide special social commentary on Nigerian society. Its English has a vigour and style of its own that will distinguish Nigerian English from the original in the same way that the idioms of American English have grown apart from those of the original.

The relationship between press and government is an uneasy yet on the whole healthy one of tensions and pressures. There are wide press criticisms of all aspects of government as well as consistent calls for changes—a return to civilian rule being one of the most important of these calls. From time to time the government has put a variety of pressures upon the press; sometimes its reporters have been jailed; once a state governor had a member of the press beaten; and sometimes the press finds it wise to say nothing. In July 1975—shortly before the coup—the Federal Military Government announced that it was to give financial support to newspaper organisations to encourage wider circulation so that all papers could be seen throughout the country. Six weeks later the new government took control of the country's largest independent newspaper, the *Daily Times* and *Sunday Times*, as well as the *New Nigerian* which had previously been owned by the six northern states. These two are generally considered to be the country's best produced and most influential newspapers.

In 1974 the press played a major role in bringing about the resignation of the Commissioner for Communications, Joseph Tarka. It was attacked by the then Inspector-General of Police, Alhaji Kam Selem, for

mounting a campaign of blackmail against the ruling Federal Military Government by publishing inciting articles, books and pamphlets capable of whipping up sectional sentiments or disrupting law and order.

But Alhaji Lateef Jakande, the Chairman of the Newspaper Proprietors' Association, said:

> the Nigerian press is not against and will never work at variance with the objectives of the Federal Military Government. Rather, the Press which at the moment is the parliament of the people, should not only report the activities of the government but also supply the feed-backs from the people. Those who attack the Press do so out of misunderstanding.

His claim that the press at the moment was 'the parliament of the people' had real justification in both the range of discussion at a time when political parties were banned and a military regime ruled and in the comments and feedback to the government. Certainly in the months before the July 1975 coup the press was acting as the forum of the people—and most effectively too.

In a period of especially sharp public concern in Nigeria—July and August 1975—the month before and the month after the coup that toppled Gowon, the role of the press merits examination in some depth for it gives an excellent flavour of Nigerian political thinking.

The mounting criticism by the press during the weeks of July 1975 reflected a nationwide frustration with the military government that appeared more and more difficult to contain. Techniques of attack were varied. One article in the *Nigerian Tribune*[1] for example, started off: 'Today, our discussions will take us to Dahomey [Benin]. . . .' The writer then went on: 'Our reason for skipping Nigerian affairs today is NOT that our editor has been under police harassment for the past few weeks because some people want to know more about the writer of this column.' He then proceeded to attack police harassment of the press, to call for the Head of State to fulfill his promise to change the state governors, to remind the government that the census was causing unrest, that it would be better to create new states; he attacked what he called a 'lopsided teachers' harmonisation in the Western State', called for an end of the detention of those alleged to have fabricated figures for the new army salary scales and asked for their open trial; he referred to the failure of the government to deal with corruption and called upon the Head of State for a new timetable for a return to civilian rule. In effect he mentioned all the main problems then worrying the country before returning to his ostensible subject of Dahomey. Much of the writing is of an elemental type; it is extremely effective. In the same edition of the *Nigerian Tribune*, on the subject of corruption, one paragraph reads: 'Of course nobody can accuse any member of the Government of corruption. Nobody that is, who wishes to avoid being thrown into jail.'[2]

Nigeria in July 1975 may have been under a military regime and politics may not then have been allowed; reading the following piece makes this seem hardly credible:

> General Gowon may not be a very old soldier, but the time has come for him to fade away. We are now in the position to ask ourselves — why are we in the total darkness of today? The reason is simple. We never had a course to steer.[3]

On a quite different subject the same paper attacked conspicuous extravagance. Discussing socialist possibilities for Nigeria, the writer referred to the import of shire horses from Britain:

> When Governor Bako of Kano State bought from Britain 12 durbar horses which were flown on a charter plane in preparation for the grand durbar at the Black Arts Festival he certainly could not have thought he was buttressing a programme in a socialist state. The cost of each horse was N-800.00. With their flight the figure could not have been less than N-100 000. The 12 horses all died in a month and N-100 000 evaporated like the puff of smoke from a cigar smoker. It hurts when one thinks that till today under 5 per cent of Kano State school children are in school.[4]

There could be few more effective ways of mounting political and social criticism.

Later in the same article the writer returned to the theme that dominated the press in the run-up to the coup: a return to civilian rule. General Gowon might have said in his speech of October 1974 that the country was not ready to return to civilian rule as originally promised in 1976; that, however, did not stop the debate, the demands or the criticisms. The article proceeded:

> The question on the lips of everybody today is, how do we get out of this rot? How do we get the Nigerian society re-charged and so re-start a new life of buoyancy and creativity? . . . The army, we should be told is made up of individual fellow Nigerians from all over the place. We, civilians would be wrong to think these soldiers have come from a different planet with special powers to resolve all our difficulties for us. Their weaknesses we know. Their strength — for what it is worth — is visible everywhere.

The article then suggested that the Head of State should broadcast and the army retire and hand over to the civilians.[5]

Another subject of debate at that time was why the state governors had not been changed. The press advanced sarcastic excuses for the delay. A leading article in the *Sunday Times*, for example, suggested:

> All sorts of reasons have been given for the delay in the re-assignment of the governors — the current being that they wanted to

be around to shake Her Majesty the Queen's hand in October (the Queen was to make a state visit to Nigeria at that time). I suppose anybody who shakes the lady's hand has an enhanced social status. This should entitle him to use the initials—SOQEH (Shaker of Queen Elizabeth's Hand). Another school of thought puts the governors' reassignment to the period after the Black Arts Festival (then scheduled for the November).[6]

A week before the coup the Nigerian Commissioner for Information became the prime target for most of the press and their pursuit of him was relentless (see above p. 18). In the *Nigerian Observer* he was attacked, as elsewhere, for failing to see that 'the ship of state was heading towards a cataclysm':

> All Nigerian homes talk of nothing else today and all except Edwin Clark are in a hurry to see something done to staunch a total national eclipse.[7]

When, a week before his fall, Gowon addressed Regimental Sergeants Major at Dodan Barracks he again promised that the state governors were to be changed. The *Nigerian Tribune* welcomed his scotching the ugly rumours that the governors were to stay on indefinitely and after a passage of great sarcasm, finished up:

> Last week's statement from Dodan Barracks must have been intended to scorch these ugly rumours and reassure the nation that the promise still stands. The 'Nigerian Tribune' heartily welcomes the reassurance. But it is only action, not words that can reassure the nation.[8]

In theory politics are banned in Nigeria; in practice its society remains one of the most political in Africa. The techniques employed to bring political discussion before the public were varied and if one method became overused another would be employed but the same topic would remain under review. Thus, in the *Daily Times* of 25 July 1975, a priest who was also a political scientist was interviewed:

> QUESTION: As a political scientist, how suitable generally do you find the army as a government?
> Father Ejiofor: It is a pointed question.

He went on to give some pointed answers. Then came the coup and the new regime of Brigadier Mohammed.

Five days later on 4 August 1975, the *Times International* could, with justice, begin an editorial by saying:

> Hardly have the citizens of any one country been more embroiled in a spirited and long-winded debate on who should wield political power in the country as have Nigerians in the past four years.[9]

The press had played a major part in making that possible.

The press also exhibits a pardonable caution on occasions—not without its tongue in its cheek. On coup day plus two—Thursday 31 July 1975—the *Daily Times*, Nigeria's leading paper which, it might have been supposed, would then be editorialising upon the coup and the challenges facing the new government, did nothing of the kind. Instead the Opinion Column had a splendidly dull piece headed: 'Promoting Safety at Work' which started: 'Industrialisation is a necessary pre-requisite to economic growth and development of any nation, hence our national struggle to become industrialised. . . .'[10]

But soon enough the press were at it: commenting upon the new regime's programme and style; offering advice; and asking questions about those topics that were not yet clarified—which meant, as usual, a return to civilian rule. The *Sunday Times* said the weekend after the coup: 'Whatever programme is decided upon, the return to democratic rule must be given a prominent place. . . . The Nigerian public is anxiously waiting.[11] It went on to offer advice about policy— that the government should make public who owned what in major companies, for example, and tilting at the Nigerian practice of pomp, it said: 'There should be less siren blowing, but more action.' In a different editorial the *New Nigerian* of 4 August 1975, said:

> But perhaps the most important reason for a return to civil rule is that a government which emerges from popular involvement is directly accountable to the people. It can be changed peacefully without a coup when in the opinion of the citizenry, the government has lost the will to rule in their interest.[12]

The same editorial discussed the kind of civil rule that should be reinstated.

The ability to poke fun and ridicule is an essential and much used weapon of the Nigerian press. Ten days after the coup a *Sunday Chronicle* article began:

> So we had the THIRD COMING in which the order which had grown nauseatingly old was bloodlessly changed, and we have on our hands new prefixes to go along with. We are thus the ex-this, ex-that, ex-these, ex-those, the 'former', the 'erstwhile' . . . Even if you were yearning for the men in 'agbada' and you woke up one rainy day to find another set of men in khaki, and you had no choice, you may want to give them a chance. . . . If someone said that the new men need some luck, someone else would say that they need it plenty.[13]

And in the *Nigeria Herald* of 18 August another article began:

> The queue of men and women waiting to give some advice to the new Head of State, Brigadier Murtala Mohammed, must be really long by now, but I will not allow that fact to restrain me from

submitting a list of things that must go or (be) changed as they were or were to be, according to the regime that crashed under its own weight on Tuesday, July 29, 1975.

The advice followed.[14]

The press were generous to the fallen Gowon. Although it had been attacking him and his regime before the coup for their failings—which were many—and continued to say that these justified his fall afterwards, the press also paid tribute to his achievements and sought to reach a balanced judgement—as well as pointing out that the new had yet to prove themselves. In an article that attempted to assess the Gowon years the *Sunday Times* of 3 August started off:

> Perhaps it is rather premature to start running commentaries and issuing elegies on the now-overthrown regime. For one thing, nobody can say with any certainty what is up the sleeves of the new rulers.[15]

Speaking of the indigenisation exercise which had received much critical comment in Nigeria for not having done anything of the sort, the same article went on sarcastically:

> Nigerians were successfully (and thanks to the power that be then) entrenched to take over the sale of gari, palm oil, akara loaves, tuwo and other specialised jobs that required primitive brawn and native intelligence.

Having divided the regime's years into a number of scenes the article concluded:

> It was not accidental that the former regime wanted to herald in its 10th anniversary with a colossal festivity tagged World Black and African Festival of 'awards and contracts'? It is, I guess, in keeping with this dramatic spirit that the first official reaction of General Gowon to his overthrow was seeking refuge in William Shakespeare. 'All the world is a stage,' he was quoted as saying, 'and all men and women are actors . . .'.

A week later in a far from unkind appraisal of Gowon a writer in the same paper said:

> For my own part, I am sorry to see General Gowon miss a golden opportunity for immortalising his name. He ran a beautiful race but pulled a muscle as he was approaching the tape. He prepared a delicious dish but overturned the pot at the service table. He wrote an excellent speech but lost his voice at the time of delivery.[16]

While the *Nigerian Observer* said:

> There was no doubt that General Yakubu Gowon made serious mistakes particularly by surrounding himself with lots of dead

weights and tolerating some immatured military governors who dismissed commissioners at will, ordered caning of journalists, degraded university intellectuals and insulted elders, but he was a gentleman. Even though many went to his detention camps but he was never a tyrant.[17]

Another paper, the *New Nigerian*, said of Gowon:

But it will be interesting to see how future historians judge the man against the background of the circumstances under which he had to work. One thing is clear however: anyone who thinks only himself can rule and sits tight in office is a sitting duck for overthrow.[18]

There also was a warning for Gowon's successor.

When three weeks after the coup Lagos City Council decided to change the names of streets—Yakubu Gowon and Mobolaji Johnson (named after the ex-governor of Lagos State)—back to their old colonial ones, the press attacked such pettiness. The *Nigerian Herald* began an editorial: 'No word would be too strong to describe the weekend decision of Lagos City Council to revert the names . . .'; and went on '. . . this action which, in our considered opinion, smells much of the proverbial "Hosanna" "Crucify Him" deafening chorus on cars everywhere.'[19]

And the *Daily Times* headed its Opinion Column 'Too Petty' and after slating the pettiness of the decision the editorial went on:

Facts in our history include this: Gowon was the Head of State of this country for nine years; he was a compromise candidate and his compromise nature carried this nation through during the civil war; his external policy placed Nigeria on the world map. Most importantly his African policy yielded result such as the formation of ECOWAS. This is not to say that General Gowon did not have his weaknesses and these are numerous too. He was a leader who started well but towards the end of his rule became too powerful and isolated from the yearnings of the people he governed. His major error was human. He erred by not knowing when to quit with honour.[20]

Not a bad political epitaph all things considered.

Nigerian papers have brought to a fine art a special mixed quality of invective, sarcasm and witchhunting. One of the great problems which infuriated Nigerians in 1975 was the lack of petrol round the country, despite the fact that Nigeria had recently leapt into seventh place in the world as an oil producer. It was a question of both refining capacity and distribution.

If any Nigerian has a penchant for celebrating obscure anniversaries the NIGERIAN HERALD declares every July 1 one such occasion to be remembered. It is the national anniversary of the

BROKEN PROMISE. Last April, a very seasoned civil servant and effective boss of the Ministry of Petroleum and Energy, Mr. P. C. Asiodu; made the solemn pledge that this country would be relieved of the ridiculous petroleum shortages by June ending.

It was not, of course, and thereafter the editorial attacked the whole system of supply.[21] Other papers took up the refrain until Mr Asiodu must have regretted ever giving a deadline for anything. The *Nigerian Tribune* had a 2 000-word article taking the luckless Asiodu to task for his rash promises. High or low, those who make public statements in Nigeria are liable to have them taken up, examined, dissected, and, if they are found wanting those responsible are harried mercilessly for their failings—although always with humour.

The press constantly deals with major themes of public life—education, the universities, the spread of oil wealth, agriculture, how the Third Plan can be made to succeed, communications, the quality of life, the need for political direction and guiding principles in public life. This is the function of any press anywhere. In Nigeria, where a large proportion of people are still illiterate and where an essential part of the press' task is to make its papers lively, this has been achieved to a quite remarkable degree. The punch is there; the criticisms; the seeking out of the incompetent, the stuffy and pompous or corrupt. It is also done with panache and humour so that the pursuit of an erring civil servant, for example, becomes a kind of game in which readers return each day to see what point the chase has reached. A subject of particular and continuing public concern during 1975 was that of the constant congestion of Nigeria's ports with all the consequences this had for development. The *Sunday Punch* of 13 July carried the following:

> May I warm your hearts this Sunday morning with a poignant example of optimism. . . . Last Saturday the Federal Commissioner for Transport Navy Captain Olufemi Olumide revealed that 167 ships were waiting to berth as against 78 when General Yakubu Gowon visited the port in April. The statement is in sharp contrast to this advertisement copy inserted by Nigerian Ports Authority in the London *Times* of June 30 1975: Nigeria's Ports Are Being Planned For The Eighties [there followed a screed about modernisation and containers]: We ensure rapid turn-round of international shipping by providing 24-hour labour force. . . .

The piece ended: 'Correct interpretation: The ports are being planned so that we can clear in the 80's all the goods required in the 70's.'[22]

The press speaks well for Nigeria. In 1975, a vital year for Africa's greatest nation, half a generation of independence was celebrated; a peaceful and bloodless coup changed the government after nine years;

and the mammoth development plan, made possible by the oil boom, was launched. The year should represent a turning point in the country's history. Writing in the *Nigerian Tribune* on 2 August 1975, Olukayode Bakre said:

> It does not matter what people say of Mother Nigeria. She is not bereft of able children. See the new faces staring at me from Dodan Barracks. See them with brass buttons, with Military pips and police batons. I can see them with Naval cape and hear their high-sounding names. Sure, Mother Nigeria is blessed. . . . Having said so much of Mother Nigeria, let's offer a simple prayer:
>
>> Oh Mother Nigeria
>> Thou who gave
>> To thy Children
>> The power to hire and fire
>> Be thou our guidance
>> Now that we have fired a set
>> And hired another
>> To choose aright
>> The path of rectitude
>> To pursue that
>> Which will lead us
>> To the promised land
>> Where no man is oppressed
>> And justice reigns supreme.[23]

Notes

1   *Nigeria Tribune*, 10 July 1975
2   *Ibid.*
3   *Ibid.*
4   *Ibid.*
5   *Ibid.*
6   *Sunday Times*, 20 July 1975
7   *Nigerian Observer*, 23 July 1975
8   *Nigerian Tribune*, 25 July 1975
9   *Times International*, 4 August 1975
10 *Daily Times*, 31 July 1975
11 *Sunday Times*, 3 August 1975
12 *New Nigerian*, 4 August 1975
13 *Sunday Chronicle*, 10 August 1975
14 *Nigerian Herald*, 18 August 1975
15 *Sunday Times*, 3 August 1975
16 *Sunday Times*, 10 August 1975
17 *Nigerian Observer*, 14 August 1975
18 *New Nigerian*, 14 August 1975
19 *Nigerian Herald*, 18 August 1975

20   *Daily Times*, 18 August 1975
21   *Nigerian Herald*, 8 July 1975
22   *Sunday Punch*, 13 July 1975
23   Olukayode Bakre, *Nigerian Tribune*, 2 August 1975

Appendix 1

Text of speech to the Nation by Brigadier Murtala Mohammed the day after assuming power, 30 July 1975

Fellow Nigerians,
Events of the past few years have indicated that despite our great human and material resources, the Government has not been able to fulfil the legitimate expectations of our people. Nigeria has been left to drift.
This situation, if not arrested, would inevitably have resulted in chaos and even bloodshed.
In the endeavour to build a strong, united and virile nation, Nigerians have shed much blood; the thought of further bloodshed, for whatever reasons, must, I am sure, be revolting to our people. The Armed Forces, having examined the situation, came to the conclusion that certain changes were inevitable.
After the civil war, the affairs of State, hitherto a collective responsibility, became characterised by lack of consultation, indecision, indiscipline and even neglect. Indeed, the public at large became disillusioned and disappointed by these developments. This trend was clearly incompatible with the philosophy and image of a corrective regime.
Unknown to the general public, the feeling of disillusion was also evident among members of the Armed Forces whose administration was neglected but who, out of sheer loyalty to the Nation, and in the hope that there would be a change, continued to suffer in silence. Things got to a stage where the head of the administration became virtually inaccessible even to official advisers; and when advice was tendered, it was often ignored.
Responsible opinion, including advice by eminent Nigerians, traditional rulers, intellectuals etc., was similarly discarded. The leadership, either by design or default, had become too insensitive to the true feelings and yearnings of the people. The nation was thus being plunged inexorably into chaos.
It was obvious that matters could not and should not, be allowed to continue in this manner, and in order to give the nation a new lease of

life, and a sense of direction, the following decisions were taken:

The removal of General Yakubu Gowon as Head of the Federal Military Government and commander-in-chief of the Armed Forces.

The retirement of General Yakubu Gowon from the Armed Forces in his present rank of general with full benefits, in recognition of his past services to the nation.

General Gowon will be free to return to the country as soon as conditions permit; he will be free to pursue any legitimate undertakings of his choice in any part of the country. His personal safety and freedom and those of his family will be guaranteed.

The following members of the Armed Forces are retired with immediate effect.

Vice-Admiral J. E. A. Wey, Chief of Staff, Supreme Headquarters

Major-General Hassan Katsina, Deputy Chief of Staff, Supreme Headquarters

Major-General David Ejoor, Chief of Staff (Army)

Rear-Admiral Nelson Soroh, Chief of Naval Staff

Brigadier E. E. Ikwue, Chief of Air Staff

and all other officers of the rank of Major-General (or equivalent) and above.

Alhaji Kam Salem, Inspector-General of Police

Chief T. A. Fagbola, Deputy Inspector-General of Police.

Also, with immediate effect, all the present Military Governors, and the Administrator of the East-Central State, have been relieved of their appointments and retired.

As you are already aware, new appointments have been made as follows:

Brigadier Olusegun Obasanjo, Chief of Staff, Supreme Headquarters; Brigadier T. Y. Danjuma, Chief of Army Staff; Colonel John Yisa Doko, Chief of Air Staff; Commodore Adelanwa, Chief of Naval Staff; Mr M. D. Yusufu, Inspector-General of Police.

New Military Governors have also been appointed for the states as follows:

Lieutenant-Colonel Muhammed Buhari—North-East;

Colonel George Innih—Mid-West;

Lieutenant-Colonel Sani Bello—Kano;

Captain Lawal (NN)—Lagos;

Lieutenant-Colonel Paul Omu—South-East;

Colonel Ibrahim Taiwo—Kwara;

Captain Akin Aduwo (NN)—West;

Colonel Anthony Ochefu—East-Central;

Lieutenant-Colonel Usman Jibrin—North-Central;

Colonel Abdullahi Mohammed—Benue-Plateau;

Lieutenant-Colonel Umaru Mohammed—North-West;

Lieutenant-Colonel Zamani Lekwot—Rivers.

The structure of government has been re-organised. There will now be

three organs of government, at the Federal level, namely:
The Supreme Military Council;
The National Council of States; and
The Federal Executive Council.
There will, of course, continue to be Executive Councils at the State level.
The reconstituted Supreme Military Council will comprise the following:
The Head of State and C-in-C of the Armed Forces
Brigadier Olusegun Obasanjo, Chief of Staff, Supreme Headquarters
Brigadier T. Y. Danjuma, Chief of Army Staff
Commodore Adelanwa, Chief of Naval Staff
Colonel John Yisa Doko, Chief of Air Staff
Mr M. D. Yusufu, Inspector-General of Police
GOCs—1st Division, Brigadier Julius Alani Akinrade
          2nd Division, Brigadier Martin Adamu
          3rd Division, Brigadier Emmanuel Abisoye
          LGO, Brigadier John Obade
Colonel Joseph Garba
Lieutenant-Colonel Shehu Yar Aduwa
Brigadier James Oluleye
Brigadier Iliya Bisalla
Colonel Ibrahim Babangida
Lieutenant-Colonel Muktar Mohammed
Colonel Dan Suleman
Captain Olufemi Olumide (NN)
Captain H. Husaini Abdullahi (NN)
Mr Adamu Suleiman, Commissioner of Police
Lieutenant-Colonel Alfred Aduloji
Lieutenant-Commander Godwin Kanu (NN)
All civil commissioners in the Federal Executive Council are relieved of their appointment with immediate effect. The composition of the new council will be announced shortly.
We will review the political programme and make an announcement in due course. In the meantime, a panel will be set up to advise on the question of new states. A panel will also be set up to advise on the question of the Federal Capital.
With regard to the 1973 population census, it is now clear that whatever results are announced will not command general acceptance throughout the country. It has therefore been decided to cancel the 1973 population count. Accordingly, for planning purposes, the 1963 census figures shall continue to be used.
A panel will be set up to advise on the future of the Interim Common Services Agency (ICSA) and the Eastern States Interim Assets and Liabilities Agency (ESIALA).
The Second World Black and African Festival of Arts and Culture is

postponed in view of the obvious difficulties in providing all the necessary facilities. Consultations will be held with the other participating countries with a view to fixing a new date.

Finally, we reaffirm this country's friendship with all countries. Foreign nationals living in Nigeria will be protected. Foreign investments will also be protected. The Government will honour all obligations entered into by the previous Governments of the Federation. We will also give continued active support to the Organisation of African Unity, the United Nations Organisation and the Commonwealth.

Fellow countrymen, the task ahead of us calls for sacrifice and self-discipline at all levels of our society. This Government will NOT tolerate indiscipline. This Government will NOT condone abuse of office.

I appeal to you all to cooperate with the Government in our endeavour to give this nation a new lease of life. This change in Government has been accomplished without shedding any blood; and we intend to keep it so.

Long live the Federal Republic of Nigeria.

Good night.

Appendix 2

The Federal Executive Council appointed following the coup of 29 July 1975:

Brigadier Ilyasu Bisalla, Defence; Colonel Joseph Garba, External Affairs; Mr B. O. W. Mafeni, Agriculture; Brigadier James J. Oluleye, Establishments; Lieutenant-Colonel Ahmadu Ali, Education; Mr A. E. Ekukinam, Finance; and Alhaji Umaru Mutallab, Economic Development; Colonel Dan Suleiman, Health; Alhaji Umaru Shinkafi, Internal Affairs; Mr Justice Daniel Ibekwe, Justice and Attorney-General; Mr Effiong Otu-Ekong, Mines and Power; Brigadier Mohammed Shuwa, Trade; Lieutenant-Colonel Shehu Yar'Adua, Transport; Captain Olufemi Olumide, Works; Colonel M. Inua Wushishi, Industries; Brigadier Ibrahim B. M. Haruna, Information; Brigadier Henry Adefope, Ministry of Labour; Mr S. O. Williams, Communications; Dr T. O. Akobo, Petroleum and Energy; Mr M. A. Ajose-Adeogun, Co-operatives and Supplies; Dr R. A. Adeleye, Housing, Urban Development and Environment; Dr I. V. William Osisiogu, Water Resources; Alhaji Shaibu Kazaure, Aviation; Brigadier Olufemi Olutoye, Youth and Sports; and Commander O. P. Fingesi, Special Duties (Black Arts Festival).

Appendix 3

Census comparisons

	1952–53 census (millions)	1963 census (millions)	1973 census (millions (provisional)
Lagos	0.50	1.44	2.47
Western	4.36	9.49	8.92
Mid-Western	1.49	2.54	3.24
Rivers	0.75	1.54	2.23
East-Central	4.57	7.23	8.06
South-Eastern	1.90	3.62	3.46
Benue-Plateau	2.30	4.01	5.17
Kwara	1.19	2.40	4.64
North-Western	3.40	5.73	8.50
North-Central	2.35	4.10	6.79
Kano	3.40	5.77	10.90
North-Eastern	4.20	7.79	15.38
Total	30.41	55.66	79.76

Appendix 4

The States: New names and divisions

OLD NAMES	NEW NAMES		
UNCHANGED	*New States*	*Capitals*	*Boundary adjustments*
North Central	Kaduna	Kaduna	None
Kano	Kano	Kano	None
Rivers	Rivers	Port Harcourt	None
Mid-Western	Bendel	Benin	None
South-Eastern	Cross River	Calabar	
Kwara	Kwara	Ilorin	Add Igala area to Benue
Lagos	Lagos	Ikeja	
CHANGED			
Western	Ogun	Abeokuta	Abeokuta and Ijebu Provinces
	Ondo	Akure	Ondo Province
	Oyo	Ibadan	Oyo, Ibadan, Oshun, Ife, Ijesha, Ibarapa
East Central	Imo	Owerri	Afikpo, Oguta, Nkwere, Mbano, Mbaise, Bende, Arechuku, Umuahia, Okigwe, Orlu, Etiti, Ohafia, Northern Ngwa, Owerri, Aba, Ukwa, Mbaitolu/Ikeduru divisions
	Anambra	Enugu	Enugu, Isiuzo, Uzo-Uwani, Udi, Abakiliki, Njikoka, Idemili, Nsukka, Aguata, Onitsha, Ihiala, Nnewi, etc.
North Western	Niger	Minna	Niger province excluding Zuru
	Sokoto	Sokoto	Sokoto province including Zuru
Benue Plateau	Benue	Makurdi	Gboko, Makurdi, Katsina Ala, Oturkpo, Igala, Dekina, Ida and Ankpa divisions
	Plateau	Jos	Jos, Pankshin, Akwanga, Laktang, Shendam, Nassarawa, Lafia and Jarawa district in Bauchi division
North Eastern	Bauchi	Bauchi	Bauchi province less Jarawa district
	Borno	Maiduguri	Borno provinces less Shani district, etc.
	Gongola	Yola	Sarduana and Adamawa provinces plus Whari division (in Benue Plateau) and Shani

Source: *African Development*

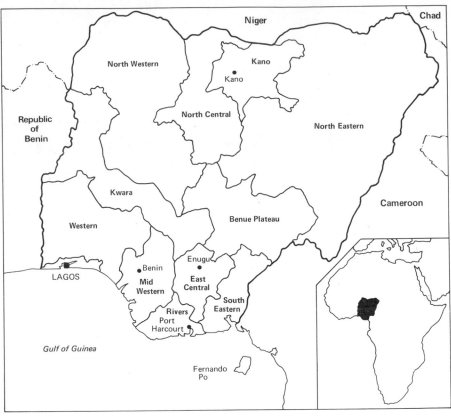
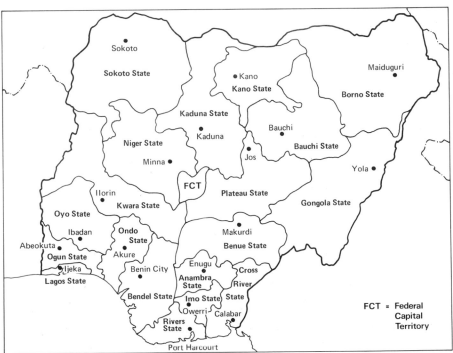

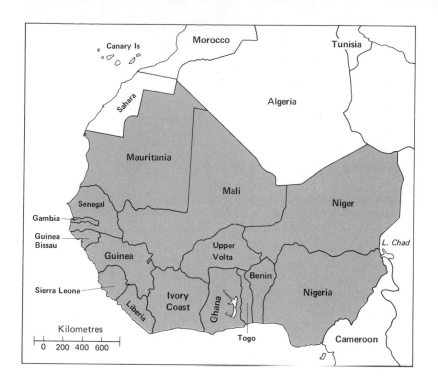

How the states have changed: from twelve (above left) under Gowon's regime to nineteen (left) formulated by Mohammed's administration and carried out under Obasanjo's

The member countries of the Economic Community of West African States (above). Nigeria took the lead in establishing ECOWAS

Appendix 5

Nigerian crude oil production

('000 barrels per day)

	1st qtr. 1975	1974	1973	1972
SBP/NNOC	1,204,186	1,398,500	1,293,706	1,208,184
Gulf	226,978	366,550	364,559	325,415
Mobil	158,923	247,526	222,384	166,594
Agip/Phillips	163,704	155,146	100,515	51,648
Elf	78,452	83,666	63,919	55,136
Texaco		2,680	8,318	10,177
Total	1,832,243	2,254,068	2,053,401	1,817,154

Appendix 6

Nigeria's Merchant Banks
Who owns what

Nigerian Acceptances (1963)
Capital Increased to N2.5m (1974)
60% owned by:

Financial Holdings	—Hill Samuel	40%	
	—John Holt	26.6%	60%
	—Grindlays	20%	
	—Credit Lyonnais	13.3%	

Has issued shares to:

National Insurance Company of Nigeria	25	
NNDC	10%	40%
Private Interests	5%	

Icon Securities (1975) Capital N1.5m

Baring Brothers	15%
Morgan Guarantee Trust	25%
NICON (National Insurance Company of Nigeria)	15%
National Development Investment Bank	45%

UDT (1974) Capital N1.5m
Wholly owned by UDT London through Bentworth Finance

First National City Bank New York (1974) Capital N1.5m
Wholly owned subsidiary of FNCB-NY

First National Bank of Chicago
Wholly owned by parent company in US

Chase Securities Capital N1.5m

Chase Manhattan	75%
Standard and Chartered	20%
Mitsubishi Trust and Banking Corporation	5%

Source: *African Development*, March 1975

Appendix 7

Growth rates of demand and production—commodities

(annual growth rate %)

Commodity	Consumer Demand	Farm Production*
Maize	3.8	8.0
Millet	3.8	8.0
Sorghum	3.8	8.0
Rice	5.7	11.5
Wheat	10.4	11.5
Cassava	1.9	5.5
Potatoes (sweet)	1.9	6.0
Yams	1.9	6.0
Cocoyams	0.9	5.5
Plantains	1.9	5.5
Groundnuts	2.8	7.5
Beans (cowpea)	2.8	7.5
Soya beans	2.8	7.5
Melon seeds	2.8	7.5
Vegetables	5.7	10.4
Fruits	6.6	12.8
Palm oil	4.7	9.5
Groundnut oil	4.7	9.5
Melon Seed oil	4.7	9.5

* This is intended to take into account seed rates, processing and storage losses, except requirements for exports and plate wastes.

Source: *African Development*, March 1975

Appendix 8

The new Head of State and Commander-in-Chief of the Armed Forces, Lieutenant-General Olusegun Obasanjo, broadcast to the nation on the situation in the country on 14 February 1976 as follows:

Fellow Citizens

We are once again passing through a critical period in the history of this country.

For me personally, this has been one of the saddest moments in my life. The Supreme Military Council has already announced the assassination of His Excellency General Murtala Muhammed.

We all mourn the passing away of one of the greatest sons of Nigeria.

I had the privilege of serving as the Chief of Staff, Supreme Headquarters, under him. And I have no doubt in my mind that the late General Muhammed gave this country a unique sense of direction and purpose.

We are all now obliged to continue with this policy laid down by the Supreme Military Council under the dynamic leadership of the late General Muhammed.

From the account of the tragic incident gathered so far, the late Head of State was shot yesterday on his way to the office.

His ADC, Lieutenant Akinfenwa, his orderly and the driver who were with him in the car were also killed.

The Governor of Kwara State, Col. Ibrahim Taiwo, who was abducted yesterday, was shot dead and his body was found dead in a shallow grave outside Ilorin.

Colonel Dumuje was shot and wounded in another location in Lagos on his way to the office.

This dastardly act was committed by a few dissident troops organised by Lieutenant-Colonel G. S. Dimka of the Nigerian Army Physical Training Corps.

Many arrests have already been made and the Supreme Military Council has set up a Military Board of Inquiry to carry out full-scale investigation into the incident and the planning of the assassination.

I wish to assure the nation that the Supreme Military Council has taken a firm decision that all those found to be guilty will be summarily dealt with in a military way.

I, therefore, appeal to all sections of Nigerians not to take the law into their hands but to rest assured that the Federal Military Government will see to it that justice is done.

As we have heard in the statement by the Supreme Military Council, I have been called upon, against my personal wish, and desire, to serve as the new Head of State.

But I have accepted this honour in the interest of the nation and in memory of the late Head of State.

I know that he will have wished that somebody should continue the task of nation building from where he left off.

I have worked very closely with him and I shared his beliefs and commitment to Federal Military Government's policies and actions.

I believe I feel strongly committed to all he had been doing and I can pay him no better tribute than to continue in the spirit with which he had led this country—that of complete dedication.

All policies of Federal Military Government continue as before and all ministries should continue their usual duties.

This tragic incident can only lead to a greater dedication to the upliftment and progress of this nation.

This situation was brought so swiftly under control because of the loyalty and dedication of the Armed Forces and the Police.

The Armed Forces and the Police deserve praise and appreciation from the government and the people of this country.

Reports have also reached me from all over the country of public support from various sections of the community. The Federal Military Government is very gratified by this demonstration of loyalty and support.

At the end of the seven-day mourning period which was announced earlier, Friday February 20th, 1976, is hereby declared a public holiday to enable all Nigerians to offer special prayers in all places of worship.

Finally, I would like to appeal to all of you for calm and .to avoid any action that might cause a breach of the peace.

This is a period that calls for continuous vigilance and it is the duty of one and all to maintain this vigilance in order to preserve the stability of the nation.

Goodnight.

Three new military governors were later appointed by the Supreme Military Council (SMC): Colonel Dan Suleiman of the Air Force for Plateau State; Lieutenant-Colonel M. A. Amin, also of the Air Force, for Borno State and Captain Husaini Abdullahi of the Navy for Bendel State.

Formerly Federal Commissioner for Health, Colonel Suleiman succeeded Colonel Abdullahi Muhammed who was posted to the Supreme Headquarters.

Lieutenant-Colonel Amin succeeded Lieutenant-Colonel Muhammadu Buhari who became Federal Commissioner for Petroleum and Energy.

Captain Abdullahi succeeded Colonel George Innih, who was reassigned as Military Governor of Kwara State in succession to the late Colonel Ibrahim Taiwo who was killed during the abortive coup of 13 February.

Five new commissioners were named by the SMC in a major cabinet reshuffle.

They were Major-General O. E. Obada, former General Officer commanding 4 Infantry Division (Works); Lieutenant-Colonel Muktar Mohammed, a member of the SMC (Housing, Urban Development and Environment); Lieutenant–Colonel Muhammadu Buhari, former Military Governor of Borno State (Petroleum and Energy); Lieutenant-Colonel M. Magoro (Transport) and Alhaji Kafaru Tinubu, former Commissioner of Police, Anambra State (Health).

The Head of State, Lieutenant-General Olusegun Obasanjo, also reassigned three federal commissioners to new ministries.

Malam U. A. Muttalab moved from the Ministry of Economic Development to the Ministry of Co-operatives and Supply; Dr R. A. Adeleye moved from Ministry of Housing, Urban Development and Environment to the Ministry of Industries, and Dr M. T. O. Akobo, Commissioner for Petroleum and Energy, moved to the Ministry of Economic Development.

Index

Aba Textile Mills, 44
Abashiya, Dr Chris S., 113
Abdullahi, Capt. Husaini, 3, 175, 184, 185
Abisoye, Brigadier Emmanuel, 2, 9, 30, 145, 175
Achebe, Chinua, 155
Action Group, x, xi, xii
Adamu, Brigadier Martin, 2, 175
Adebayo, Brigadier Robert, 24
Adebo Commission/award (1971), 120
Adedji, Prof. Adebayo, 51
Adekun, Col Peter, 127
Adelanwa, Commodore, 2, 174, 175
Adeleye, Dr R. A., 177, 185
Adetunji, Alhaji Adebayo, 94
Adua, Lieut-Col Shehu Yar, 2
Aduloju, Lieut-Col Alfred 3, 175
African Development Bank (ADB), 67
African Development Fund, 67
African Groundnuts Council, 67
Agip-Phillips, 52, 53, 61, 180
agriculture and rural development, 31, 42, 45, 46, 52, 58, 65, 68, 69–71, 72, 73, 74, 76, 80, 91–102, 112, 182
Aguda, Mr Justice, 30
Aguiyi-Ironsi, Major-General, xiii
Ahmadu Bello University, 105, 108, 111, 153
Air Force, 40, 137
air transport, 68, 71–2, 124, 125, 131
Ajaokuta steel plant, 157, 158–9
Akinrinade, Brigadier Julius Alani, 2, 7, 175
Akintola, Chief S. L., x, xii, xiii
Akoba, Dr M. T. O., 177, 185
Akporugo, Andy, 19
Aluko, Prof., 149–50
Aluko, Sam, 79
Amalgamated Tin Mines of Nigeria, 85
Amin, Lieut-Col M. A., 184, 185

Angola, 136–8
Animashaun, Alhaji Babs, 117
Apapa, 28–9, 60
Apena Declaration (1974), 119
Arikpo, Dr Okoi, 135, 141
Army, armed forces 23, 24, 37–40, 76, 146, 174, 184
Ashe, Arthur, 7
Asiodu, Philip, 53, 59, 155, 170
Assets Investigation Panel, 33, 42
Association of African Central Banks, 67
Awolowo, Chief Obafemi, x, xi, xii, 19, 23, 78
Awoonor, Kofi, 155
Ayida, Allison, 11
Azikiwe, Dr Nnamdi, ix, x, xi, xii–xiii

Bacita sugar mill, 97
Baikie, Prof. Adamu, 108
Bakolari dam, 81
Bakre, Olukayode, 171
Balewa, Sir Abubakar Tafawa, x, xi, xiii, 138
Babangida, Col Ibrahim, 2
Bamigboye, David, 17
Bassey, Sam, 117
Bello, Sir Ahmadu, ix
Benin Kingdom, viii
    (now: Benue and Plateau),
Benue Plateau State 44, 47, 174, 178
Benue River Basin Development Authority, 96
Biafra, xiii, 41, 52, 89, 134, 135
Bissala, Brigadier I. D., 2, 9, 175,177
Black Arts Festival (FESTAC), 3, 5, 17, 23, 26, 160–1, 165, 166, 168, 175–6
Bonny natural gas plant, 61
Botswana, 135, 139
brewing industry (beer and soft drinks), 43, 46, 74, 84, 87
Britain, British, colonialism, viii–ix; post-Independence relations with Nigeria,